AQUAMAN
THE WATERBEARER

DAN DIDIO VP-EDITORIAL
DAN RASPLER AND **IVAN COHEN** EDITORS-ORIGINAL SERIES
VALERIE D'ORAZIO ASSISTANT EDITOR-ORIGINAL SERIES
ANTON KAWASAKI EDITOR-COLLECTED EDITION
ROBBIN BROSTERMAN SENIOR ART DIRECTOR
PAUL LEVITZ PRESIDENT & PUBLISHER
GEORG BREWER VP-DESIGN & RETAIL PRODUCT DEVELOPMENT
RICHARD BRUNING SENIOR VP-CREATIVE DIRECTOR
PATRICK CALDON SENIOR VP-FINANCE & OPERATIONS
CHRIS CARAMALIS VP-FINANCE
TERRI CUNNINGHAM VP-MANAGING EDITOR
ALISON GILL VP-MANUFACTURING
LILLIAN LASERSON SENIOR VP & GENERAL COUNSEL
JIM LEE EDITORIAL DIRECTOR-WILDSTORM
DAVID MCKILLIPS VP-ADVERTISING & CUSTOM PUBLISHING
JOHN NEE VP-BUSINESS DEVELOPMENT
CHERYL RUBIN VP-BRAND MANAGEMENT
BOB WAYNE VP-SALES & MARKETING

AQUAMAN: THE WATERBEARER

PUBLISHED BY DC COMICS.
COVER AND COMPILATION COPYRIGHT © 2003 DC COMICS.
ALL RIGHTS RESERVED.

ORIGINALLY PUBLISHED IN SINGLE MAGAZINE FORM IN AQUAMAN #1-4, AQUAMAN
SECRET FILES #1 AND JLA/JSA SECRET FILES #1. COPYRIGHT © 2002, 2003 DC COMICS.
ALL RIGHTS RESERVED. ALL CHARACTERS, THEIR DISTINCTIVE LIKENESSES AND RELATED
INDICIA FEATURED IN THIS PUBLICATION ARE TRADEMARKS OF DC COMICS. THE STORIES,
CHARACTERS AND INCIDENTS FEATURED IN THIS PUBLICATION ARE ENTIRELY FICTIONAL.
DC COMICS DOES NOT READ OR ACCEPT UNSOLICITED SUBMISSIONS OF IDEAS, STORIES
OR ARTWORK.

DC COMICS, 170 0 BROADWAY, NEW YORK, NY 10019
A WARNER BROS. ENTERTAINMENT COMPANY
PRINTED IN CANADA. FIRST PRINTING.
ISBN: 1-4012-0088-5
COVER ILLUSTRATION BY J.G. JONES
COVER COLOR BY PAUL MOUNTS
PUBLICATION DESIGN BY TOSH THOMAS HALL

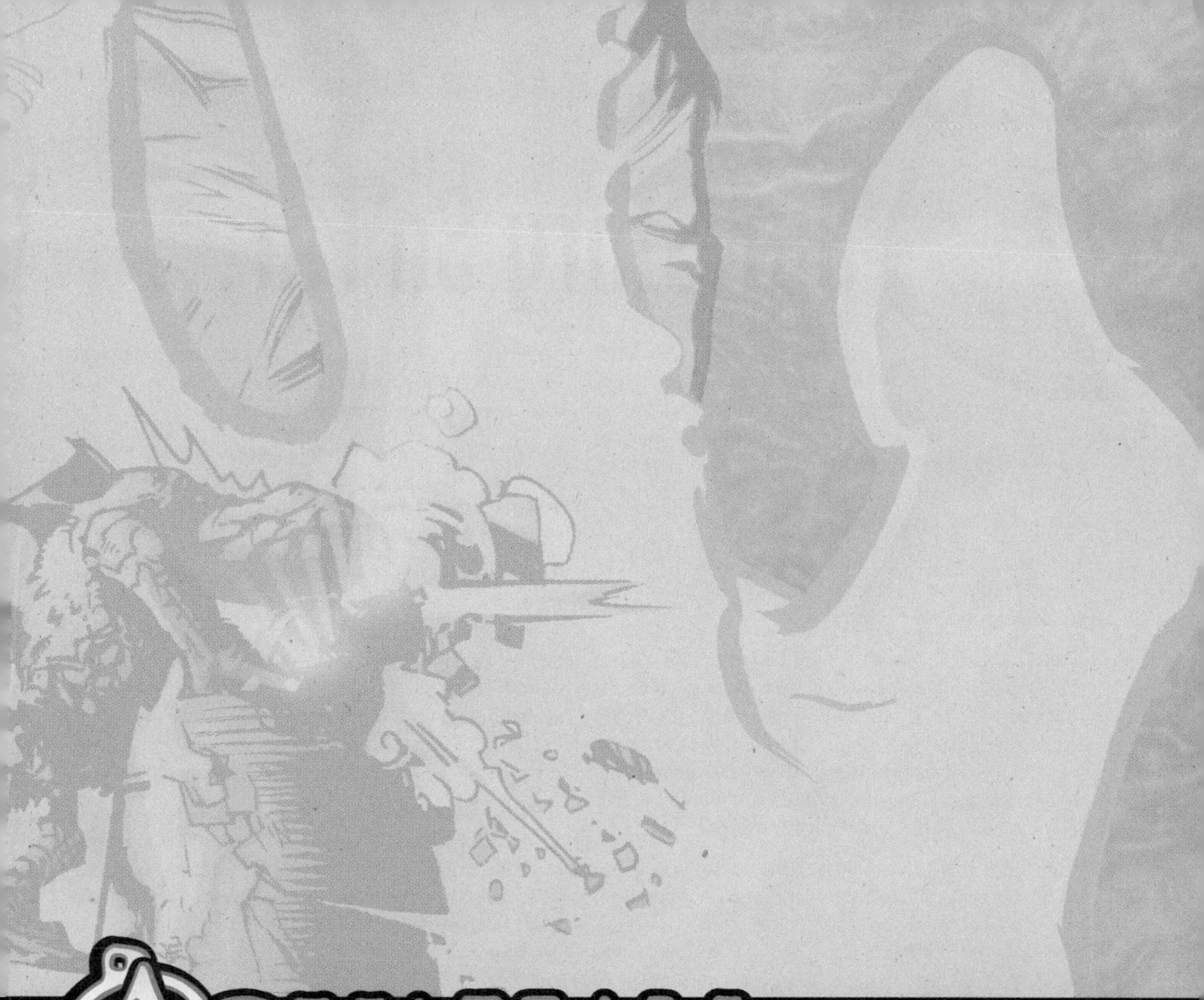

AQUAMAN THE WATERBEARER

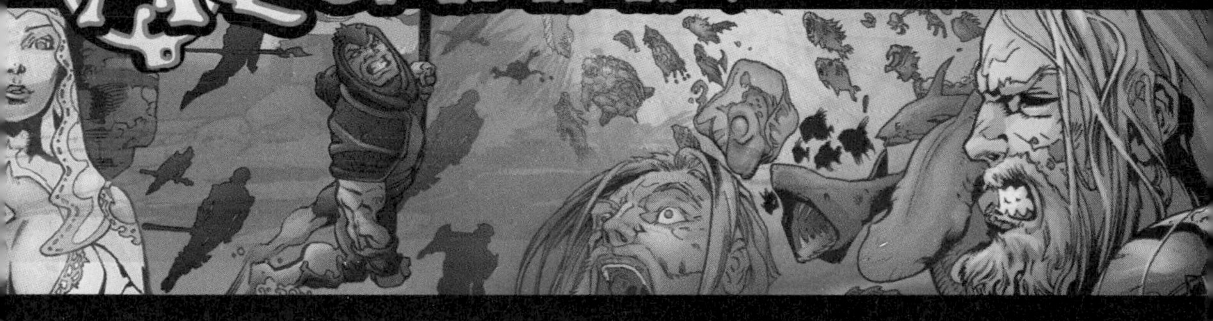

RICK VEITCH WRITER

YVEL GUICHET NORM BREYFOGLE JOSHUA HOOD DIETRICH SMITH PENCILLERS

MARK PROPST DENNIS JANKE SEAN PARSONS INKERS

NATHAN EYRING TOM MCCRAW COLORISTS

MIKE HEISLER KURT HATHAWAY LETTERERS

ALEX MALEEV YVEL GUICHET MARK PROPST ORIGINAL SERIES COVERS

AQUAMAN CREATED BY PAUL NORRIS

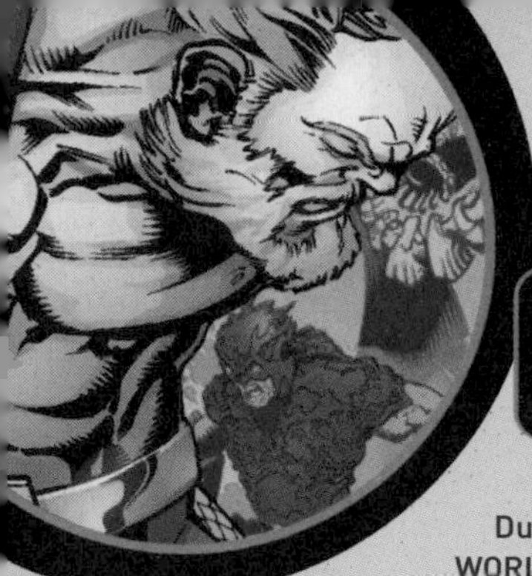

Our Story So Far...

During the events of OUR WORLDS AT WAR, Aquaman, the king of Atlantis and a founding member of the Justice League of America, died brutally at the hands of Imperius Rex. At the same time the entire underwater civilization of Atlantis also disappeared.

The world mourned and the JLA's core was profoundly affected by the tragic loss of their most steadfast member.

Months later, however, clues surfaced that hinted the King of the Seven Seas might have been alive. In the end it was discovered that instead of being vaporized, Aquaman, along with the city of Atlantis, had been sent backwards in time 3000 years by a magic spell cast by his trusted companion Garth (also known as the super-hero Tempest).

Knowledge of this era in Atlantean history (known as the Obsidian Age) had been lost to the winds of time, but soon Aquaman discovered the truth. The current-day Atlantis had been sent back in time by the evil sorceress, Gamemnae, where it would take its rightful place above the water instead of below. At the same time, thousands of modern-day citizens of Atlantis were also sent back in time, and enslaved by the people of the Obsidian Age's Atlantis. Aquaman was dealt an even harsher fate as his body was imprisoned for 15 years, believed dead by all the Atlanteans he had once ruled over.

Eventually the JLA (thanks to Tempest's magic) journeyed back in time to defeat Gamemnae, rescue the people of modern-day Atlantis, and find their comrade Aquaman.

Unfortunately, victory had its price, and while modern-day Atlantis was restored to its proper place in time, the island was once again sunk beneath the sea — this time by Aquaman himself, who made the painful decision to save his people by relegating their home beneath the waves of the Atlantic. Once again, Atlantis was lost to the ocean. Only this time, the people of Atlantis knew who was responsible.

Now Aquaman (known also by his Atlantean name, Orin, and by his human name, Arthur Curry) must pay the price for rescuing a civilization that has become so blinded by its archaic laws and traditions that it no longer trusts those who would lead it to greatness.

It's a dark day in Atlantis, and its favorite son is lost to us once more.

And so begins a new chapter in the story of Aquaman...

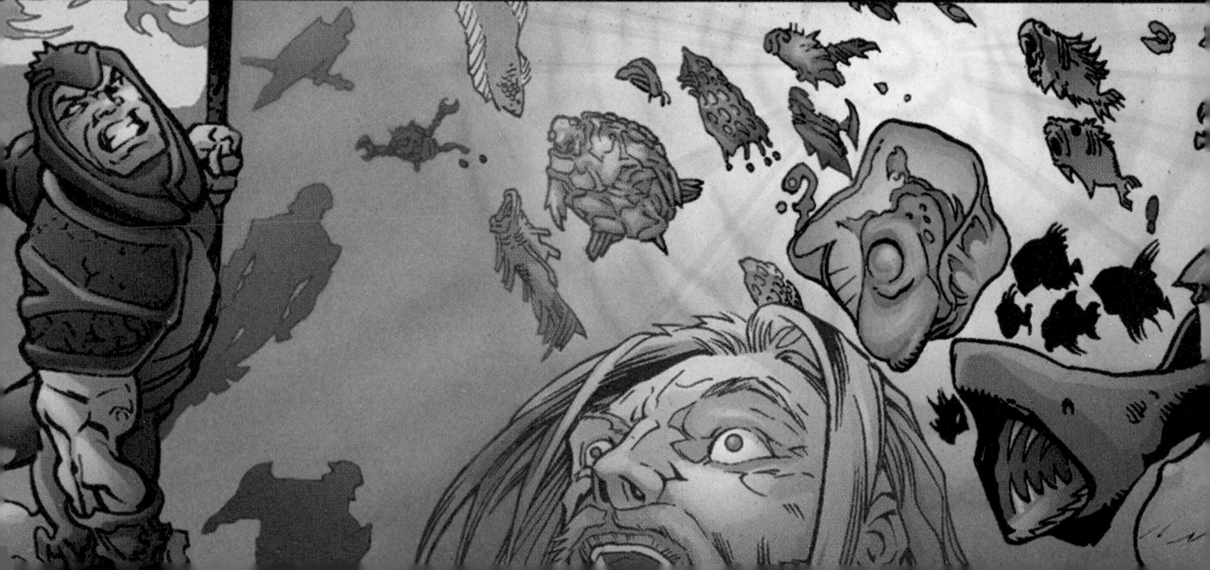

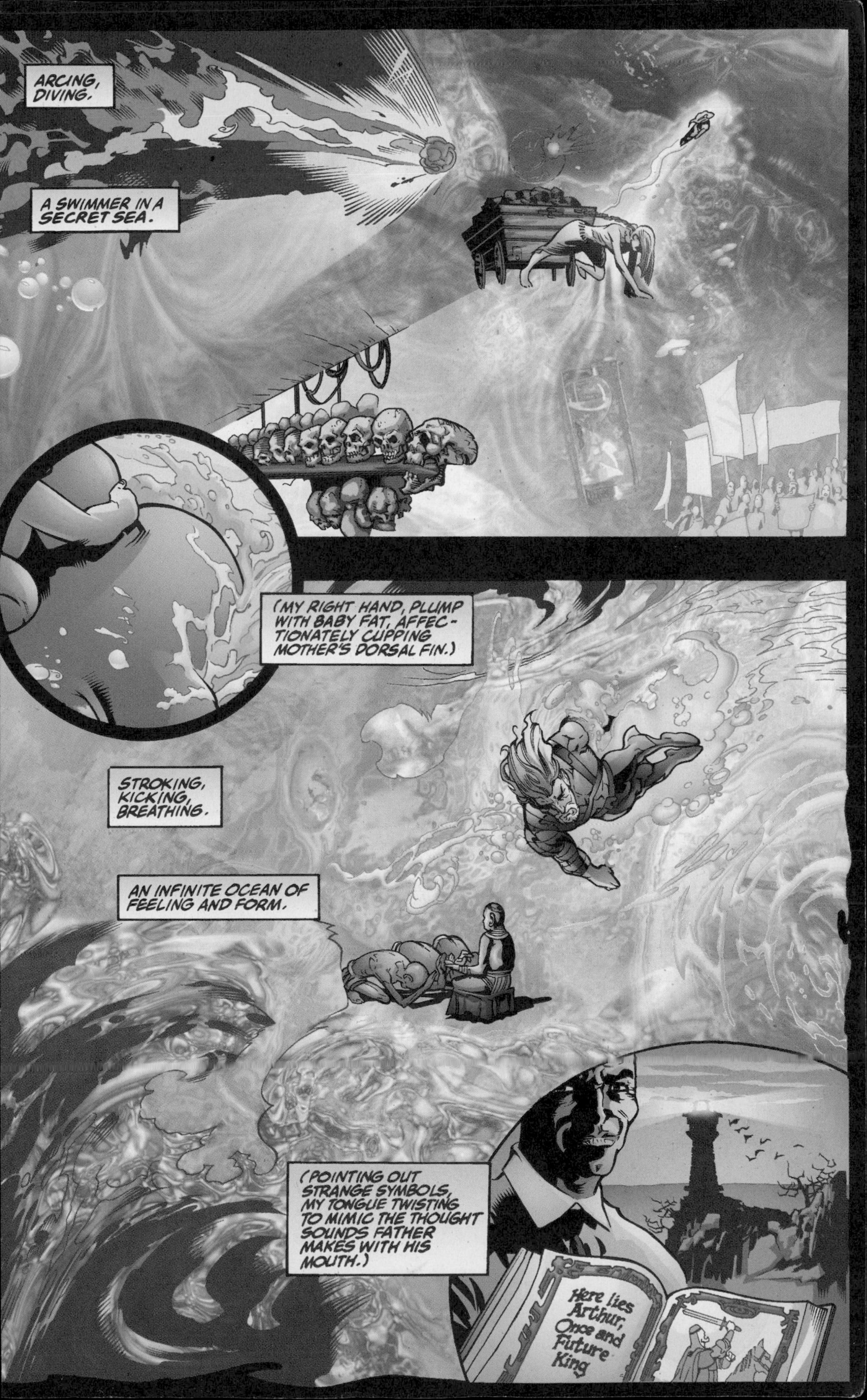
ARCING, DIVING.
A SWIMMER IN A SECRET SEA.
(MY RIGHT HAND, PLUMP WITH BABY FAT, AFFEC-TIONATELY CUPPING MOTHER'S DORSAL FIN.)
STROKING, KICKING, BREATHING.
AN INFINITE OCEAN OF FEELING AND FORM.
(POINTING OUT STRANGE SYMBOLS, MY TONGUE TWISTING TO MIMIC THE THOUGHT SOUNDS FATHER MAKES WITH HIS MOUTH.)
Here lies Arthur, Once and Future King

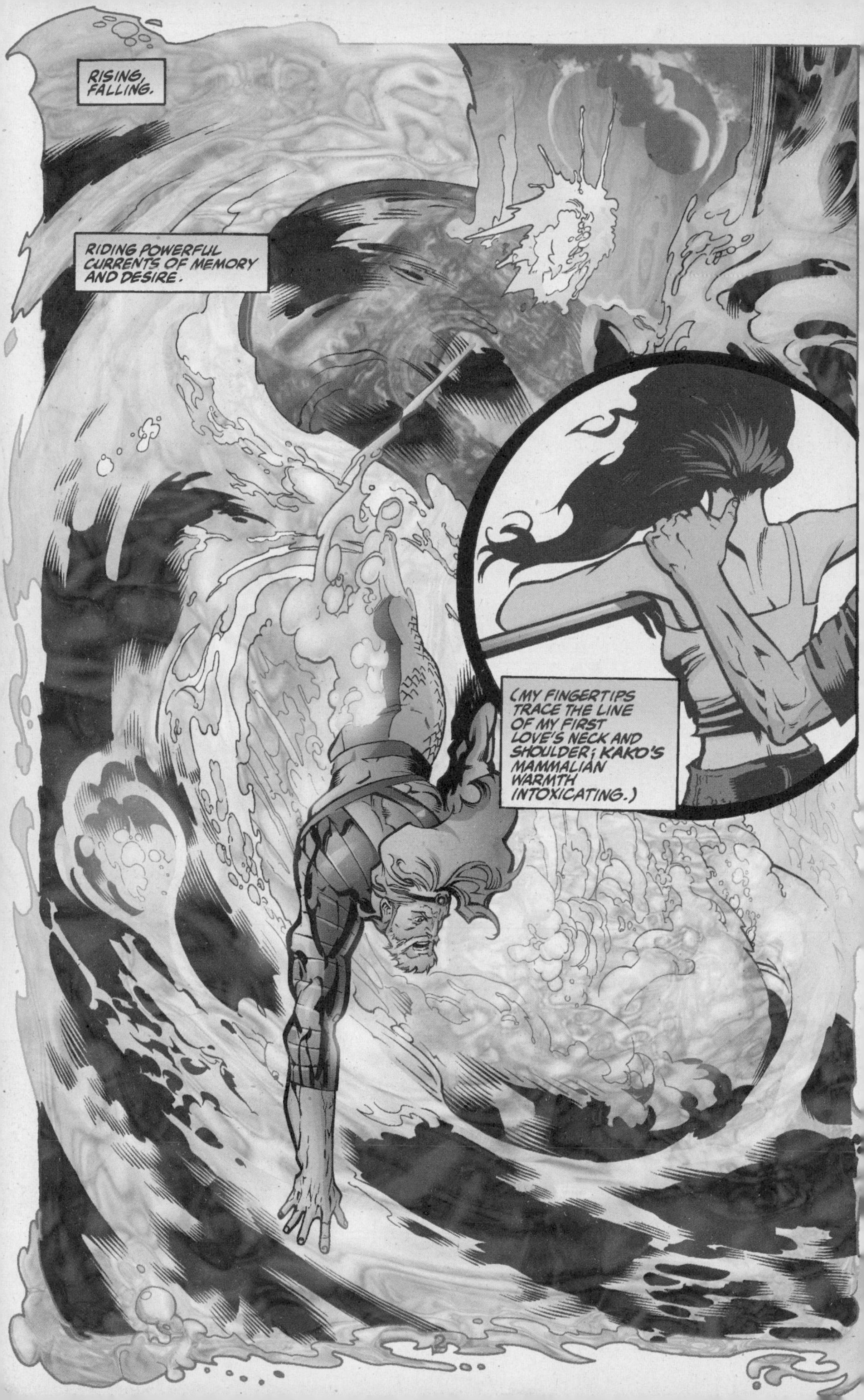
RISING, FALLING.
RIDING POWERFUL CURRENTS OF MEMORY AND DESIRE.
(MY FINGERTIPS TRACE THE LINE OF MY FIRST LOVE'S NECK AND SHOULDER; KAKO'S MAMMALIAN WARMTH INTOXICATING.)

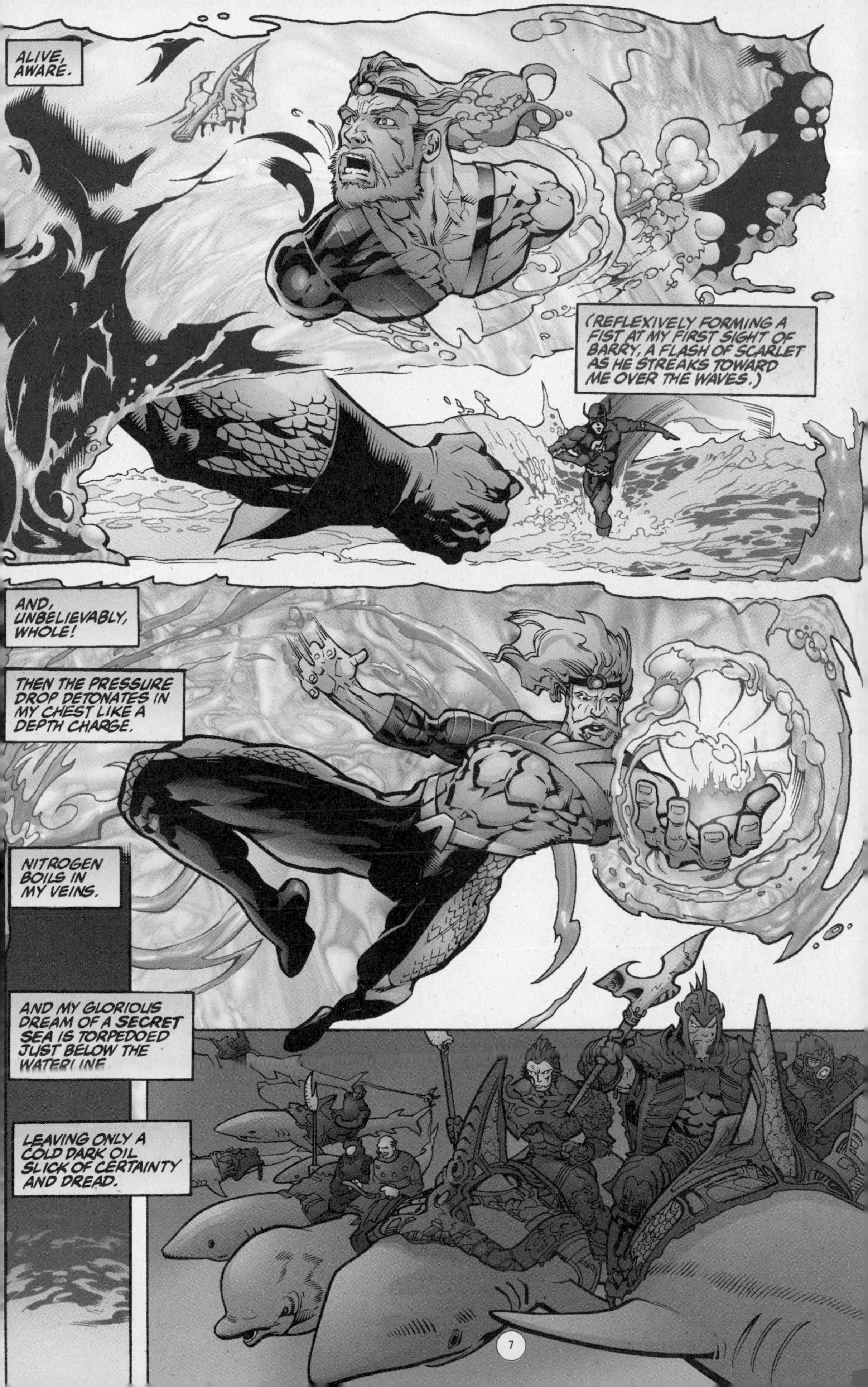
ALIVE, AWARE.
(REFLEXIVELY FORMING A FIST AT MY FIRST SIGHT OF BARRY, A FLASH OF SCARLET AS HE STREAKS TOWARD ME OVER THE WAVES.)
AND, UNBELIEVABLY, WHOLE!
THEN THE PRESSURE DROP DETONATES IN MY CHEST LIKE A DEPTH CHARGE.
NITROGEN BOILS IN MY VEINS.
AND MY GLORIOUS DREAM OF A SECRET SEA IS TORPEDOED JUST BELOW THE WATERLINE.
LEAVING ONLY A COLD DARK OIL SLICK OF CERTAINTY AND DREAD.

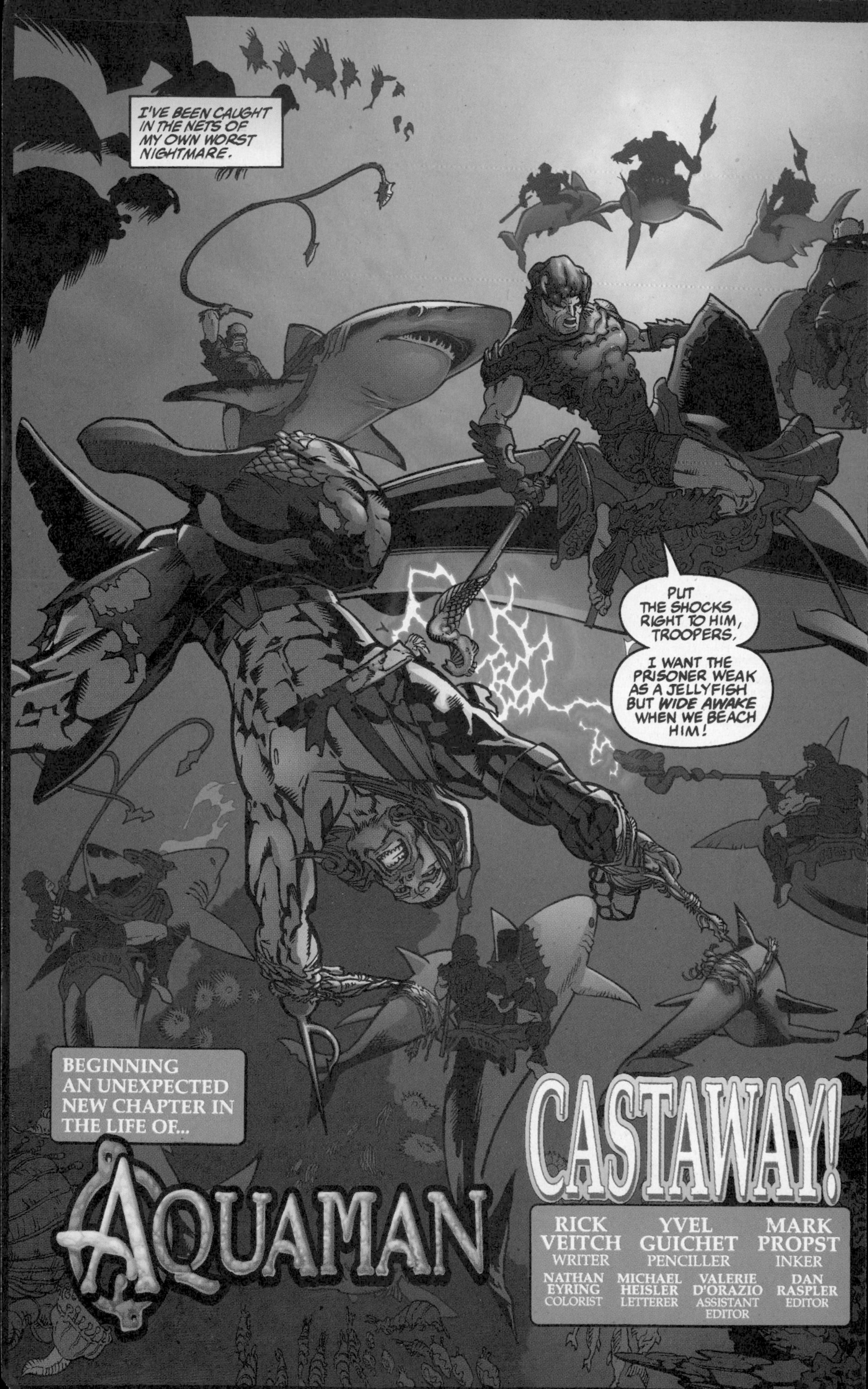

I'VE BEEN CAUGHT IN THE NETS OF MY OWN WORST NIGHTMARE.
PUT THE SHOCKS RIGHT TO HIM, TROOPERS.
I WANT THE PRISONER WEAK AS A JELLYFISH BUT WIDE AWAKE WHEN WE BEACH HIM!
BEGINNING AN UNEXPECTED NEW CHAPTER IN THE LIFE OF...
AQUAMAN
CASTAWAY!
RICK VEITCH WRITER
YVEL GUICHET PENCILLER
MARK PROPST INKER
NATHAN EYRING COLORIST
MICHAEL HEISLER LETTERER
VALERIE D'ORAZIO ASSISTANT EDITOR
DAN RASPLER EDITOR

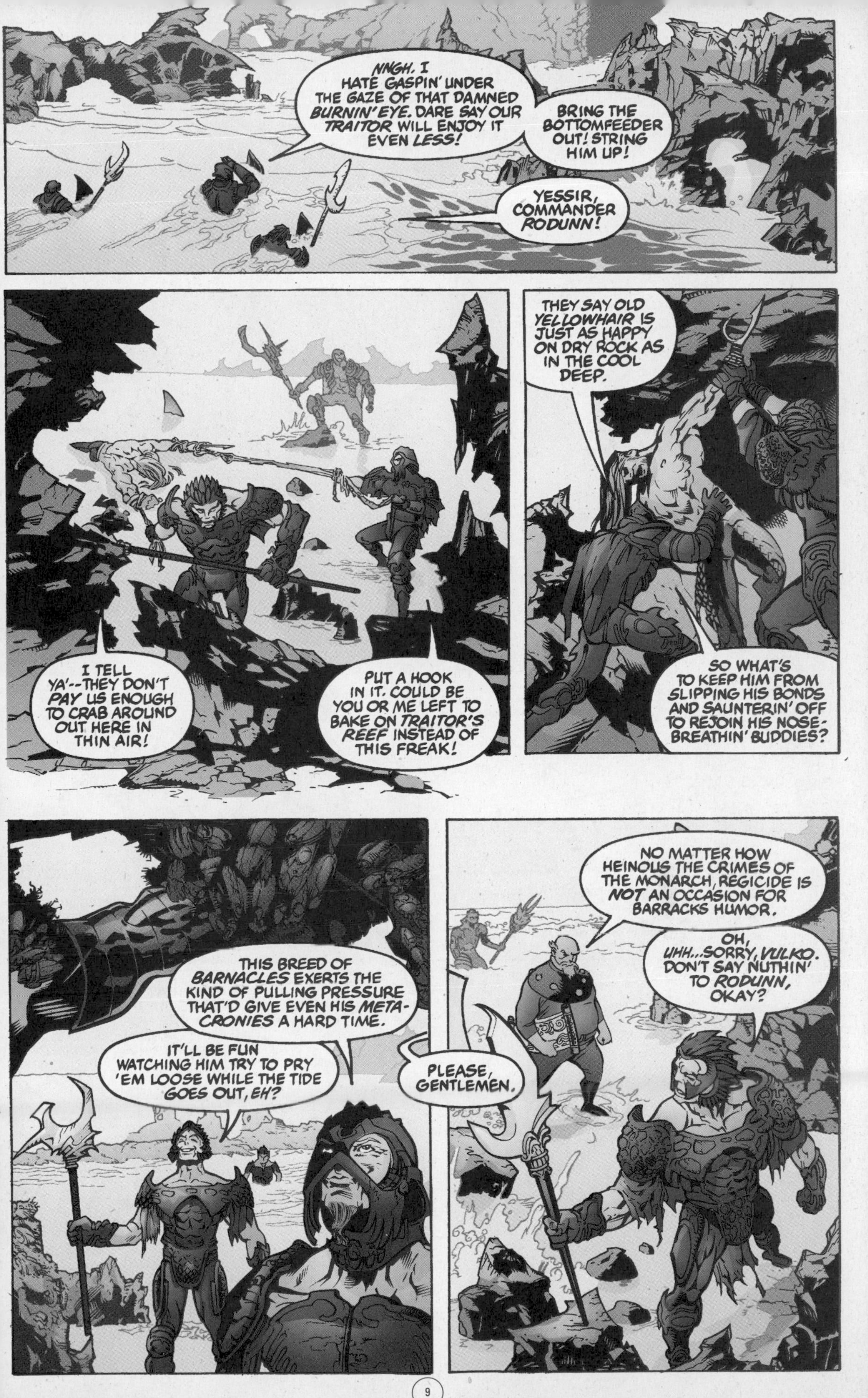
NNGH. I HATE GASPIN' UNDER THE GAZE OF THAT DAMNED BURNIN' EYE. DARE SAY OUR TRAITOR WILL ENJOY IT EVEN LESS!
BRING THE BOTTOMFEEDER OUT! STRING HIM UP!
YESSIR, COMMANDER RODUNN!
I TELL YA'--THEY DON'T PAY US ENOUGH TO CRAB AROUND OUT HERE IN THIN AIR!
PUT A HOOK IN IT. COULD BE YOU OR ME LEFT TO BAKE ON TRAITOR'S REEF INSTEAD OF THIS FREAK!
THEY SAY OLD YELLOWHAIR IS JUST AS HAPPY ON DRY ROCK AS IN THE COOL DEEP.
SO WHAT'S TO KEEP HIM FROM SLIPPING HIS BONDS AND SAUNTERIN' OFF TO REJOIN HIS NOSE-BREATHIN' BUDDIES?
THIS BREED OF BARNACLES EXERTS THE KIND OF PULLING PRESSURE THAT'D GIVE EVEN HIS META-CRONIES A HARD TIME.
IT'LL BE FUN WATCHING HIM TRY TO PRY 'EM LOOSE WHILE THE TIDE GOES OUT, EH?
PLEASE, GENTLEMEN.
NO MATTER HOW HEINOUS THE CRIMES OF THE MONARCH, REGICIDE IS NOT AN OCCASION FOR BARRACKS HUMOR.
OH, UHH...SORRY, VULKO. DON'T SAY NUTHIN' TO RODUNN, OKAY?

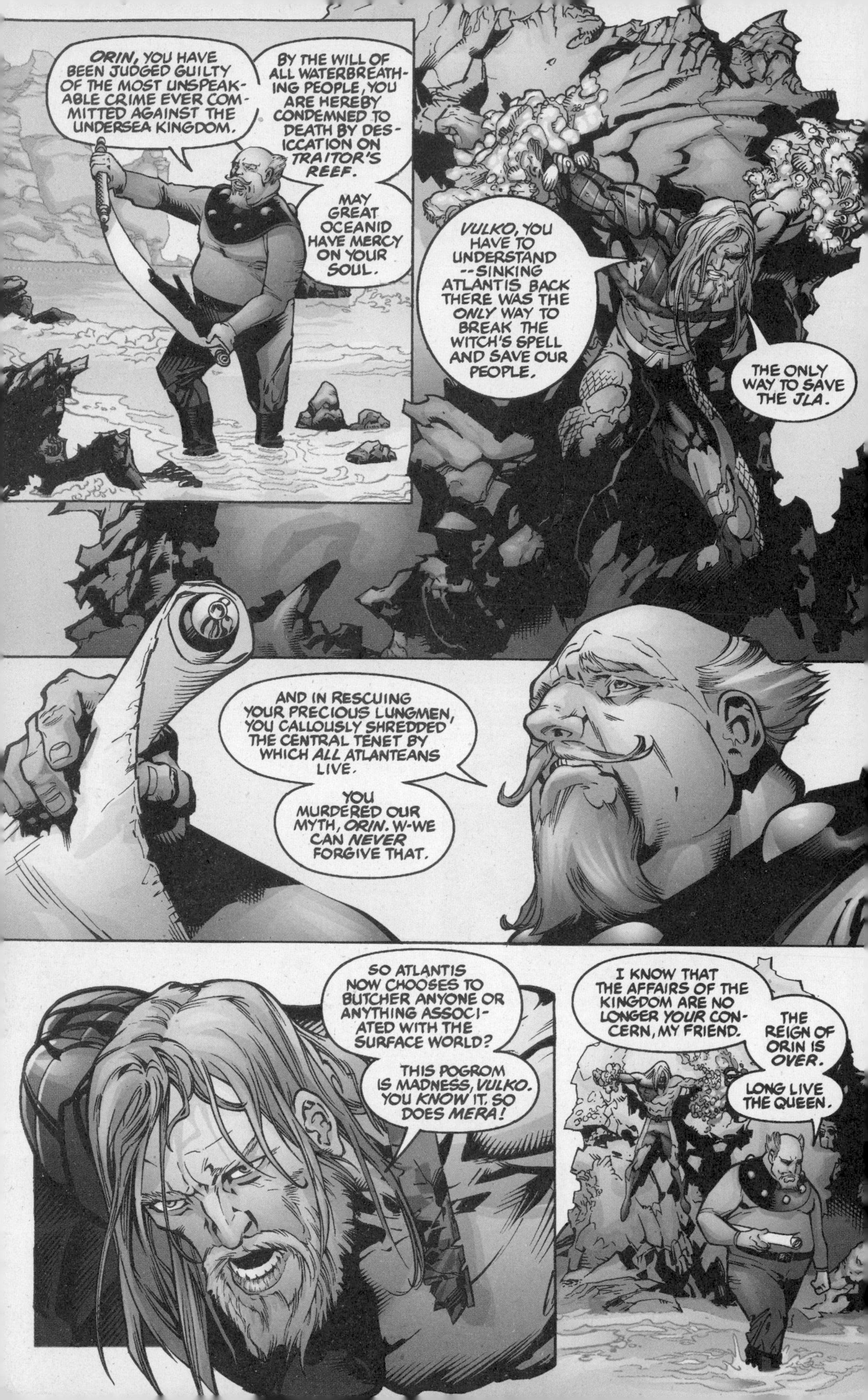
ORIN, YOU HAVE BEEN JUDGED GUILTY OF THE MOST UNSPEAKABLE CRIME EVER COMMITTED AGAINST THE UNDERSEA KINGDOM.
BY THE WILL OF ALL WATERBREATHING PEOPLE, YOU ARE HEREBY CONDEMNED TO DEATH BY DESICCATION ON TRAITOR'S REEF.
MAY GREAT OCEANID HAVE MERCY ON YOUR SOUL.
VULKO, YOU HAVE TO UNDERSTAND --SINKING ATLANTIS BACK THERE WAS THE ONLY WAY TO BREAK THE WITCH'S SPELL AND SAVE OUR PEOPLE.
THE ONLY WAY TO SAVE THE JLA.
AND IN RESCUING YOUR PRECIOUS LUNGMEN, YOU CALLOUSLY SHREDDED THE CENTRAL TENET BY WHICH ALL ATLANTEANS LIVE.
YOU MURDERED OUR MYTH, ORIN. W-WE CAN NEVER FORGIVE THAT.
SO ATLANTIS NOW CHOOSES TO BUTCHER ANYONE OR ANYTHING ASSOCIATED WITH THE SURFACE WORLD?
THIS POGROM IS MADNESS, VULKO. YOU KNOW IT. SO DOES MERA!
I KNOW THAT THE AFFAIRS OF THE KINGDOM ARE NO LONGER YOUR CONCERN, MY FRIEND.
THE REIGN OF ORIN IS OVER.
LONG LIVE THE QUEEN.

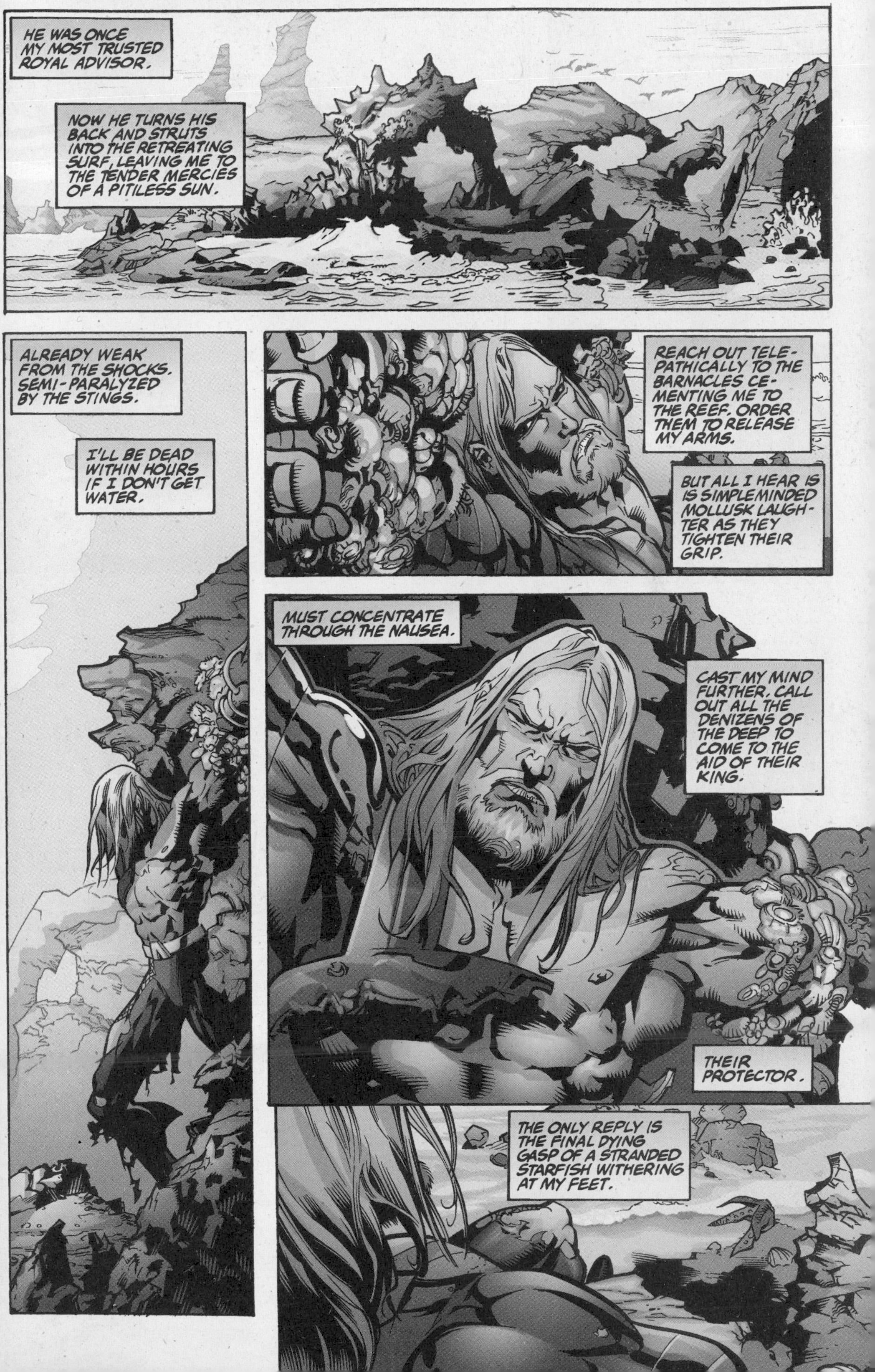
HE WAS ONCE MY MOST TRUSTED ROYAL ADVISOR.
NOW HE TURNS HIS BACK AND STRUTS INTO THE RETREATING SURF, LEAVING ME TO THE TENDER MERCIES OF A PITILESS SUN.
ALREADY WEAK FROM THE SHOCKS. SEMI-PARALYZED BY THE STINGS.
I'LL BE DEAD WITHIN HOURS IF I DON'T GET WATER.
REACH OUT TELE-PATHICALLY TO THE BARNACLES CE-MENTING ME TO THE REEF. ORDER THEM TO RELEASE MY ARMS.
BUT ALL I HEAR IS IS SIMPLEMINDED MOLLUSK LAUGH-TER AS THEY TIGHTEN THEIR GRIP.
MUST CONCENTRATE THROUGH THE NAUSEA.
CAST MY MIND FURTHER. CALL OUT ALL THE DENIZENS OF THE DEEP TO COME TO THE AID OF THEIR KING.
THEIR PROTECTOR.
THE ONLY REPLY IS THE FINAL DYING GASP OF A STRANDED STARFISH WITHERING AT MY FEET.

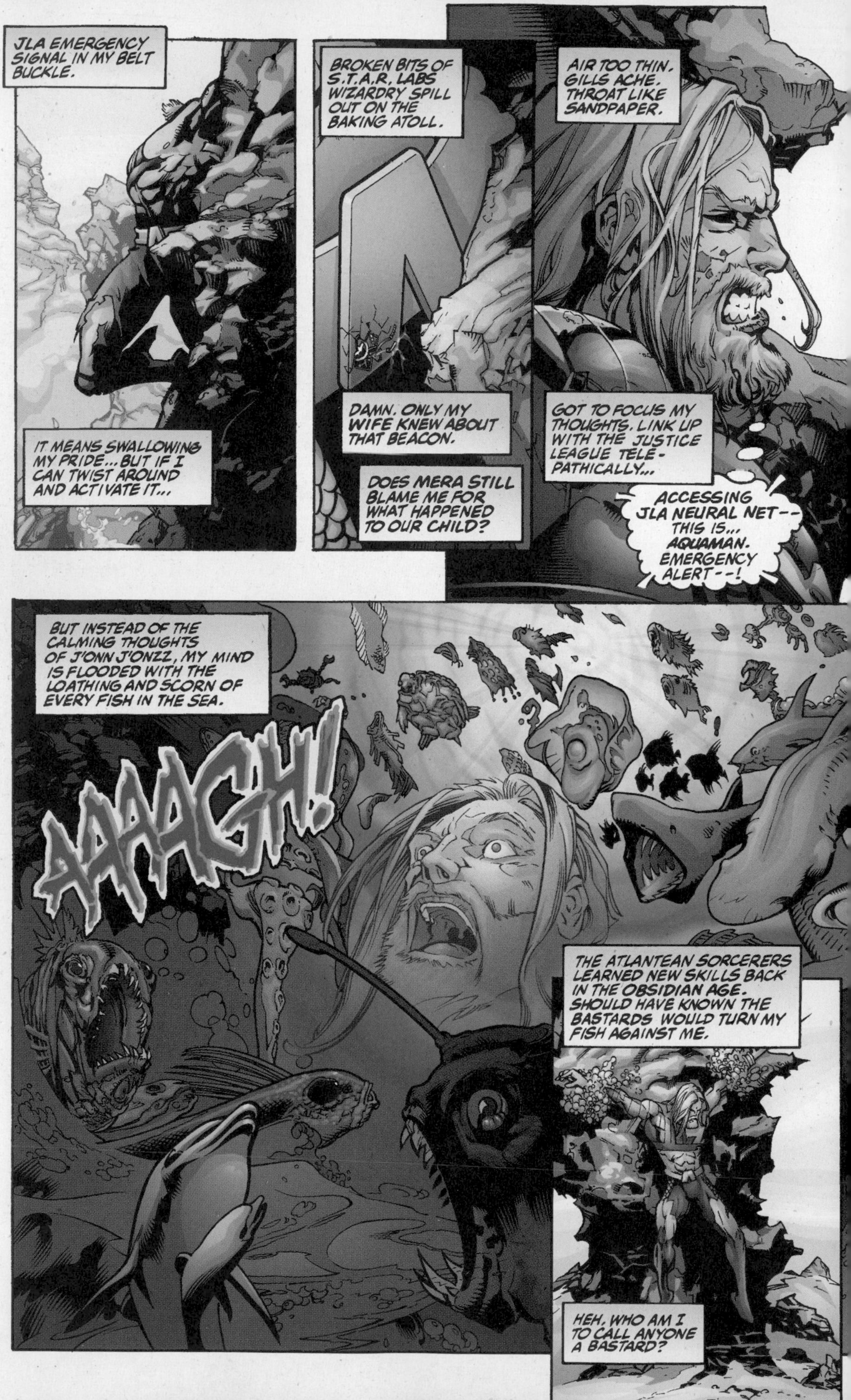
JLA EMERGENCY SIGNAL IN MY BELT BUCKLE.
IT MEANS SWALLOWING MY PRIDE... BUT IF I CAN TWIST AROUND AND ACTIVATE IT...
BROKEN BITS OF S.T.A.R. LABS WIZARDRY SPILL OUT ON THE BAKING ATOLL.
DAMN. ONLY MY WIFE KNEW ABOUT THAT BEACON.
DOES MERA STILL BLAME ME FOR WHAT HAPPENED TO OUR CHILD?
AIR TOO THIN. GILLS ACHE. THROAT LIKE SANDPAPER.
GOT TO FOCUS MY THOUGHTS. LINK UP WITH THE JUSTICE LEAGUE TELE-PATHICALLY...
ACCESSING JLA NEURAL NET-- THIS IS... AQUAMAN. EMERGENCY ALERT--!
BUT INSTEAD OF THE CALMING THOUGHTS OF J'ONN J'ONZZ, MY MIND IS FLOODED WITH THE LOATHING AND SCORN OF EVERY FISH IN THE SEA.
AAAAGH!
THE ATLANTEAN SORCERERS LEARNED NEW SKILLS BACK IN THE OBSIDIAN AGE. SHOULD HAVE KNOWN THE BASTARDS WOULD TURN MY FISH AGAINST ME.
HEH. WHO AM I TO CALL ANYONE A BASTARD?

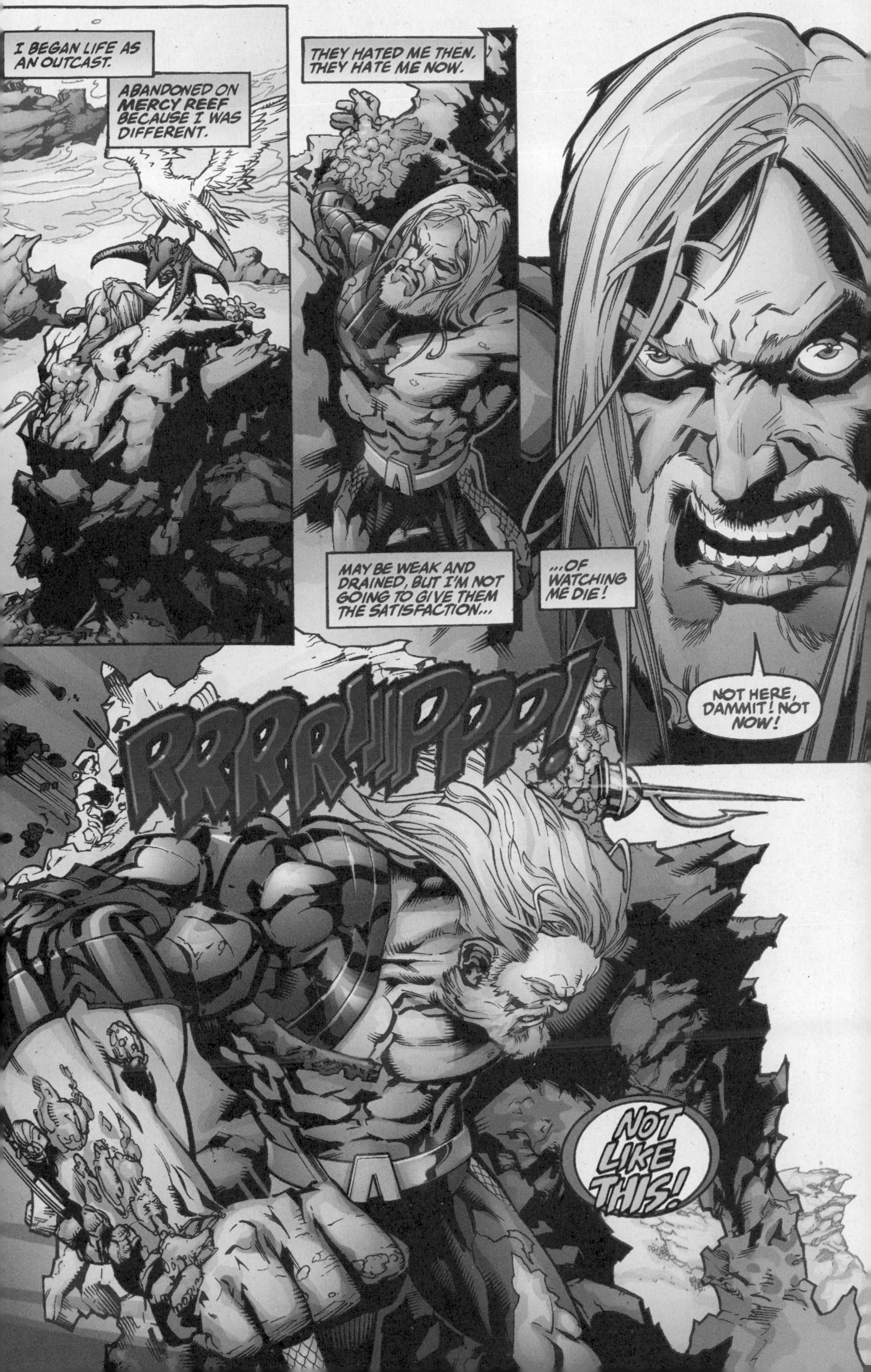
I BEGAN LIFE AS AN OUTCAST.
ABANDONED ON MERCY REEF BECAUSE I WAS DIFFERENT.
THEY HATED ME THEN, THEY HATE ME NOW.
MAY BE WEAK AND DRAINED, BUT I'M NOT GOING TO GIVE THEM THE SATISFACTION...
...OF WATCHING ME DIE!
NOT HERE, DAMMIT! NOT NOW!
RRRRIIPPP!
NOT LIKE THIS!

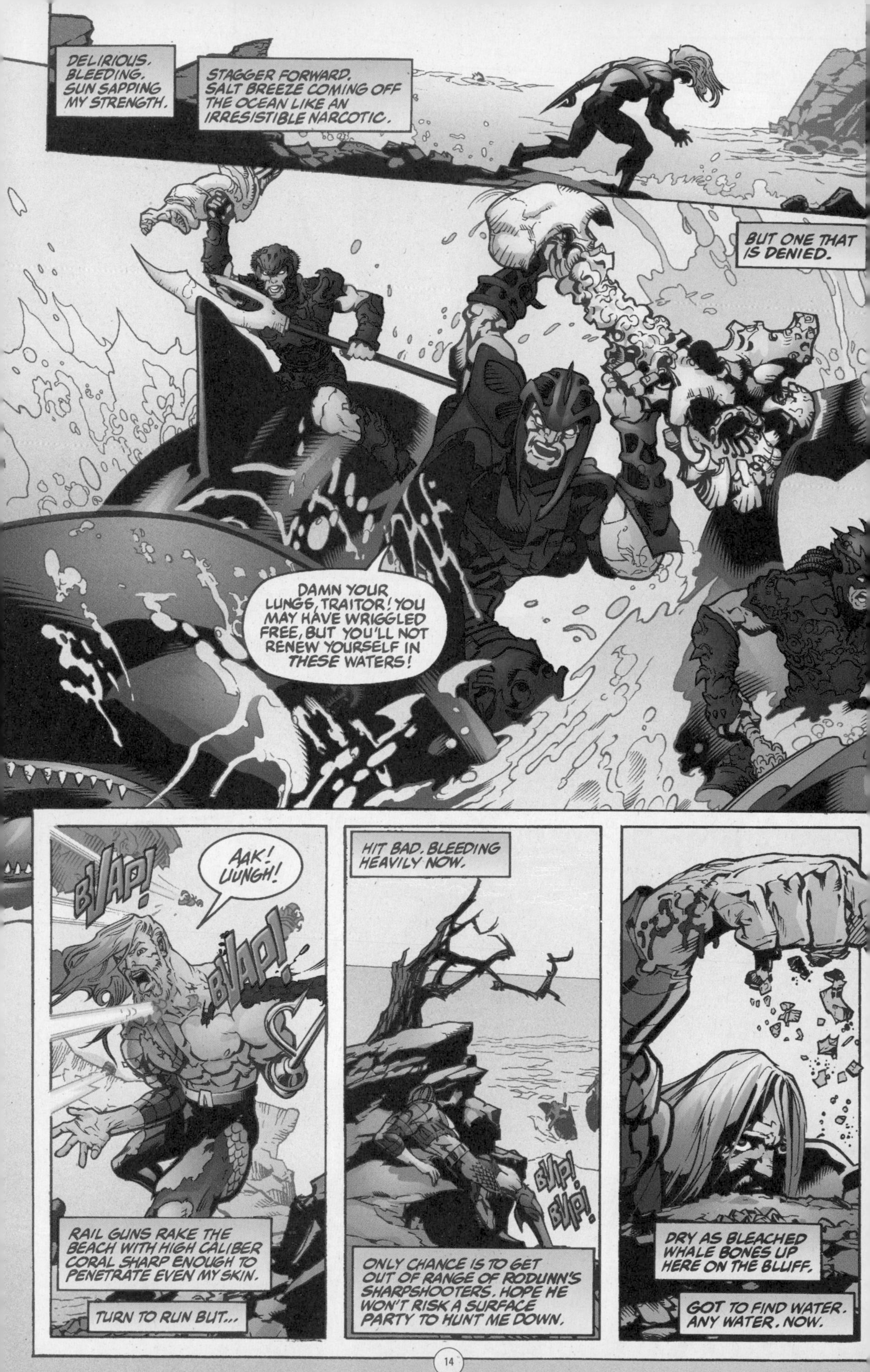

DELIRIOUS. BLEEDING. SUN SAPPING MY STRENGTH.
STAGGER FORWARD. SALT BREEZE COMING OFF THE OCEAN LIKE AN IRRESISTIBLE NARCOTIC.
BUT ONE THAT IS DENIED.
DAMN YOUR LUNGS, TRAITOR! YOU MAY HAVE WRIGGLED FREE, BUT YOU'LL NOT RENEW YOURSELF IN THESE WATERS!
BVAP!
AAK! UUNGH!
BVAP!
RAIL GUNS RAKE THE BEACH WITH HIGH CALIBER CORAL SHARP ENOUGH TO PENETRATE EVEN MY SKIN.
TURN TO RUN BUT...
HIT BAD. BLEEDING HEAVILY NOW.
BVIP! BVIP!
ONLY CHANCE IS TO GET OUT OF RANGE OF RODUNN'S SHARPSHOOTERS. HOPE HE WON'T RISK A SURFACE PARTY TO HUNT ME DOWN.
DRY AS BLEACHED WHALE BONES UP HERE ON THE BLUFF.
GOT TO FIND WATER. ANY WATER. NOW.

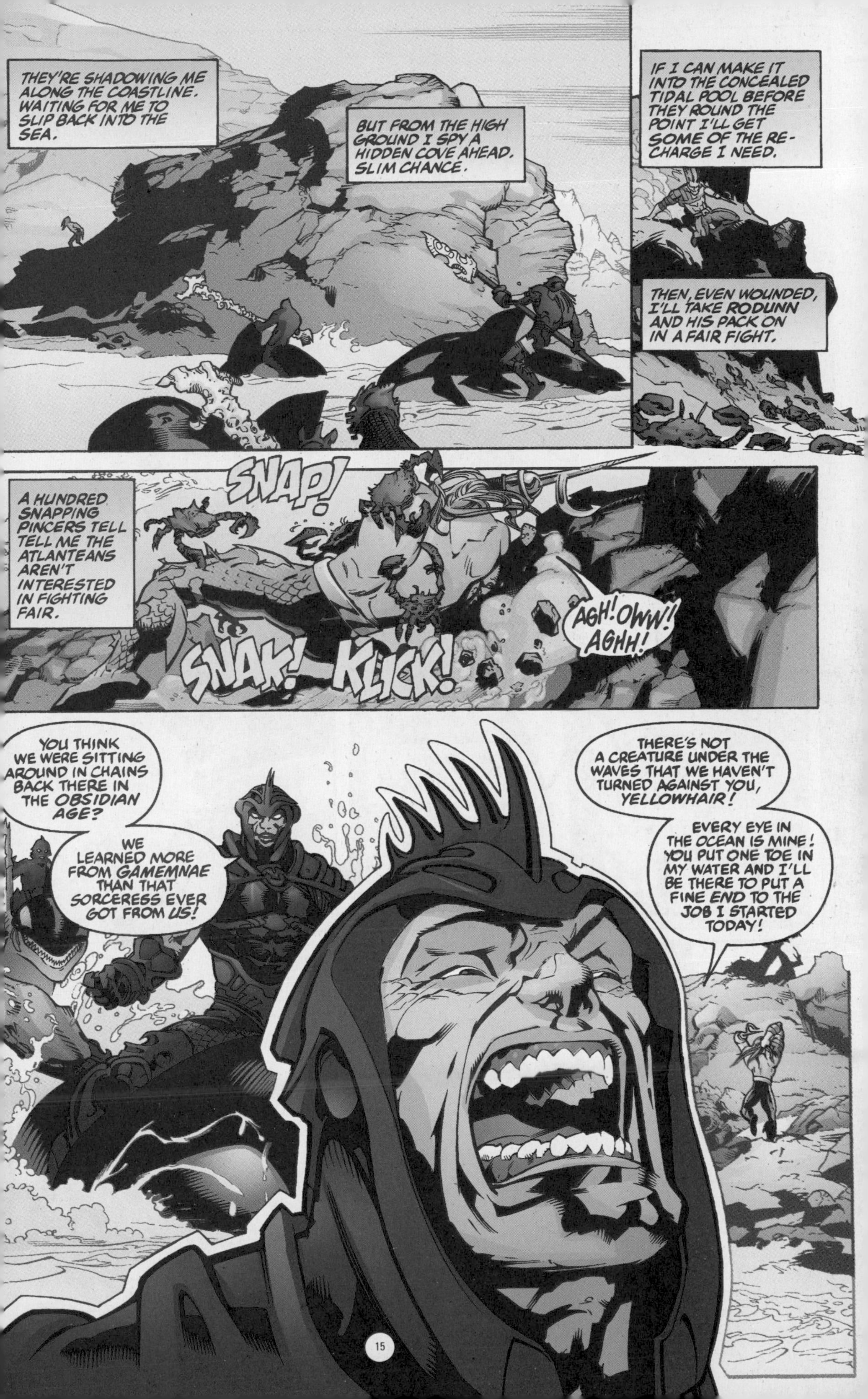
THEY'RE SHADOWING ME ALONG THE COASTLINE. WAITING FOR ME TO SLIP BACK INTO THE SEA.
BUT FROM THE HIGH GROUND I SPY A HIDDEN COVE AHEAD. SLIM CHANCE.
IF I CAN MAKE IT INTO THE CONCEALED TIDAL POOL BEFORE THEY ROUND THE POINT I'LL GET SOME OF THE RE-CHARGE I NEED.
THEN, EVEN WOUNDED, I'LL TAKE RODUNN AND HIS PACK ON IN A FAIR FIGHT.
A HUNDRED SNAPPING PINCERS TELL TELL ME THE ATLANTEANS AREN'T INTERESTED IN FIGHTING FAIR.
SNAP!
SNAK! KLICK!
AGH! OWW! AGHH!
YOU THINK WE WERE SITTING AROUND IN CHAINS BACK THERE IN THE OBSIDIAN AGE?
WE LEARNED MORE FROM GAMEMNAE THAN THAT SORCERESS EVER GOT FROM US!
THERE'S NOT A CREATURE UNDER THE WAVES THAT WE HAVEN'T TURNED AGAINST YOU, YELLOWHAIR!
EVERY EYE IN THE OCEAN IS MINE! YOU PUT ONE TOE IN MY WATER AND I'LL BE THERE TO PUT A FINE END TO THE JOB I STARTED TODAY!

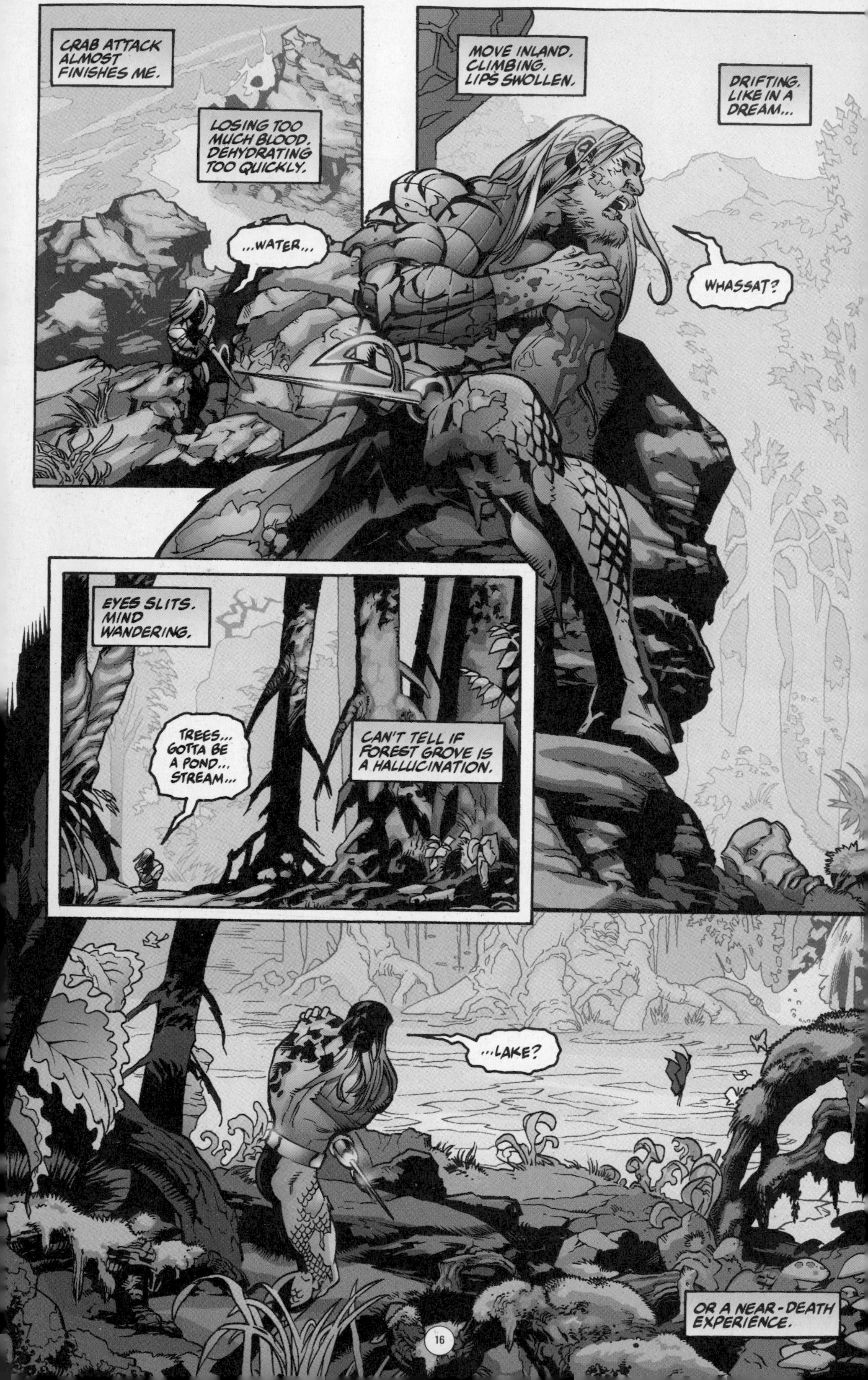
CRAB ATTACK ALMOST FINISHES ME.
LOSING TOO MUCH BLOOD. DEHYDRATING TOO QUICKLY.
...WATER...
MOVE INLAND. CLIMBING. LIPS SWOLLEN.
DRIFTING, LIKE IN A DREAM...
WHASSAT?
EYES SLITS. MIND WANDERING.
TREES... GOTTA BE A POND... STREAM...
CAN'T TELL IF FOREST GROVE IS A HALLUCINATION.
...LAKE?
OR A NEAR-DEATH EXPERIENCE.

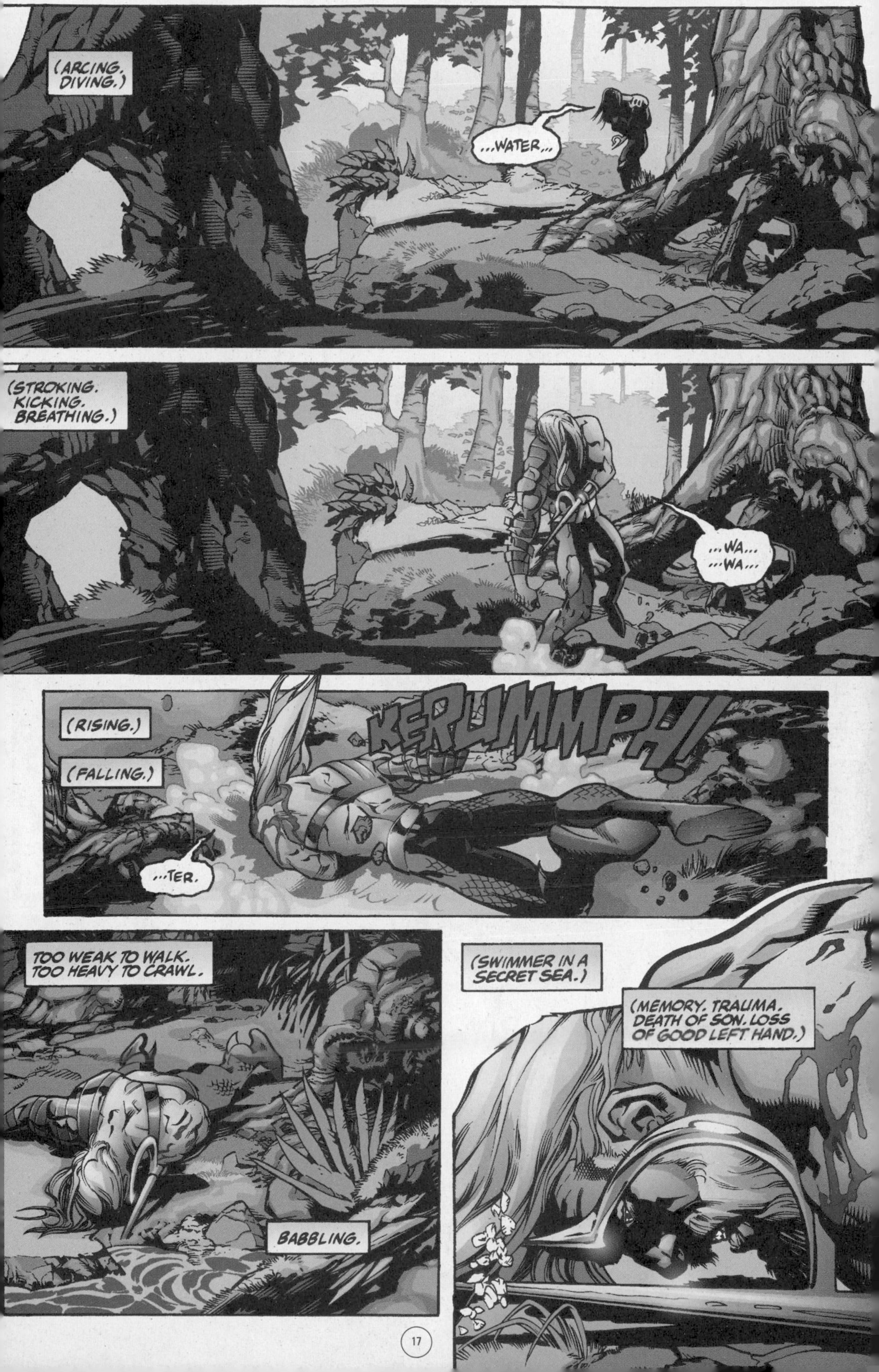
(ARCING. DIVING.)
...WATER...
(STROKING. KICKING. BREATHING.)
...WA... ...WA...
KERUMMPH!
(RISING.)
(FALLING.)
...TER.
TOO WEAK TO WALK. TOO HEAVY TO CRAWL.
BABBLING.
(SWIMMER IN A SECRET SEA.)
(MEMORY. TRAUMA. DEATH OF SON. LOSS OF GOOD LEFT HAND.)

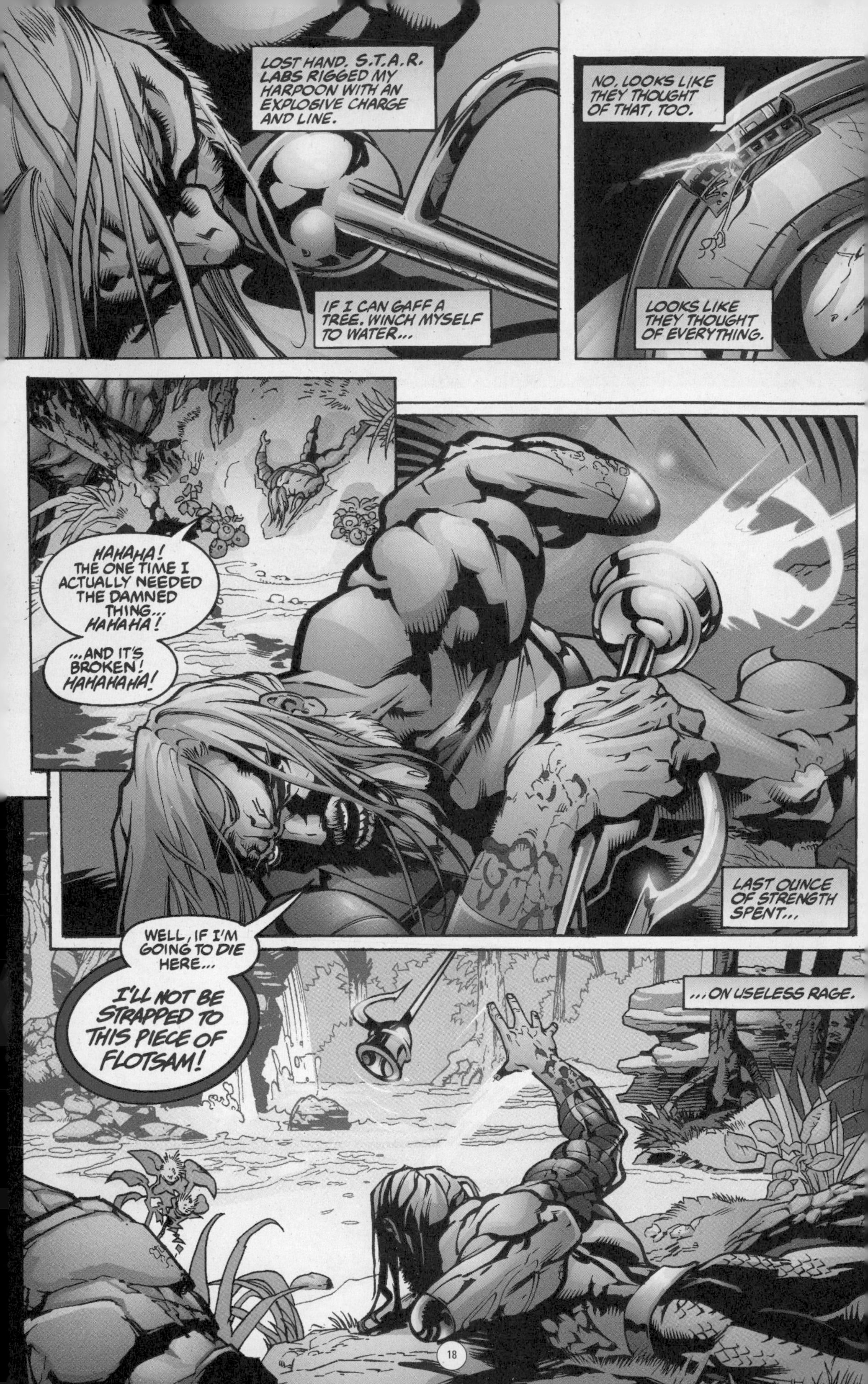
LOST HAND. S.T.A.R. LABS RIGGED MY HARPOON WITH AN EXPLOSIVE CHARGE AND LINE.
IF I CAN GAFF A TREE, WINCH MYSELF TO WATER...
NO, LOOKS LIKE THEY THOUGHT OF THAT, TOO.
LOOKS LIKE THEY THOUGHT OF EVERYTHING.
HAHAHA! THE ONE TIME I ACTUALLY NEEDED THE DAMNED THING... HAHAHA!
...AND IT'S BROKEN! HAHAHAHA!
LAST OUNCE OF STRENGTH SPENT...
...ON USELESS RAGE.
WELL, IF I'M GOING TO DIE HERE...
I'LL NOT BE STRAPPED TO THIS PIECE OF FLOTSAM!

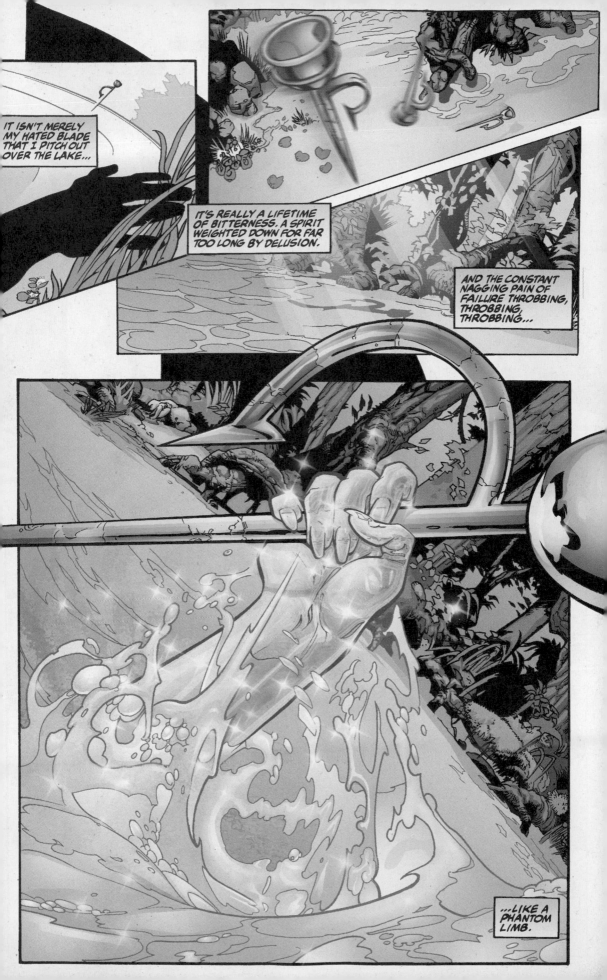

IT ISN'T MERELY MY HATED BLADE THAT I PITCH OUT OVER THE LAKE...

IT'S REALLY A LIFETIME OF BITTERNESS. A SPIRIT WEIGHTED DOWN FOR FAR TOO LONG BY DELUSION.

AND THE CONSTANT NAGGING PAIN OF FAILURE THROBBING, THROBBING, THROBBING...

...LIKE A PHANTOM LIMB.

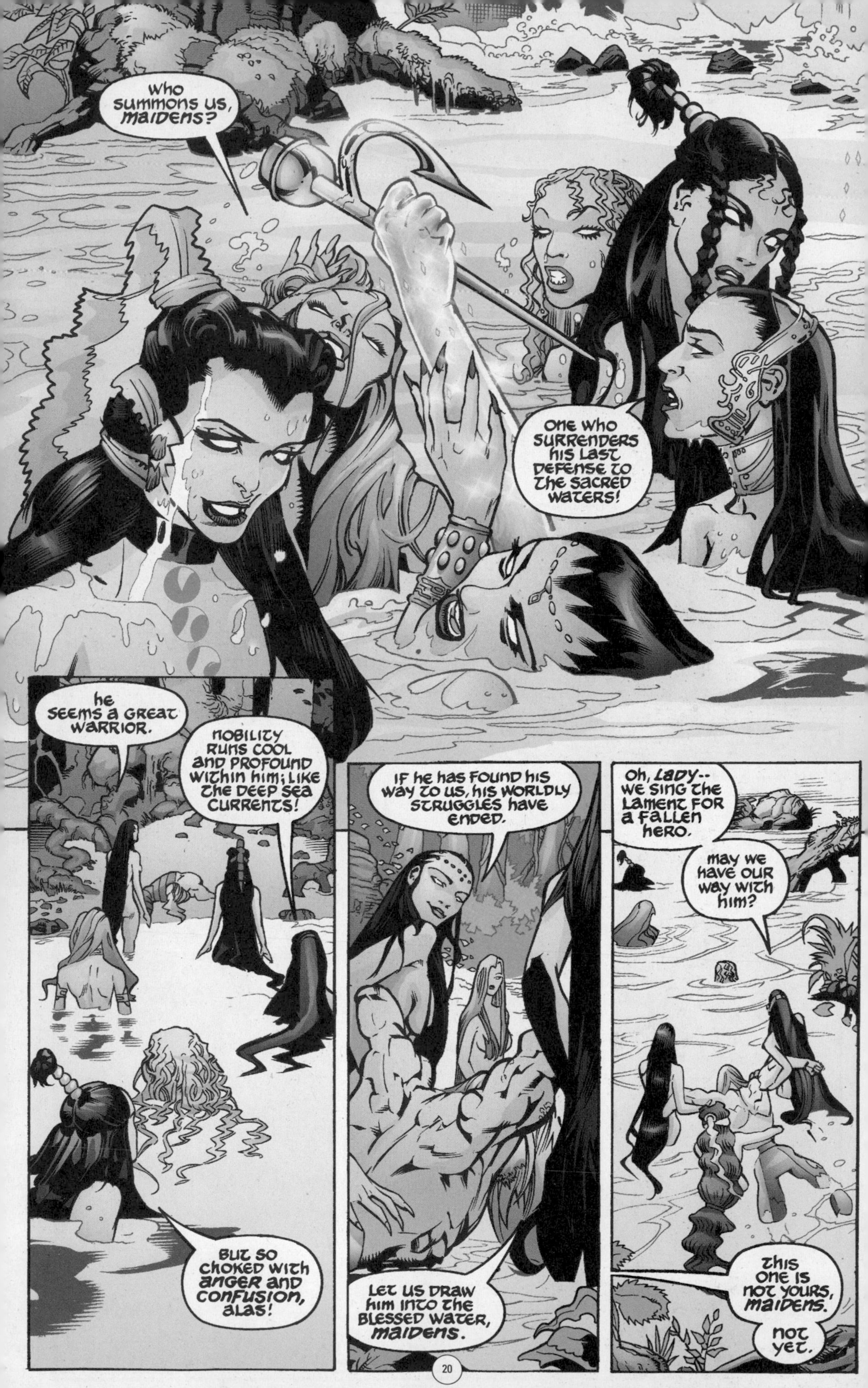

Who summons us, maidens?
One who surrenders his last defense to the sacred waters!
He seems a great warrior.
Nobility runs cool and profound within him; like the deep sea currents!
But so choked with anger and confusion, alas!
If he has found his way to us, his worldly struggles have ended.
Let us draw him into the blessed water, maidens.
Oh, Lady-- we sing the lament for a fallen hero.
May we have our way with him?
This one is not yours, maidens.
Not yet.

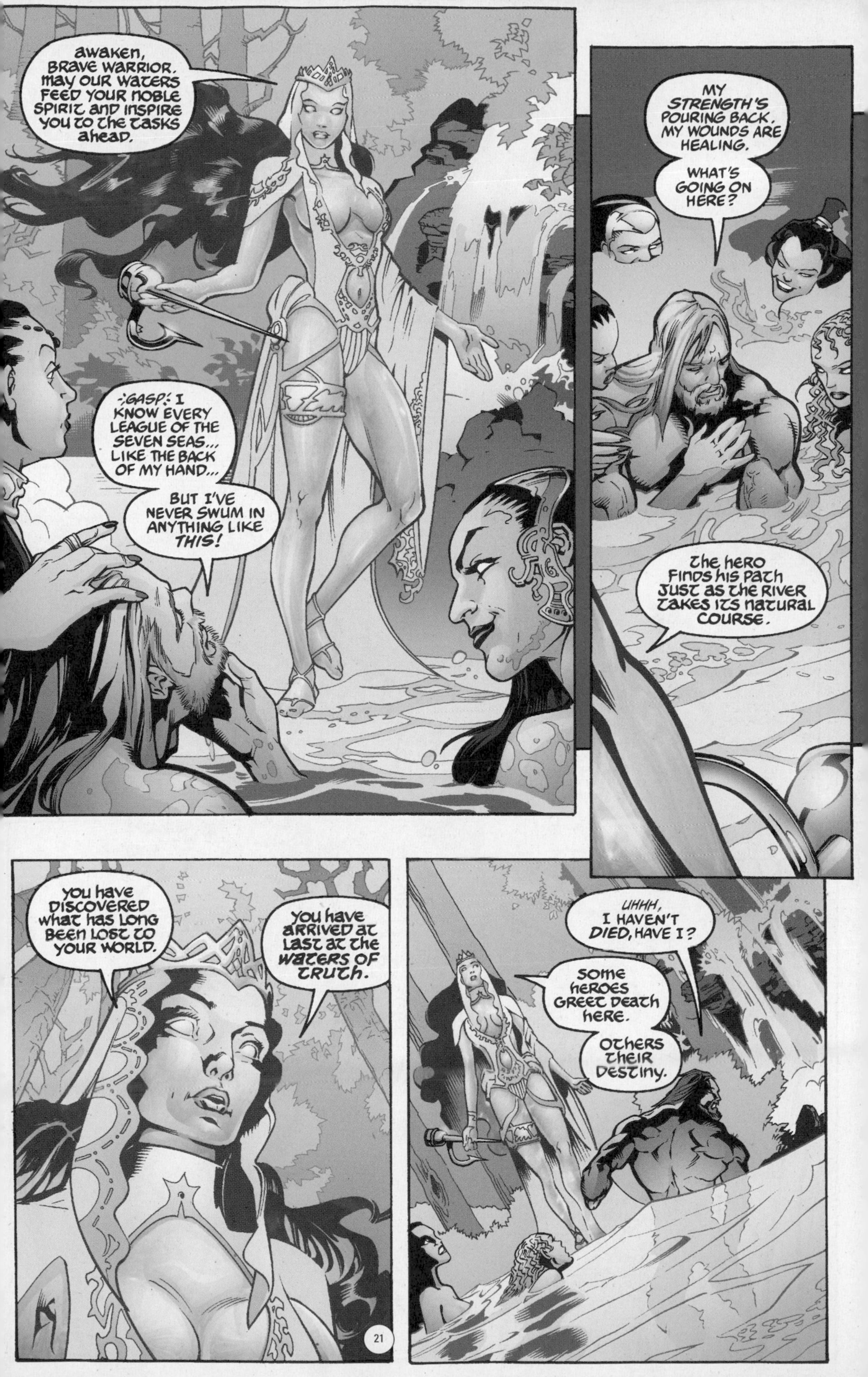
awaken, brave warrior. may our waters feed your noble spirit and inspire you to the tasks ahead.
GASP I KNOW EVERY LEAGUE OF THE SEVEN SEAS... LIKE THE BACK OF MY HAND...
BUT I'VE NEVER SWUM IN ANYTHING LIKE THIS!
MY STRENGTH'S POURING BACK. MY WOUNDS ARE HEALING.
WHAT'S GOING ON HERE?
The hero finds his path just as the river takes its natural course.
you have discovered what has long been lost to your world.
you have arrived at last at the waters of truth.
UHHH, I HAVEN'T DIED, HAVE I?
Some heroes greet death here.
Others their destiny.

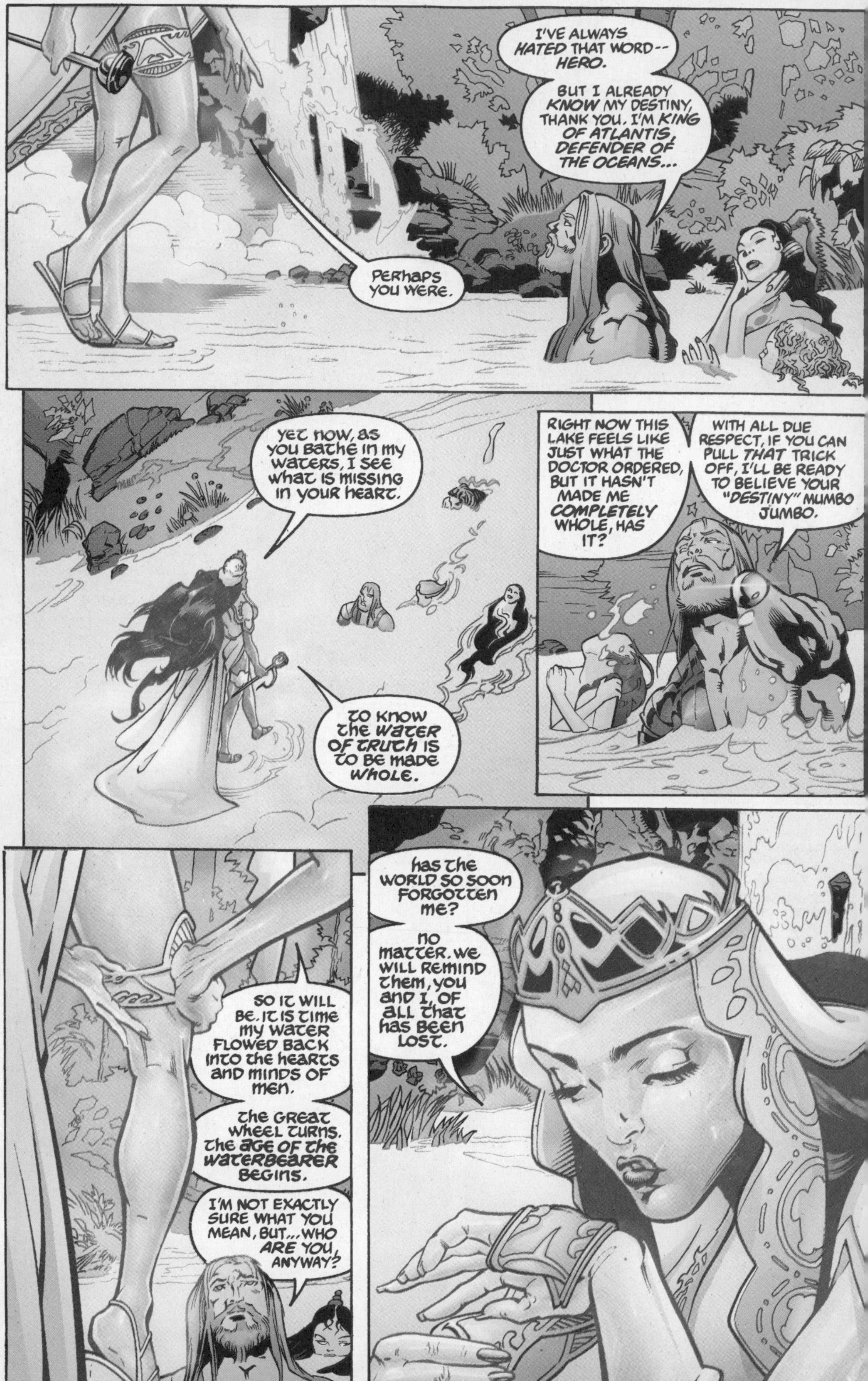
I'VE ALWAYS HATED THAT WORD-- HERO.
BUT I ALREADY KNOW MY DESTINY, THANK YOU. I'M KING OF ATLANTIS, DEFENDER OF THE OCEANS...
PERHAPS YOU WERE.
YET NOW, AS YOU BATHE IN MY WATERS, I SEE WHAT IS MISSING IN YOUR HEART.
TO KNOW THE WATER OF TRUTH IS TO BE MADE WHOLE.
RIGHT NOW THIS LAKE FEELS LIKE JUST WHAT THE DOCTOR ORDERED, BUT IT HASN'T MADE ME COMPLETELY WHOLE, HAS IT?
WITH ALL DUE RESPECT, IF YOU CAN PULL THAT TRICK OFF, I'LL BE READY TO BELIEVE YOUR "DESTINY" MUMBO JUMBO.
SO IT WILL BE. IT IS TIME MY WATER FLOWED BACK INTO THE HEARTS AND MINDS OF MEN.
THE GREAT WHEEL TURNS. THE AGE OF THE WATERBEARER BEGINS.
I'M NOT EXACTLY SURE WHAT YOU MEAN, BUT... WHO ARE YOU, ANYWAY?
HAS THE WORLD SO SOON FORGOTTEN ME?
NO MATTER. WE WILL REMIND THEM, YOU AND I, OF ALL THAT HAS BEEN LOST.

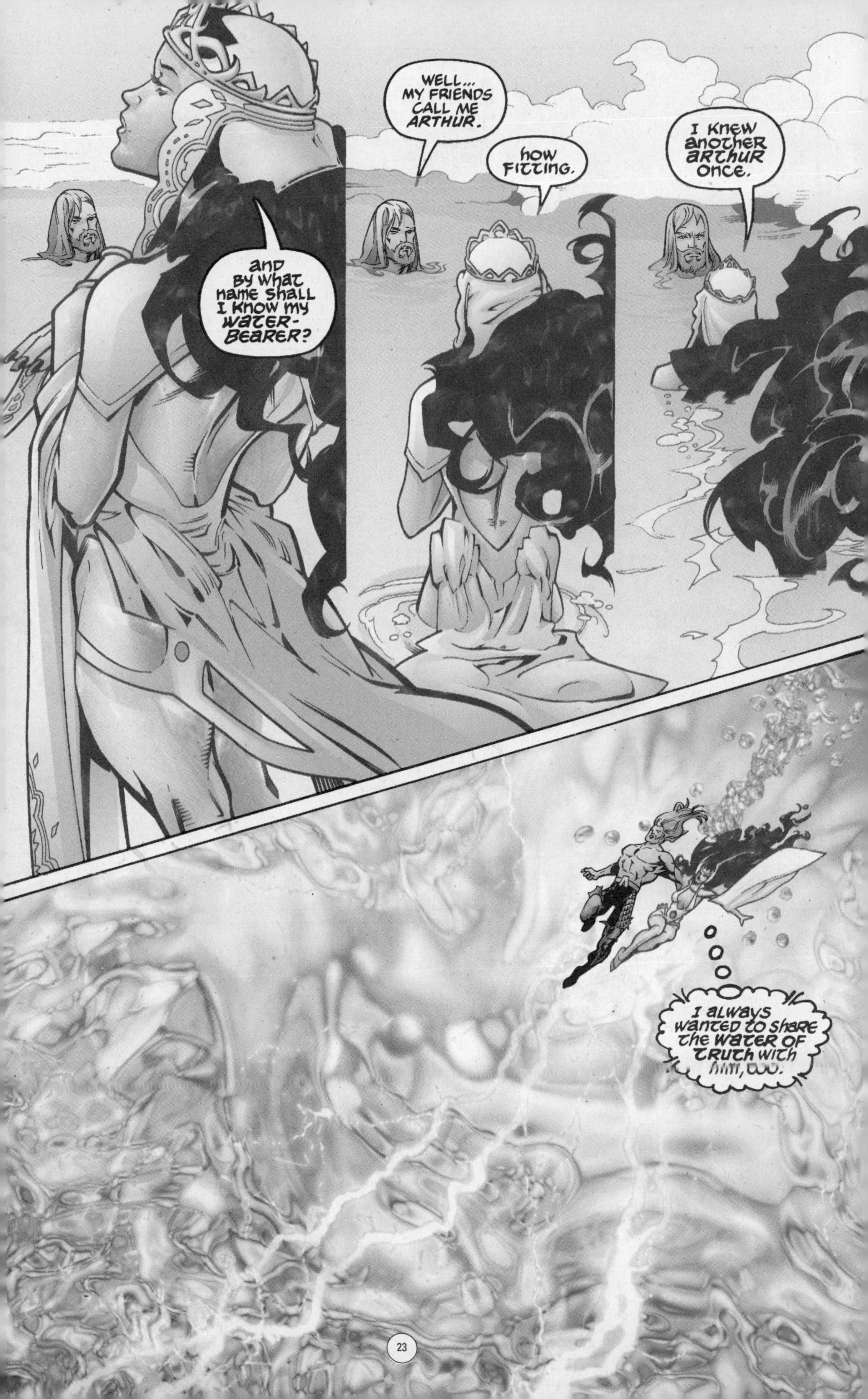
and by what name shall I know my water-bearer?
Well... my friends call me Arthur.
How fitting.
I knew another Arthur once.
I always wanted to share the water of truth with

JLA NEURAL NET ACTIVE. MARTIAN MANHUNTER, HERE. I'M CURRENTLY SEARCHING OVER THE CENTRAL ATLANTIC.

DIANA HERE, J'ONN. ANY SIGN OF ARTHUR, YET?

NOT A RIPPLE, PRINCESS. I DO WISH HE HADN'T BEEN SO HARD-SHELLED ABOUT OUR STAYING OUT OF ATLANTEAN POLITICS.

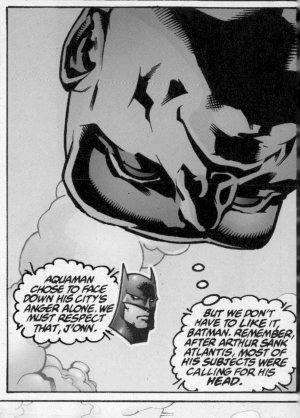

AQUAMAN CHOSE TO FACE DOWN HIS CITY'S ANGER ALONE. WE MUST RESPECT THAT, J'ONN.

BUT WE DON'T HAVE TO LIKE IT, BATMAN. REMEMBER, AFTER ARTHUR SANK ATLANTIS, MOST OF HIS SUBJECTS WERE CALLING FOR HIS HEAD.

I THINK OUR AMPHIBIAN FRIEND WOULD BE THE FIRST TO ADMIT HE CAN BE OBSTINATE SOMETIMES. WHAT'S YOUR LOCATION NOW?

CURRENTLY OVER THE ATLANTIC TRENCH, SUPERMAN. WHATEVER'S LEFT OF ATLANTIS SHOULD BE DIRECTLY BELOW ME.

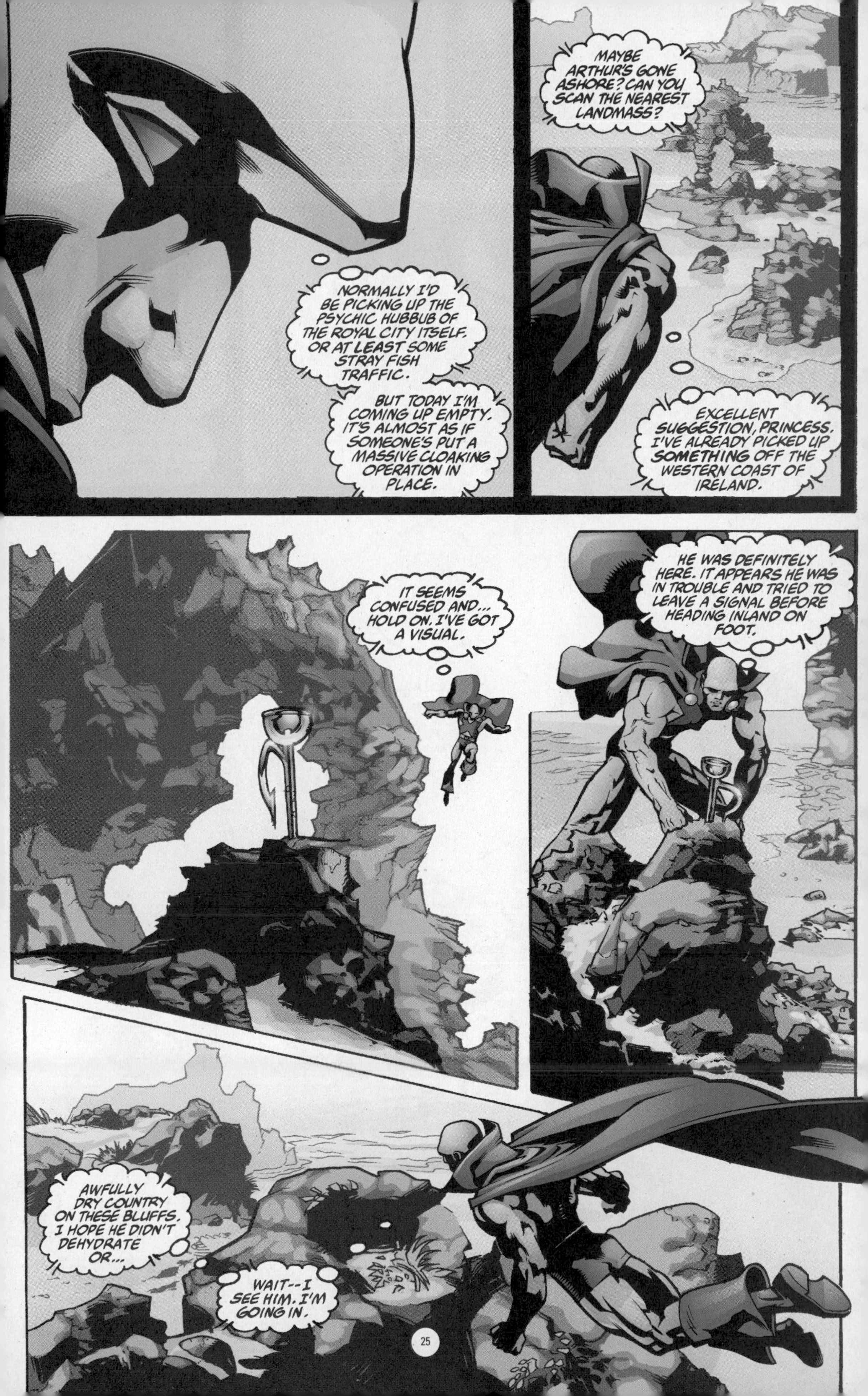
NORMALLY I'D BE PICKING UP THE PSYCHIC HUBBUB OF THE ROYAL CITY ITSELF. OR AT LEAST SOME STRAY FISH TRAFFIC.
BUT TODAY I'M COMING UP EMPTY. IT'S ALMOST AS IF SOMEONE'S PUT A MASSIVE CLOAKING OPERATION IN PLACE.
MAYBE ARTHUR'S GONE ASHORE? CAN YOU SCAN THE NEAREST LANDMASS?
EXCELLENT SUGGESTION, PRINCESS. I'VE ALREADY PICKED UP SOMETHING OFF THE WESTERN COAST OF IRELAND.
IT SEEMS CONFUSED AND... HOLD ON. I'VE GOT A VISUAL.
HE WAS DEFINITELY HERE. IT APPEARS HE WAS IN TROUBLE AND TRIED TO LEAVE A SIGNAL BEFORE HEADING INLAND ON FOOT.
AWFULLY DRY COUNTRY ON THESE BLUFFS. I HOPE HE DIDN'T DEHYDRATE OR...
WAIT--I SEE HIM. I'M GOING IN.

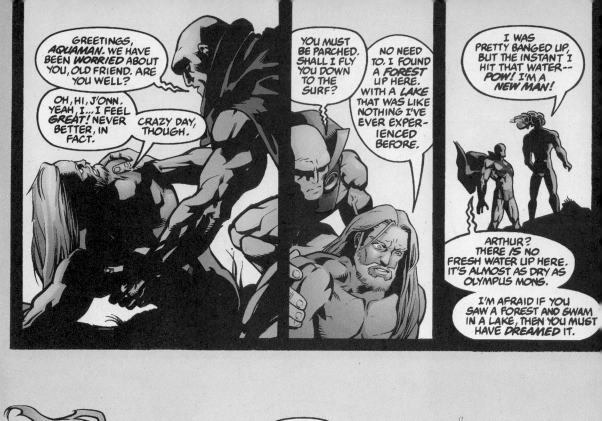

GREETINGS, AQUAMAN. WE HAVE BEEN *WORRIED* ABOUT YOU, OLD FRIEND. ARE YOU WELL?

OH, HI, J'ONN. YEAH, I... I FEEL *GREAT!* NEVER BETTER, IN FACT.

CRAZY DAY, THOUGH.

YOU MUST BE PARCHED. SHALL I FLY YOU DOWN TO THE SURF?

NO NEED TO. I FOUND A *FOREST* UP HERE. WITH A *LAKE* THAT WAS LIKE NOTHING I'VE EVER EXPERIENCED BEFORE.

I WAS PRETTY BANGED UP, BUT THE INSTANT I HIT THAT WATER-- *POW!* I'M A *NEW MAN!*

ARTHUR? THERE *IS* NO FRESH WATER UP HERE. IT'S ALMOST AS DRY AS OLYMPUS MONS.

I'M AFRAID IF YOU SAW A FOREST AND SWAM IN A LAKE, THEN YOU MUST HAVE *DREAMED* IT.

THINK SO, J'ONN?

THEN HOW DO WE EXPLAIN *THIS?*

NEXT:
TO DIE
BY THE
LIGHT OF
THE SEA!

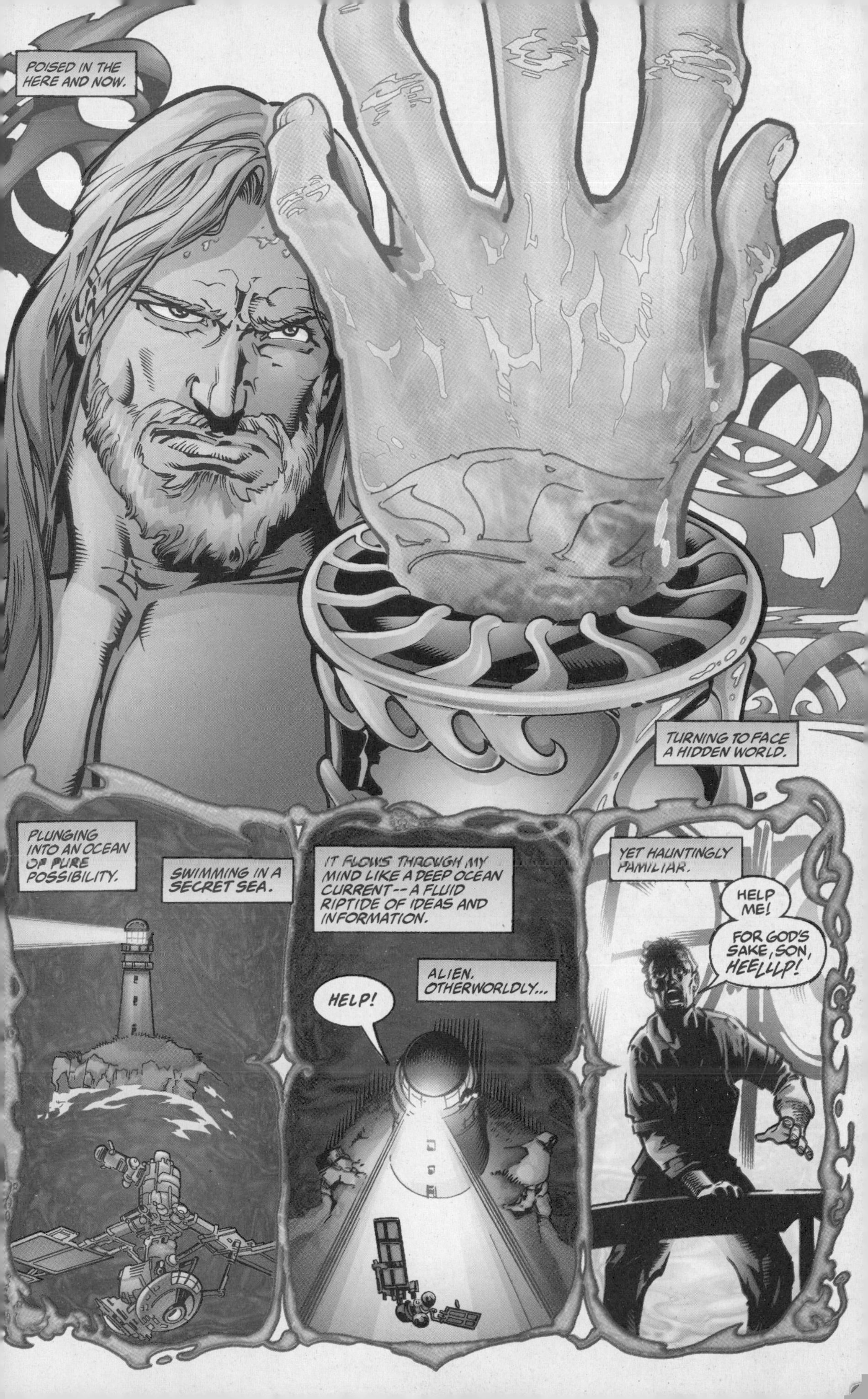
POISED IN THE HERE AND NOW.
TURNING TO FACE A HIDDEN WORLD.
PLUNGING INTO AN OCEAN OF PURE POSSIBILITY.
SWIMMING IN A SECRET SEA.
IT FLOWS THROUGH MY MIND LIKE A DEEP OCEAN CURRENT-- A FLUID RIPTIDE OF IDEAS AND INFORMATION.
ALIEN. OTHERWORLDLY...
HELP!
YET HAUNTINGLY FAMILIAR.
HELP ME!
FOR GOD'S SAKE, SON, HEELLLP!

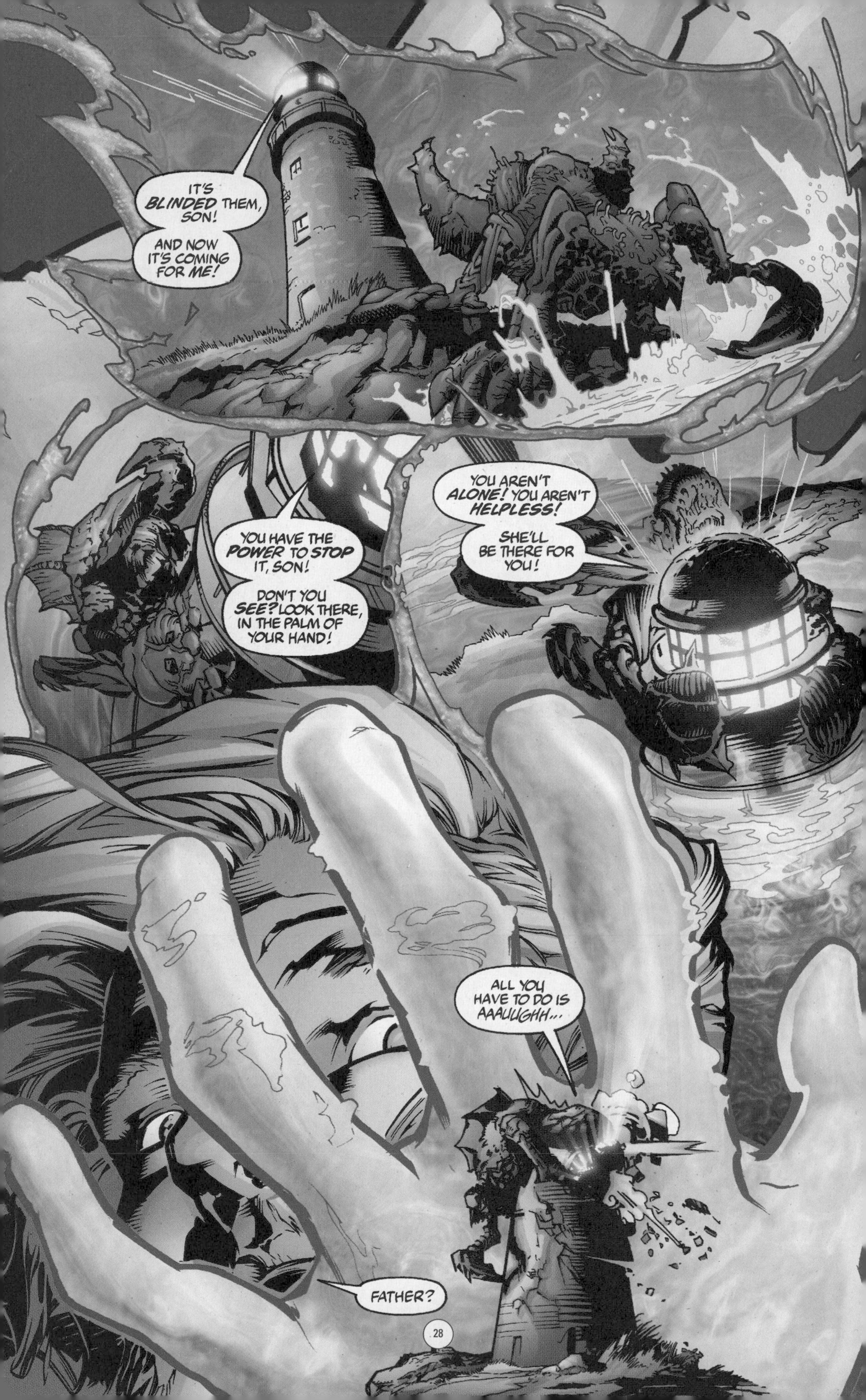

IT'S BLINDED THEM, SON!
AND NOW IT'S COMING FOR ME!
YOU HAVE THE POWER TO STOP IT, SON!
DON'T YOU SEE? LOOK THERE, IN THE PALM OF YOUR HAND!
YOU AREN'T ALONE! YOU AREN'T HELPLESS!
SHE'LL BE THERE FOR YOU!
ALL YOU HAVE TO DO IS AAAUUGHH...
FATHER?

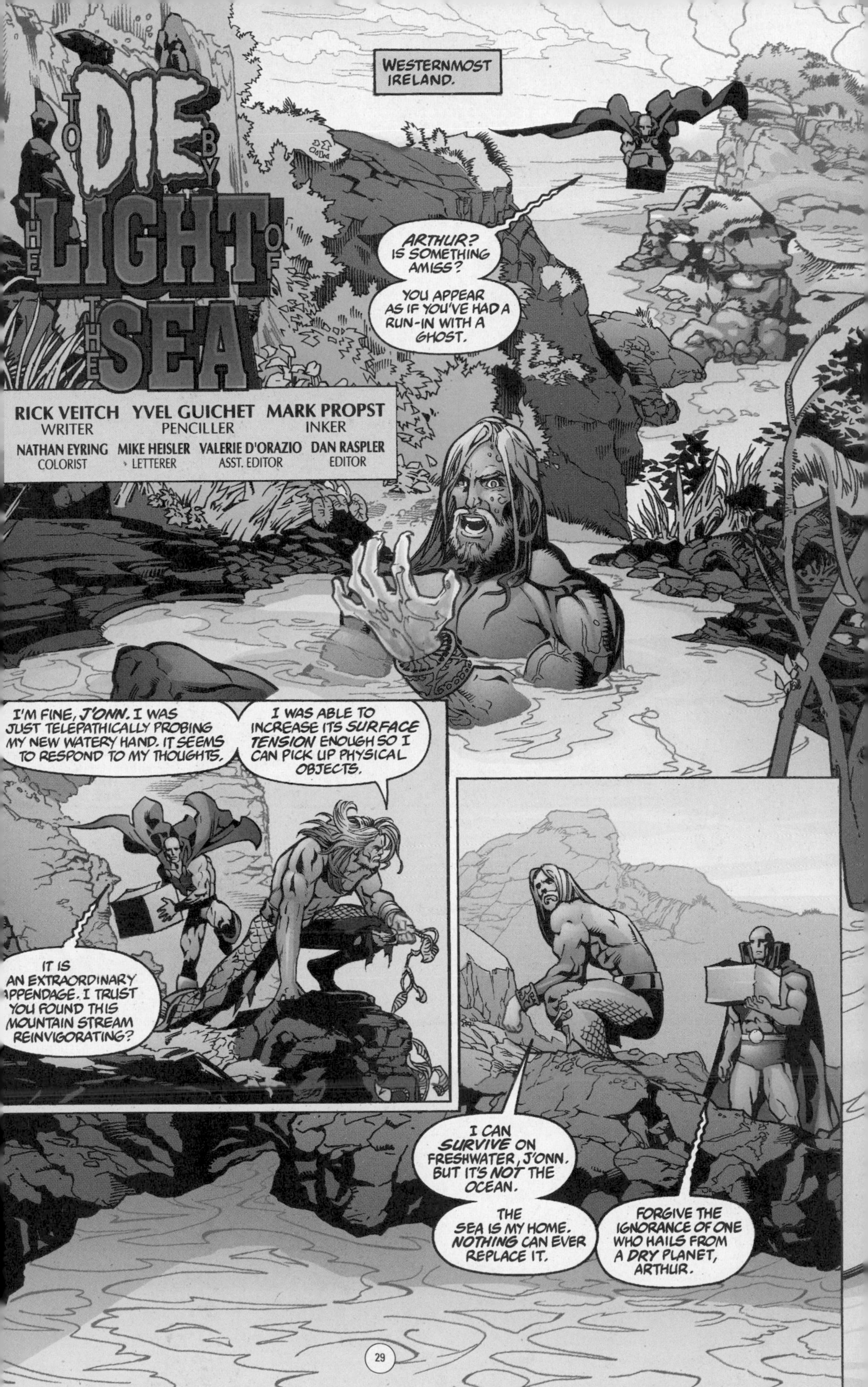
TO DIE BY THE LIGHT OF THE SEA
RICK VEITCH WRITER YVEL GUICHET PENCILLER MARK PROPST INKER
NATHAN EYRING COLORIST MIKE HEISLER LETTERER VALERIE D'ORAZIO ASST. EDITOR DAN RASPLER EDITOR
WESTERNMOST IRELAND.
ARTHUR? IS SOMETHING AMISS?
YOU APPEAR AS IF YOU'VE HAD A RUN-IN WITH A GHOST.
I'M FINE, J'ONN. I WAS JUST TELEPATHICALLY PROBING MY NEW WATERY HAND. IT SEEMS TO RESPOND TO MY THOUGHTS.
I WAS ABLE TO INCREASE ITS SURFACE TENSION ENOUGH SO I CAN PICK UP PHYSICAL OBJECTS.
IT IS AN EXTRAORDINARY APPENDAGE. I TRUST YOU FOUND THIS MOUNTAIN STREAM REINVIGORATING?
I CAN SURVIVE ON FRESHWATER, J'ONN. BUT IT'S NOT THE OCEAN.
THE SEA IS MY HOME. NOTHING CAN EVER REPLACE IT.
FORGIVE THE IGNORANCE OF ONE WHO HAILS FROM A DRY PLANET, ARTHUR.

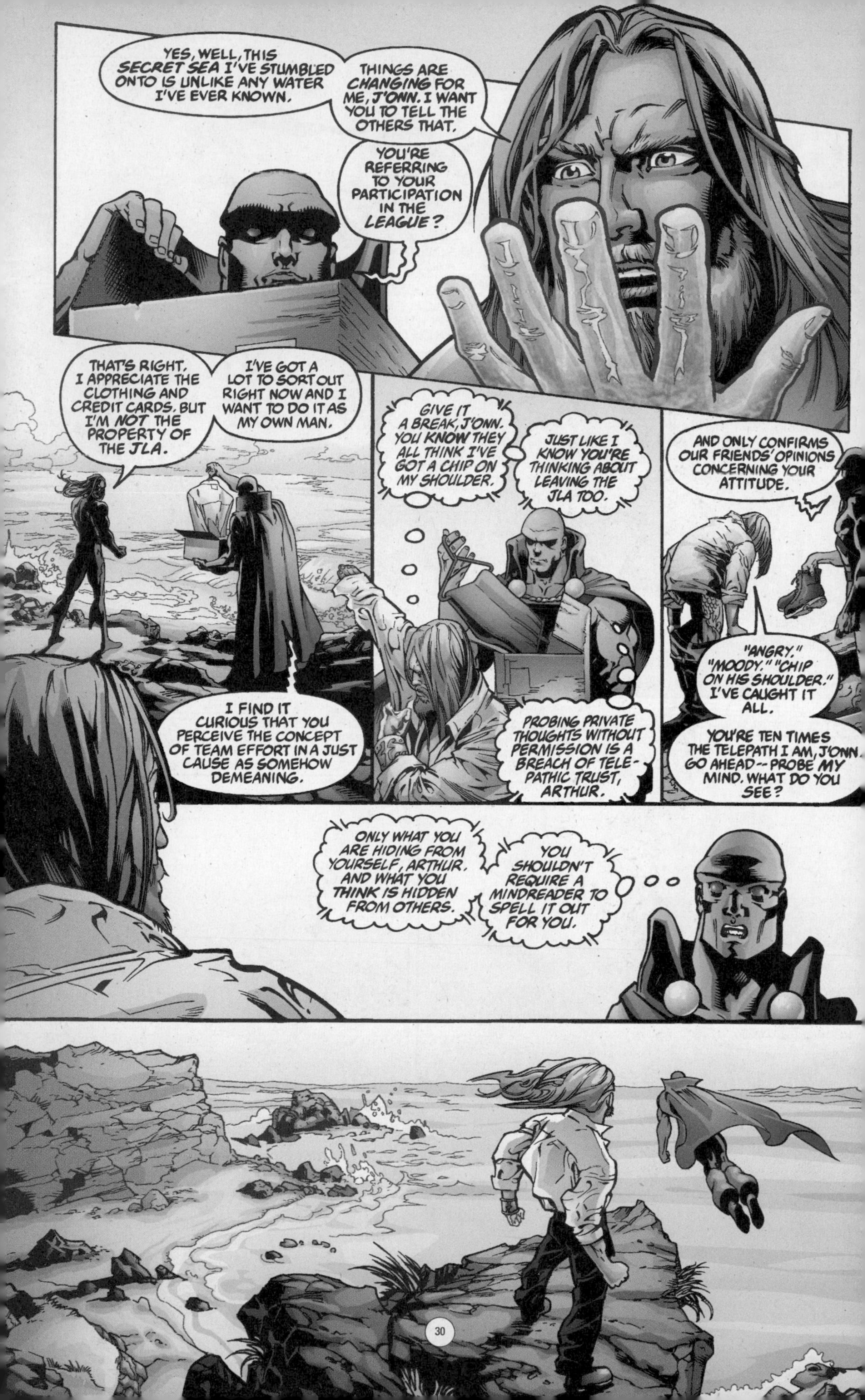

YES, WELL, THIS SECRET SEA I'VE STUMBLED ONTO IS UNLIKE ANY WATER I'VE EVER KNOWN.
THINGS ARE CHANGING FOR ME, J'ONN. I WANT YOU TO TELL THE OTHERS THAT.
YOU'RE REFERRING TO YOUR PARTICIPATION IN THE LEAGUE?
THAT'S RIGHT. I APPRECIATE THE CLOTHING AND CREDIT CARDS. BUT I'M NOT THE PROPERTY OF THE JLA.
I'VE GOT A LOT TO SORT OUT RIGHT NOW AND I WANT TO DO IT AS MY OWN MAN.
I FIND IT CURIOUS THAT YOU PERCEIVE THE CONCEPT OF TEAM EFFORT IN A JUST CAUSE AS SOMEHOW DEMEANING.
GIVE IT A BREAK, J'ONN. YOU KNOW THEY ALL THINK I'VE GOT A CHIP ON MY SHOULDER.
JUST LIKE I KNOW YOU'RE THINKING ABOUT LEAVING THE JLA TOO.
PROBING PRIVATE THOUGHTS WITHOUT PERMISSION IS A BREACH OF TELEPATHIC TRUST, ARTHUR.
AND ONLY CONFIRMS OUR FRIENDS' OPINIONS CONCERNING YOUR ATTITUDE.
"ANGRY." "MOODY." "CHIP ON HIS SHOULDER." I'VE CAUGHT IT ALL.
YOU'RE TEN TIMES THE TELEPATH I AM, J'ONN. GO AHEAD--PROBE MY MIND. WHAT DO YOU SEE?
ONLY WHAT YOU ARE HIDING FROM YOURSELF, ARTHUR. AND WHAT YOU THINK IS HIDDEN FROM OTHERS.
YOU SHOULDN'T REQUIRE A MINDREADER TO SPELL IT OUT FOR YOU.

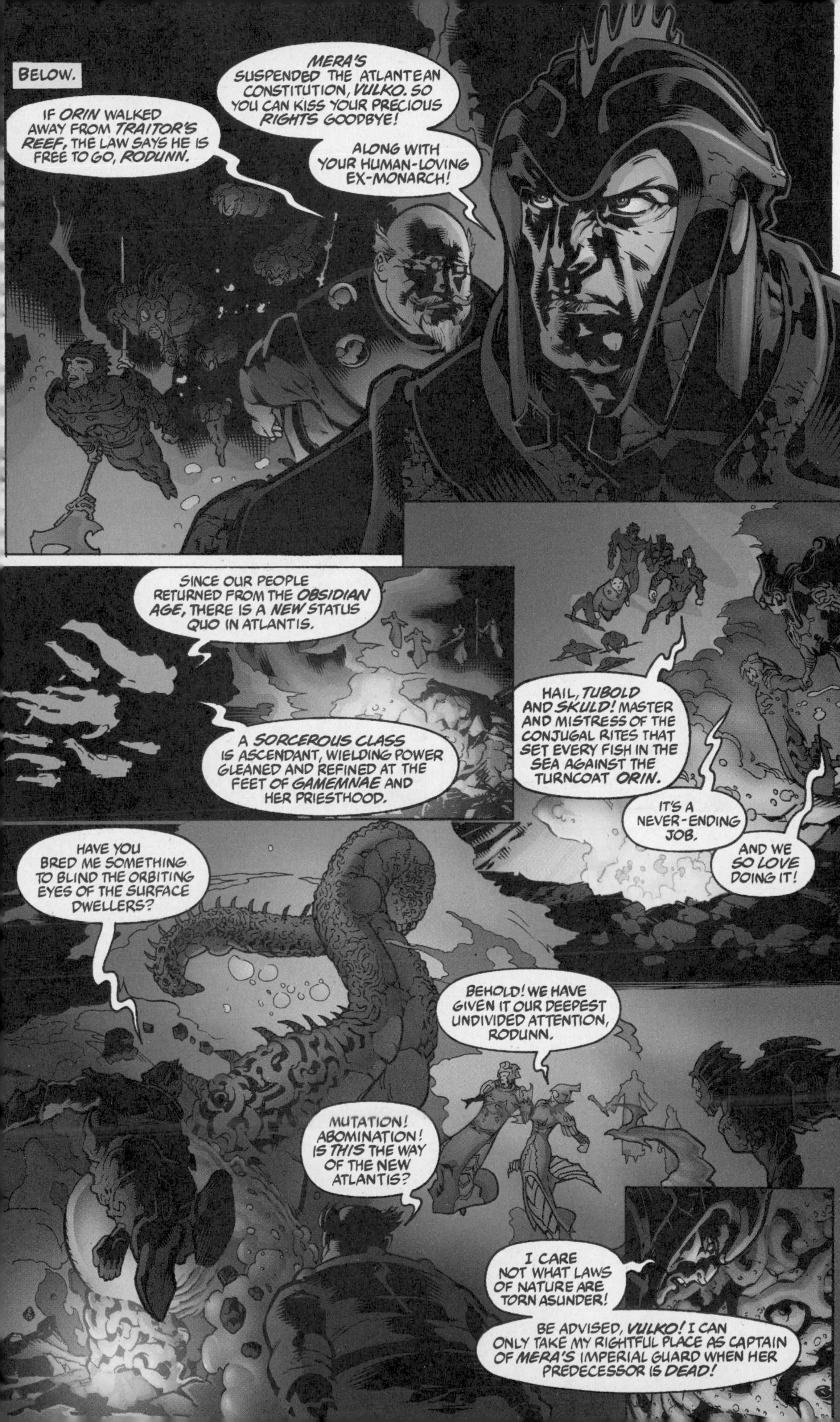
BELOW.
IF ORIN WALKED AWAY FROM TRAITOR'S REEF, THE LAW SAYS HE IS FREE TO GO, RODUNN.
MERA'S SUSPENDED THE ATLANTEAN CONSTITUTION, VULKO. SO YOU CAN KISS YOUR PRECIOUS RIGHTS GOODBYE!
ALONG WITH YOUR HUMAN-LOVING EX-MONARCH!
SINCE OUR PEOPLE RETURNED FROM THE OBSIDIAN AGE, THERE IS A NEW STATUS QUO IN ATLANTIS.
A SORCEROUS CLASS IS ASCENDANT, WIELDING POWER GLEANED AND REFINED AT THE FEET OF GAMEMNAE AND HER PRIESTHOOD.
HAIL, TUBOLD AND SKULD! MASTER AND MISTRESS OF THE CONJUGAL RITES THAT SET EVERY FISH IN THE SEA AGAINST THE TURNCOAT ORIN.
IT'S A NEVER-ENDING JOB.
AND WE SO LOVE DOING IT!
HAVE YOU BRED ME SOMETHING TO BLIND THE ORBITING EYES OF THE SURFACE DWELLERS?
BEHOLD! WE HAVE GIVEN IT OUR DEEPEST UNDIVIDED ATTENTION, RODUNN.
MUTATION! ABOMINATION! IS THIS THE WAY OF THE NEW ATLANTIS?
I CARE NOT WHAT LAWS OF NATURE ARE TORN ASUNDER!
BE ADVISED, VULKO! I CAN ONLY TAKE MY RIGHTFUL PLACE AS CAPTAIN OF MERA'S IMPERIAL GUARD WHEN HER PREDECESSOR IS DEAD!

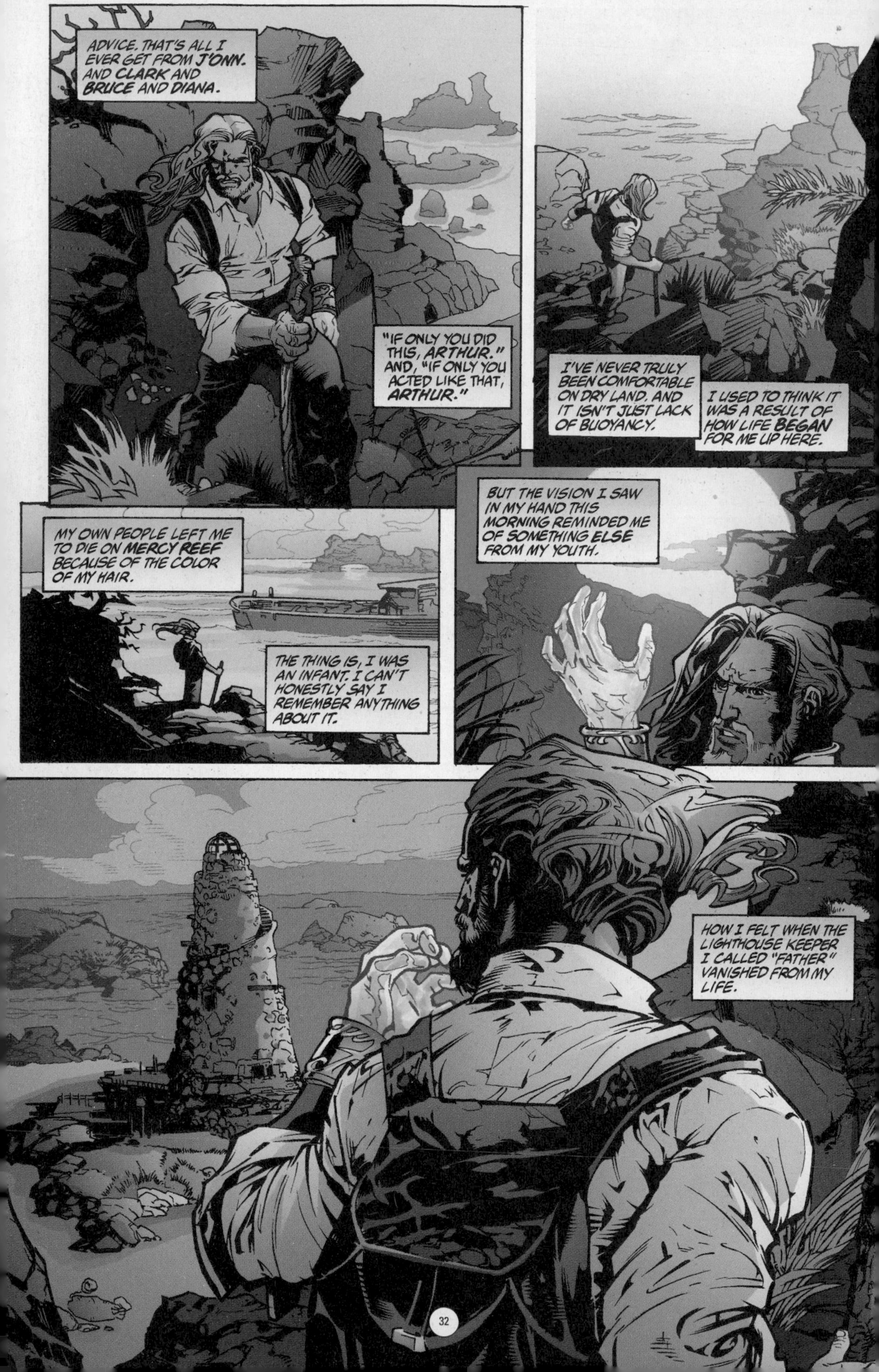

ADVICE. THAT'S ALL I EVER GET FROM J'ONN. AND CLARK AND BRUCE AND DIANA.
"IF ONLY YOU DID THIS, ARTHUR." AND, "IF ONLY YOU ACTED LIKE THAT, ARTHUR."
I'VE NEVER TRULY BEEN COMFORTABLE ON DRY LAND. AND IT ISN'T JUST LACK OF BUOYANCY.
I USED TO THINK IT WAS A RESULT OF HOW LIFE BEGAN FOR ME UP HERE.
MY OWN PEOPLE LEFT ME TO DIE ON MERCY REEF BECAUSE OF THE COLOR OF MY HAIR.
THE THING IS, I WAS AN INFANT. I CAN'T HONESTLY SAY I REMEMBER ANYTHING ABOUT IT.
BUT THE VISION I SAW IN MY HAND THIS MORNING REMINDED ME OF SOMETHING ELSE FROM MY YOUTH.
HOW I FELT WHEN THE LIGHTHOUSE KEEPER I CALLED "FATHER" VANISHED FROM MY LIFE.

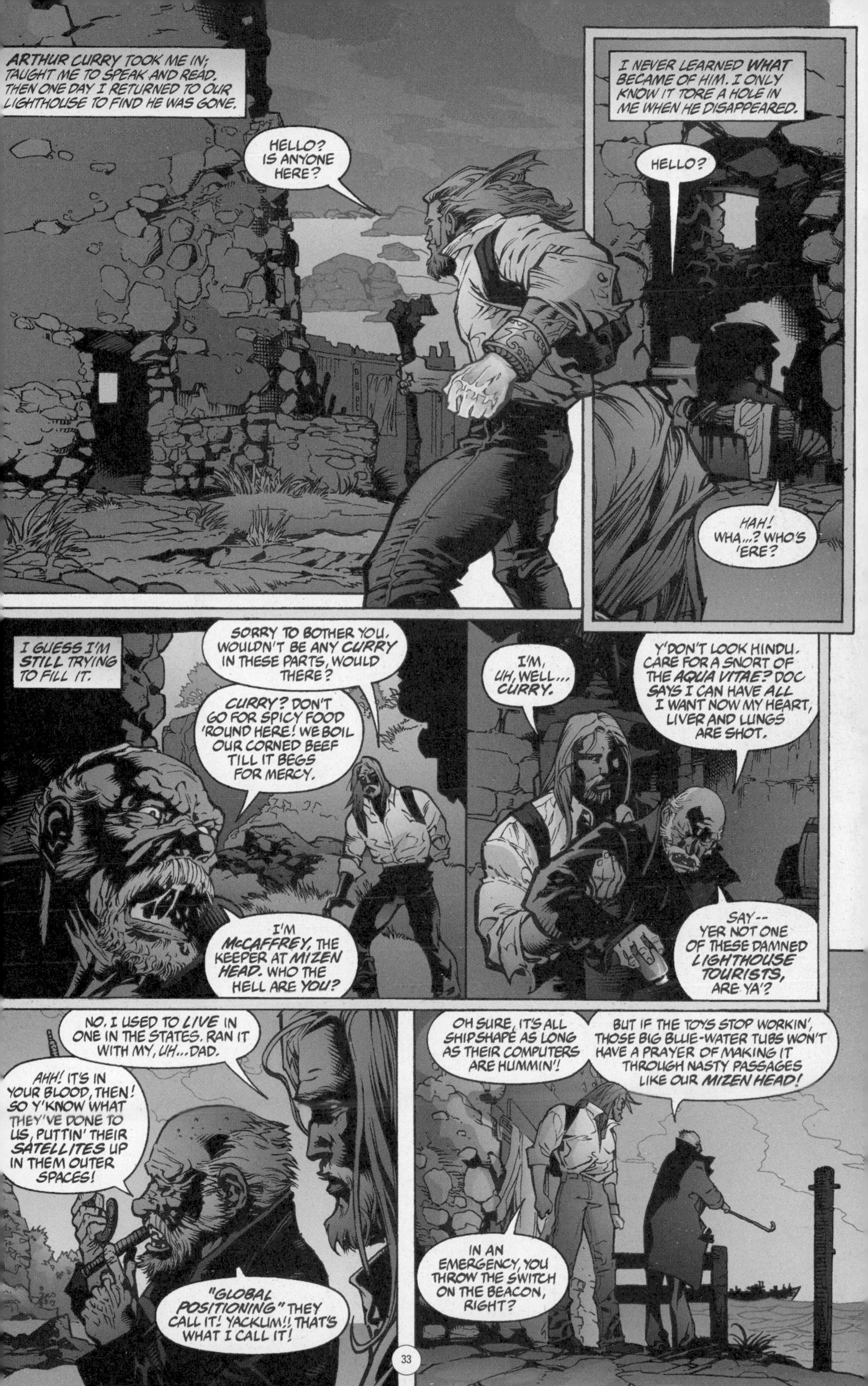

ARTHUR CURRY TOOK ME IN; TAUGHT ME TO SPEAK AND READ. THEN ONE DAY I RETURNED TO OUR LIGHTHOUSE TO FIND HE WAS GONE.
HELLO? IS ANYONE HERE?
I NEVER LEARNED WHAT BECAME OF HIM. I ONLY KNOW IT TORE A HOLE IN ME WHEN HE DISAPPEARED.
HELLO?
HAH! WHA...? WHO'S 'ERE?
I GUESS I'M STILL TRYING TO FILL IT.
SORRY TO BOTHER YOU. WOULDN'T BE ANY CURRY IN THESE PARTS, WOULD THERE?
CURRY? DON'T GO FOR SPICY FOOD 'ROUND HERE! WE BOIL OUR CORNED BEEF TILL IT BEGS FOR MERCY.
I'M McCAFFREY, THE KEEPER AT MIZEN HEAD. WHO THE HELL ARE YOU?
I'M, UH, WELL... CURRY.
Y'DON'T LOOK HINDU. CARE FOR A SNORT OF THE AQUA VITAE? DOC SAYS I CAN HAVE ALL I WANT NOW MY HEART, LIVER AND LUNGS ARE SHOT.
SAY-- YER NOT ONE OF THESE DAMNED LIGHTHOUSE TOURISTS, ARE YA'?
NO. I USED TO LIVE IN ONE IN THE STATES. RAN IT WITH MY, UH...DAD.
AHH! IT'S IN YOUR BLOOD, THEN! SO Y'KNOW WHAT THEY'VE DONE TO US, PUTTIN' THEIR SATELLITES UP IN THEM OUTER SPACES!
"GLOBAL POSITIONING" THEY CALL IT! YACKUM!! THAT'S WHAT I CALL IT!
OH SURE, IT'S ALL SHIPSHAPE AS LONG AS THEIR COMPUTERS ARE HUMMIN'!
BUT IF THE TOYS STOP WORKIN', THOSE BIG BLUE-WATER TUBS WON'T HAVE A PRAYER OF MAKING IT THROUGH NASTY PASSAGES LIKE OUR MIZEN HEAD!
IN AN EMERGENCY, YOU THROW THE SWITCH ON THE BEACON, RIGHT?

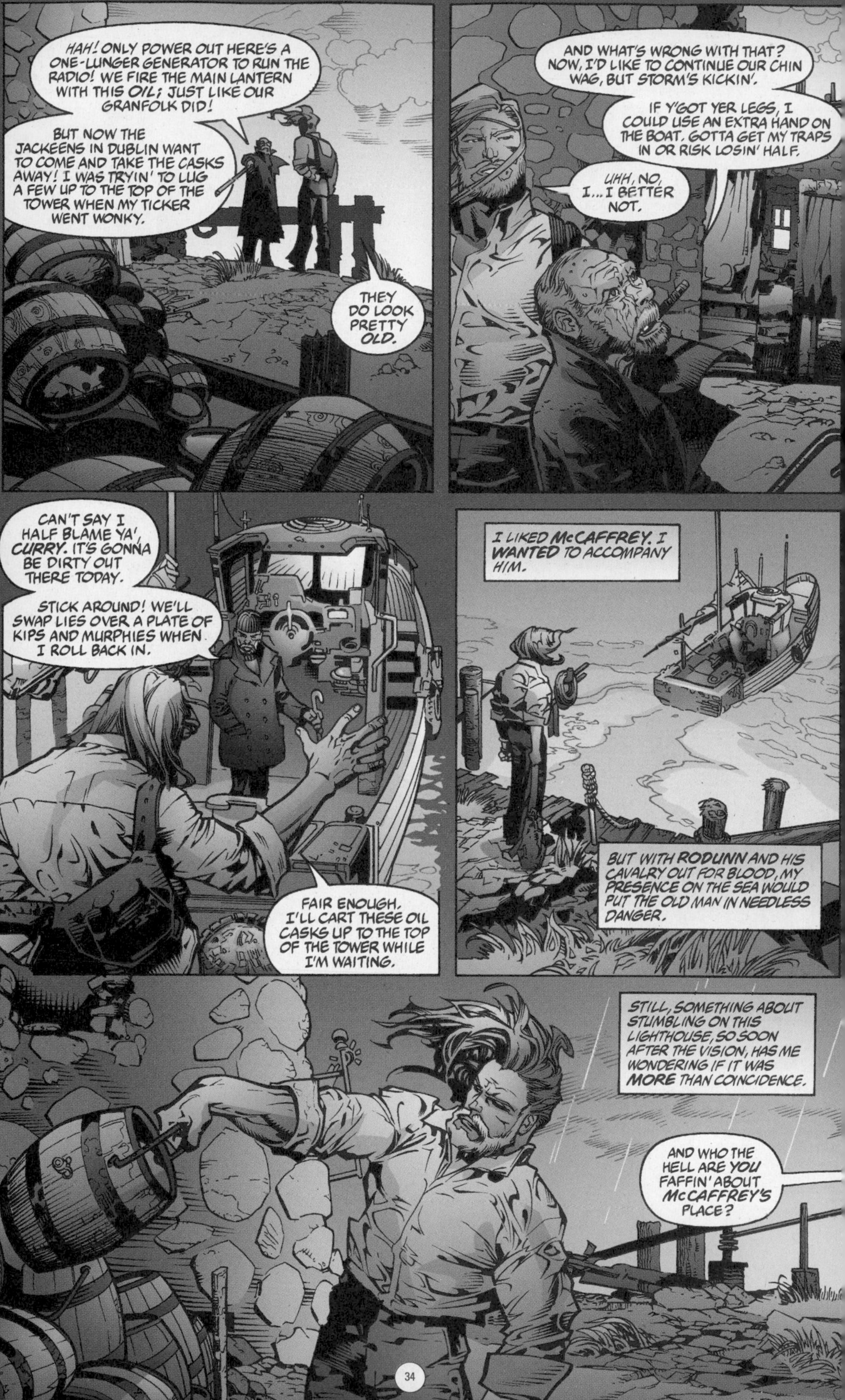
HAH! ONLY POWER OUT HERE'S A ONE-LUNGER GENERATOR TO RUN THE RADIO! WE FIRE THE MAIN LANTERN WITH THIS OIL; JUST LIKE OUR GRANFOLK DID!
BUT NOW THE JACKEENS IN DUBLIN WANT TO COME AND TAKE THE CASKS AWAY! I WAS TRYIN' TO LUG A FEW UP TO THE TOP OF THE TOWER WHEN MY TICKER WENT WONKY.
THEY DO LOOK PRETTY OLD.
AND WHAT'S WRONG WITH THAT? NOW, I'D LIKE TO CONTINUE OUR CHIN WAG, BUT STORM'S KICKIN'.
IF Y'GOT YER LEGS, I COULD USE AN EXTRA HAND ON THE BOAT. GOTTA GET MY TRAPS IN OR RISK LOSIN' HALF.
UHH, NO, I... I BETTER NOT.
CAN'T SAY I HALF BLAME YA', CURRY. IT'S GONNA BE DIRTY OUT THERE TODAY.
STICK AROUND! WE'LL SWAP LIES OVER A PLATE OF KIPS AND MURPHIES WHEN I ROLL BACK IN.
FAIR ENOUGH. I'LL CART THESE OIL CASKS UP TO THE TOP OF THE TOWER WHILE I'M WAITING.
I LIKED McCAFFREY. I WANTED TO ACCOMPANY HIM.
BUT WITH RODUNN AND HIS CAVALRY OUT FOR BLOOD, MY PRESENCE ON THE SEA WOULD PUT THE OLD MAN IN NEEDLESS DANGER.
STILL, SOMETHING ABOUT STUMBLING ON THIS LIGHTHOUSE, SO SOON AFTER THE VISION, HAS ME WONDERING IF IT WAS MORE THAN COINCIDENCE.
AND WHO THE HELL ARE YOU FAFFIN' ABOUT McCAFFREY'S PLACE?

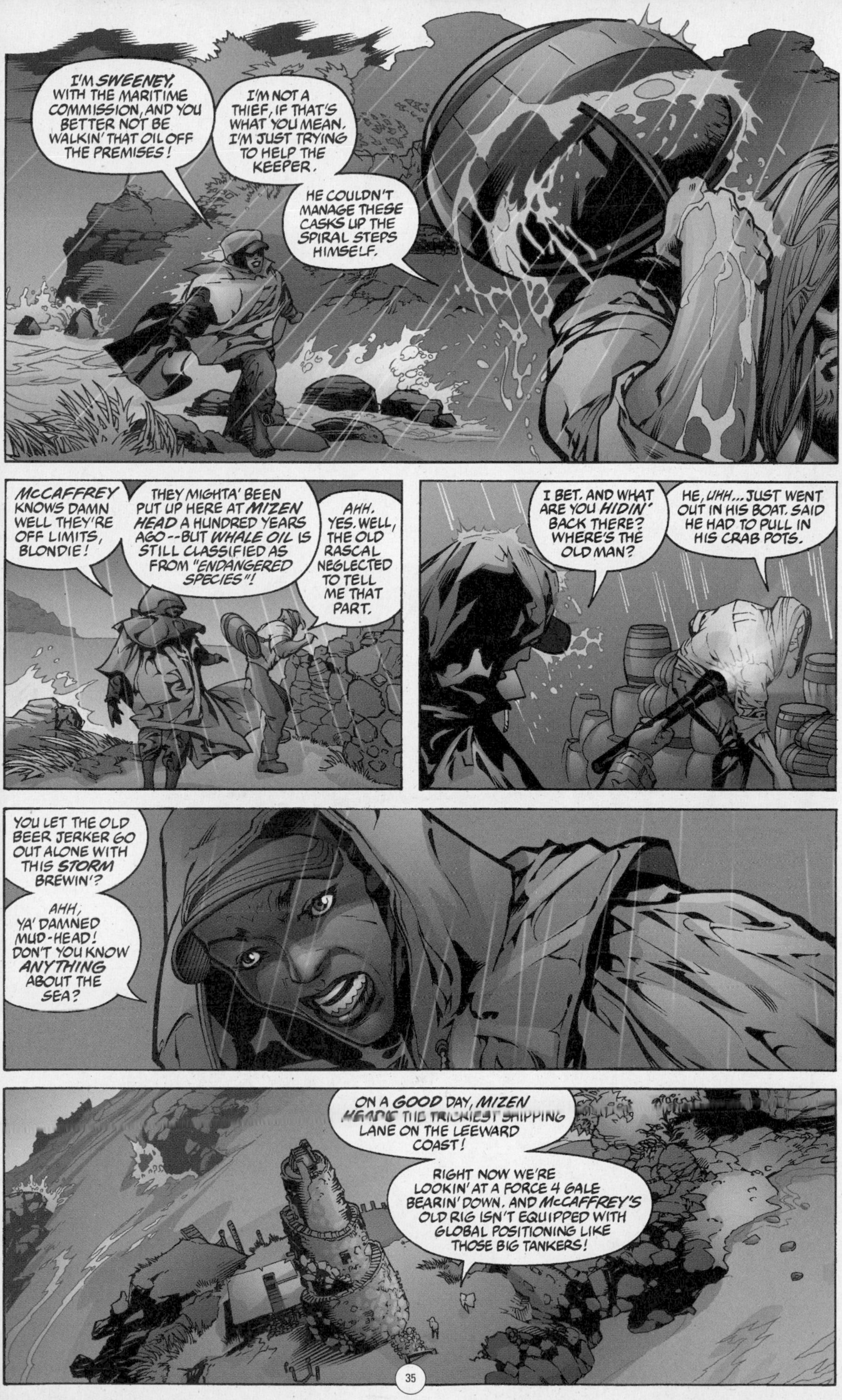
I'M SWEENEY, WITH THE MARITIME COMMISSION, AND YOU BETTER NOT BE WALKIN' THAT OIL OFF THE PREMISES!
I'M NOT A THIEF, IF THAT'S WHAT YOU MEAN. I'M JUST TRYING TO HELP THE KEEPER.
HE COULDN'T MANAGE THESE CASKS UP THE SPIRAL STEPS HIMSELF.
McCAFFREY KNOWS DAMN WELL THEY'RE OFF LIMITS, BLONDIE!
THEY MIGHTA' BEEN PUT UP HERE AT MIZEN HEAD A HUNDRED YEARS AGO--BUT WHALE OIL IS STILL CLASSIFIED AS FROM "ENDANGERED SPECIES"!
AHH. YES. WELL, THE OLD RASCAL NEGLECTED TO TELL ME THAT PART.
I BET. AND WHAT ARE YOU HIDIN' BACK THERE? WHERE'S THE OLD MAN?
HE, UHH... JUST WENT OUT IN HIS BOAT. SAID HE HAD TO PULL IN HIS CRAB POTS.
YOU LET THE OLD BEER JERKER GO OUT ALONE WITH THIS STORM BREWIN'?
AHH, YA' DAMNED MUD-HEAD! DON'T YOU KNOW ANYTHING ABOUT THE SEA?
ON A GOOD DAY, MIZEN HEAD IS THE TRICKIEST SHIPPING LANE ON THE LEEWARD COAST!
RIGHT NOW WE'RE LOOKIN' AT A FORCE 4 GALE BEARIN' DOWN. AND McCAFFREY'S OLD RIG ISN'T EQUIPPED WITH GLOBAL POSITIONING LIKE THOSE BIG TANKERS!

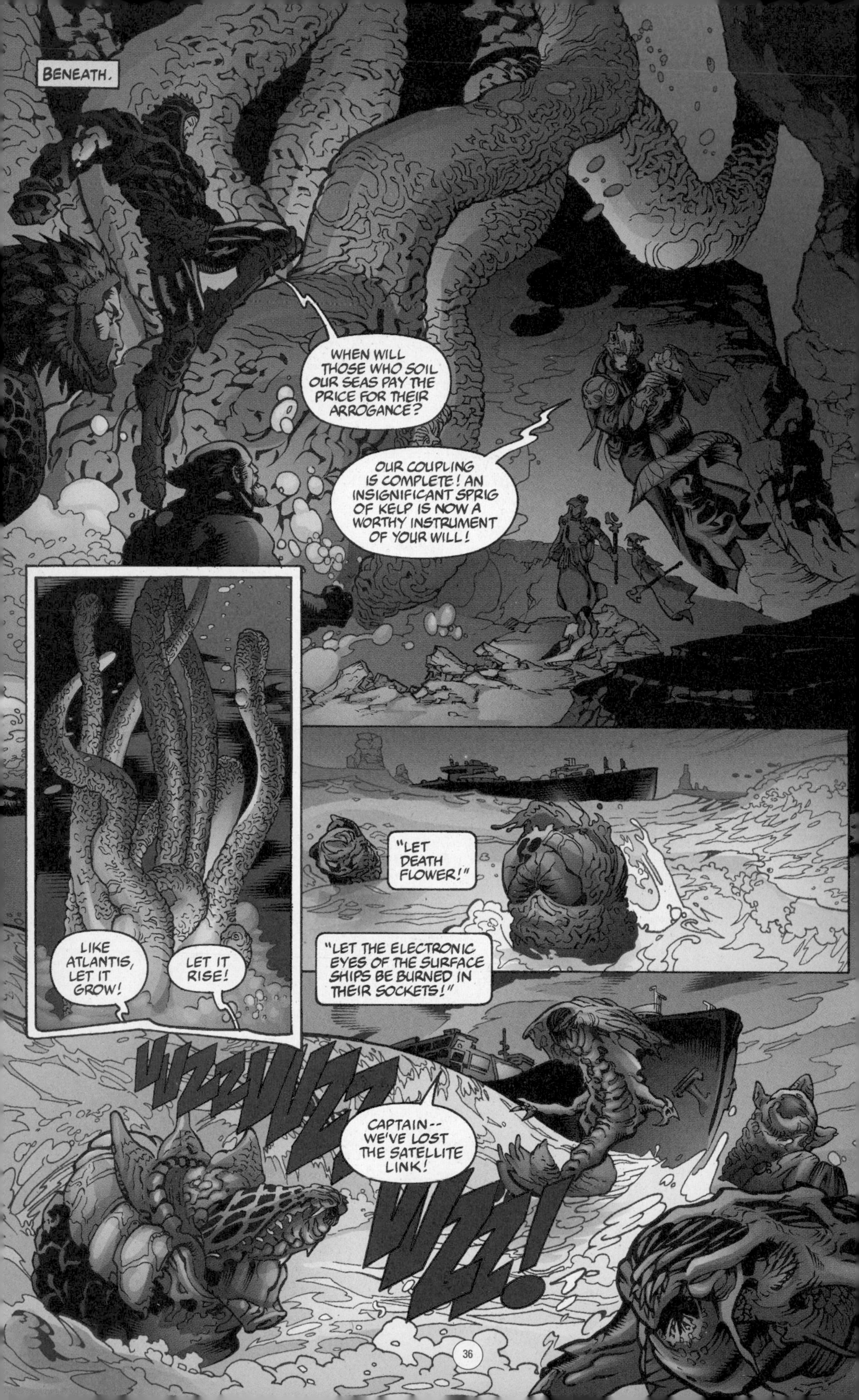
BENEATH.
WHEN WILL THOSE WHO SOIL OUR SEAS PAY THE PRICE FOR THEIR ARROGANCE?
OUR COUPLING IS COMPLETE! AN INSIGNIFICANT SPRIG OF KELP IS NOW A WORTHY INSTRUMENT OF YOUR WILL!
LIKE ATLANTIS, LET IT GROW!
LET IT RISE!
"LET DEATH FLOWER!"
"LET THE ELECTRONIC EYES OF THE SURFACE SHIPS BE BURNED IN THEIR SOCKETS!"
VVZZZVVVZZZ
CAPTAIN-- WE'VE LOST THE SATELLITE LINK!
VVZZZ!

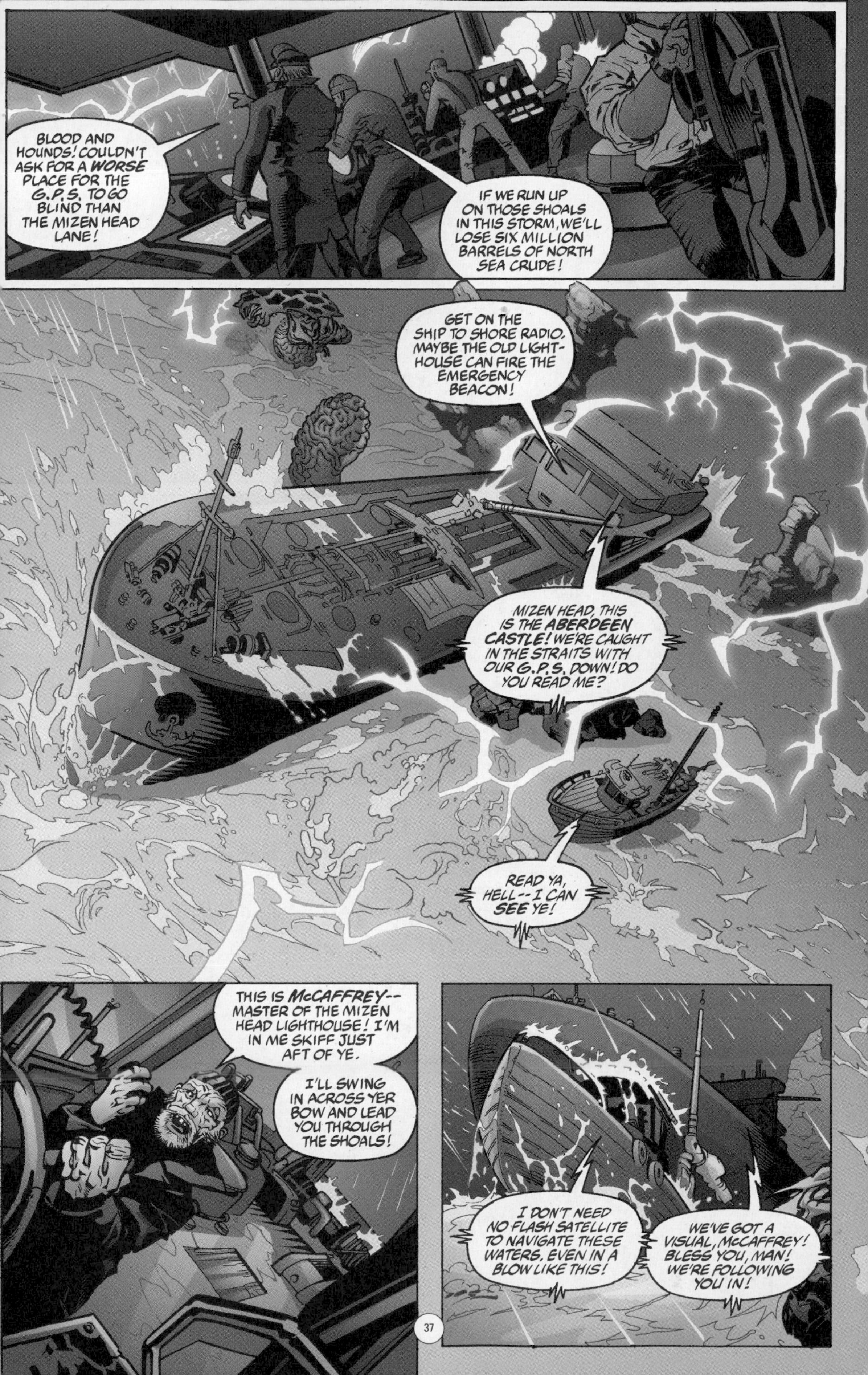
BLOOD AND HOUNDS! COULDN'T ASK FOR A WORSE PLACE FOR THE G.P.S. TO GO BLIND THAN THE MIZEN HEAD LANE!
IF WE RUN UP ON THOSE SHOALS IN THIS STORM, WE'LL LOSE SIX MILLION BARRELS OF NORTH SEA CRUDE!
GET ON THE SHIP TO SHORE RADIO. MAYBE THE OLD LIGHT-HOUSE CAN FIRE THE EMERGENCY BEACON!
MIZEN HEAD, THIS IS THE ABERDEEN CASTLE! WE'RE CAUGHT IN THE STRAITS WITH OUR G.P.S. DOWN! DO YOU READ ME?
READ YA, HELL-- I CAN SEE YE!
THIS IS McCAFFREY-- MASTER OF THE MIZEN HEAD LIGHTHOUSE! I'M IN ME SKIFF JUST AFT OF YE.
I'LL SWING IN ACROSS YER BOW AND LEAD YOU THROUGH THE SHOALS!
I DON'T NEED NO FLASH SATELLITE TO NAVIGATE THESE WATERS. EVEN IN A BLOW LIKE THIS!
WE'VE GOT A VISUAL, McCAFFREY! BLESS YOU, MAN! WE'RE FOLLOWING YOU IN!

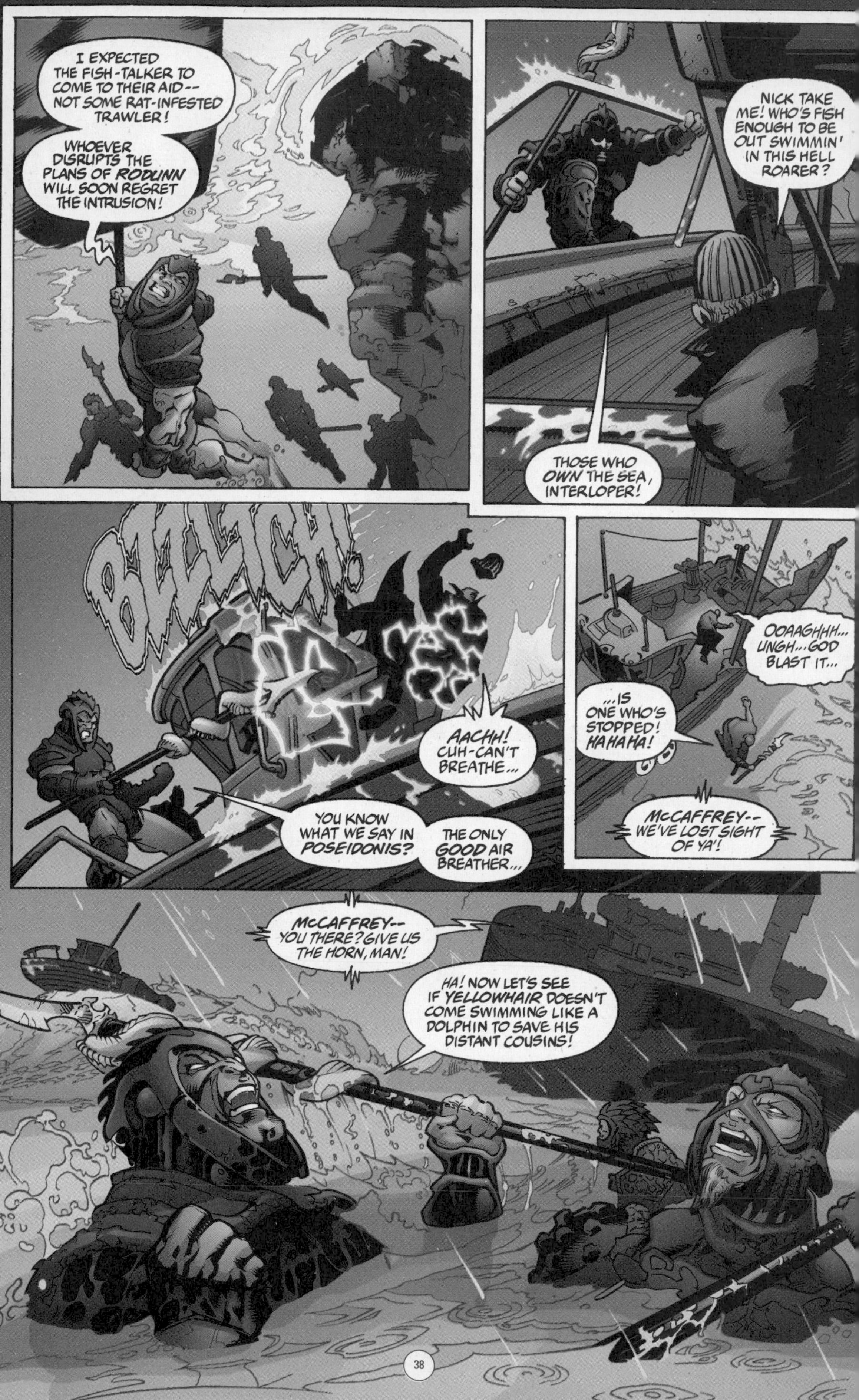
I EXPECTED THE FISH-TALKER TO COME TO THEIR AID-- NOT SOME RAT-INFESTED TRAWLER!
WHOEVER DISRUPTS THE PLANS OF RODUNN WILL SOON REGRET THE INTRUSION!
NICK TAKE ME! WHO'S FISH ENOUGH TO BE OUT SWIMMIN' IN THIS HELL ROARER?
THOSE WHO OWN THE SEA, INTERLOPER!
BZZZTCH!
AACHH! CUH-CAN'T BREATHE...
YOU KNOW WHAT WE SAY IN POSEIDONIS?
THE ONLY GOOD AIR BREATHER...
OOAAGHHH... UNGH...GOD BLAST IT...
...IS ONE WHO'S STOPPED! HAHAHA!
McCAFFREY-- WE'VE LOST SIGHT OF YA'!
McCAFFREY-- YOU THERE? GIVE US THE HORN, MAN!
HA! NOW LET'S SEE IF YELLOWHAIR DOESN'T COME SWIMMING LIKE A DOLPHIN TO SAVE HIS DISTANT COUSINS!

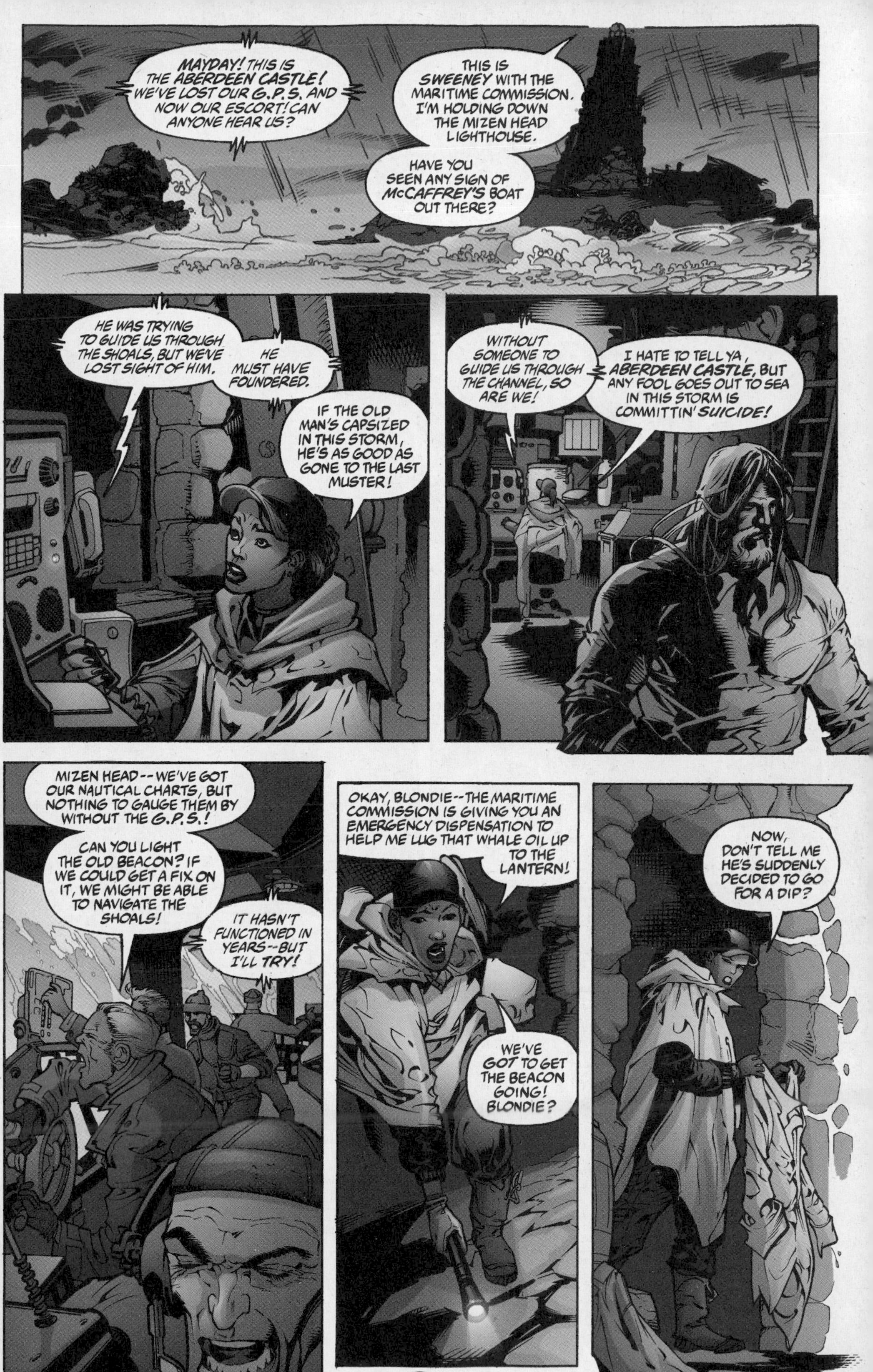
MAYDAY! THIS IS THE ABERDEEN CASTLE! WE'VE LOST OUR G.P.S. AND NOW OUR ESCORT! CAN ANYONE HEAR US?
THIS IS SWEENEY WITH THE MARITIME COMMISSION. I'M HOLDING DOWN THE MIZEN HEAD LIGHTHOUSE.
HAVE YOU SEEN ANY SIGN OF McCAFFREY'S BOAT OUT THERE?
HE WAS TRYING TO GUIDE US THROUGH THE SHOALS, BUT WE'VE LOST SIGHT OF HIM.
HE MUST HAVE FOUNDERED.
IF THE OLD MAN'S CAPSIZED IN THIS STORM, HE'S AS GOOD AS GONE TO THE LAST MUSTER!
WITHOUT SOMEONE TO GUIDE US THROUGH THE CHANNEL, SO ARE WE!
I HATE TO TELL YA, ABERDEEN CASTLE, BUT ANY FOOL GOES OUT TO SEA IN THIS STORM IS COMMITTIN' SUICIDE!
MIZEN HEAD--WE'VE GOT OUR NAUTICAL CHARTS, BUT NOTHING TO GAUGE THEM BY WITHOUT THE G.P.S.!
CAN YOU LIGHT THE OLD BEACON? IF WE COULD GET A FIX ON IT, WE MIGHT BE ABLE TO NAVIGATE THE SHOALS!
IT HASN'T FUNCTIONED IN YEARS--BUT I'LL TRY!
OKAY, BLONDIE--THE MARITIME COMMISSION IS GIVING YOU AN EMERGENCY DISPENSATION TO HELP ME LUG THAT WHALE OIL UP TO THE LANTERN!
WE'VE GOT TO GET THE BEACON GOING! BLONDIE?
NOW, DON'T TELL ME HE'S SUDDENLY DECIDED TO GO FOR A DIP?

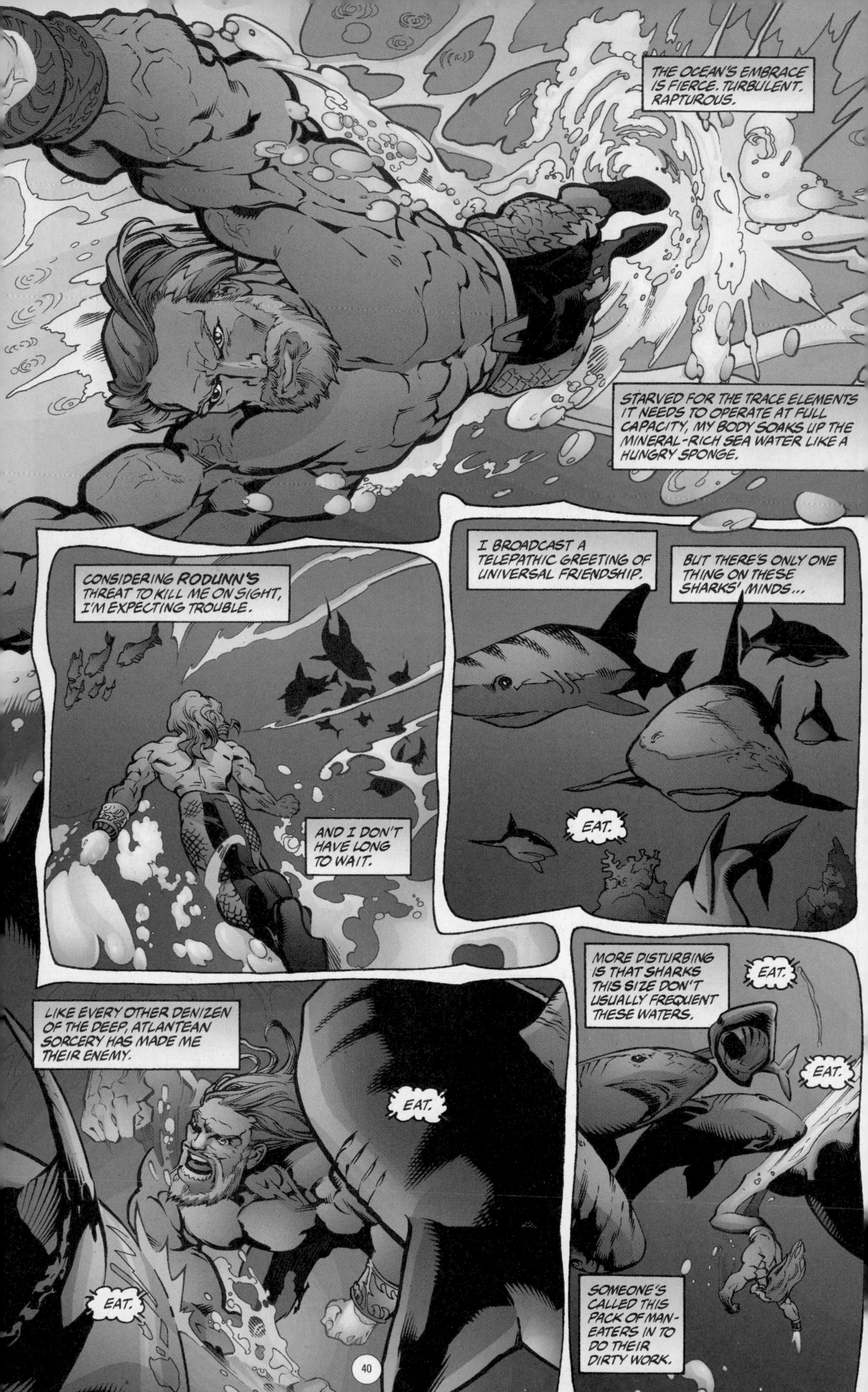
THE OCEAN'S EMBRACE IS FIERCE. TURBULENT. RAPTUROUS.
STARVED FOR THE TRACE ELEMENTS IT NEEDS TO OPERATE AT FULL CAPACITY, MY BODY SOAKS UP THE MINERAL-RICH SEA WATER LIKE A HUNGRY SPONGE.
CONSIDERING RODUNN'S THREAT TO KILL ME ON SIGHT, I'M EXPECTING TROUBLE.
AND I DON'T HAVE LONG TO WAIT.
I BROADCAST A TELEPATHIC GREETING OF UNIVERSAL FRIENDSHIP.
BUT THERE'S ONLY ONE THING ON THESE SHARKS' MINDS...
EAT.
LIKE EVERY OTHER DENIZEN OF THE DEEP, ATLANTEAN SORCERY HAS MADE ME THEIR ENEMY.
EAT.
EAT.
MORE DISTURBING IS THAT SHARKS THIS SIZE DON'T USUALLY FREQUENT THESE WATERS.
EAT.
EAT.
SOMEONE'S CALLED THIS PACK OF MAN-EATERS IN TO DO THEIR DIRTY WORK.

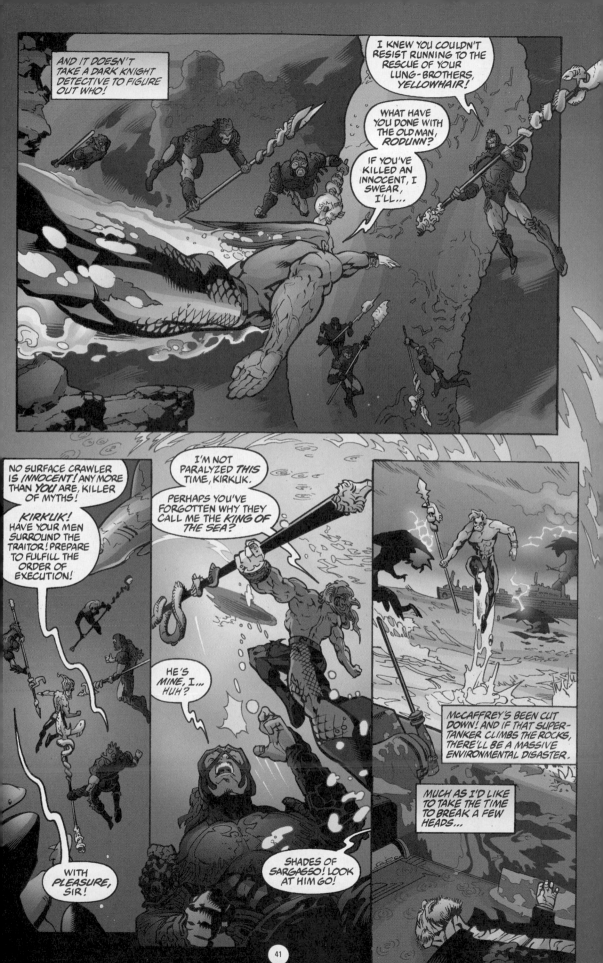

AND IT DOESN'T TAKE A DARK KNIGHT DETECTIVE TO FIGURE OUT WHO!

I KNEW YOU COULDN'T RESIST RUNNING TO THE RESCUE OF YOUR LUNG-BROTHERS, YELLOWHAIR!

WHAT HAVE YOU DONE WITH THE OLD MAN, RODUNN?

IF YOU'VE KILLED AN INNOCENT, I SWEAR, I'LL...

NO SURFACE CRAWLER IS INNOCENT! ANY MORE THAN YOU ARE, KILLER OF MYTHS!

KIRKUK! HAVE YOUR MEN SURROUND THE TRAITOR! PREPARE TO FULFILL THE ORDER OF EXECUTION!

I'M NOT PARALYZED THIS TIME, KIRKUK.

PERHAPS YOU'VE FORGOTTEN WHY THEY CALL ME THE KING OF THE SEA?

HE'S MINE, I... HUH?

WITH PLEASURE, SIR!

SHADES OF SARGASSO! LOOK AT HIM GO!

McCAFFREY'S BEEN CUT DOWN! AND IF THAT SUPER-TANKER CLIMBS THE ROCKS, THERE'LL BE A MASSIVE ENVIRONMENTAL DISASTER.

MUCH AS I'D LIKE TO TAKE THE TIME TO BREAK A FEW HEADS...

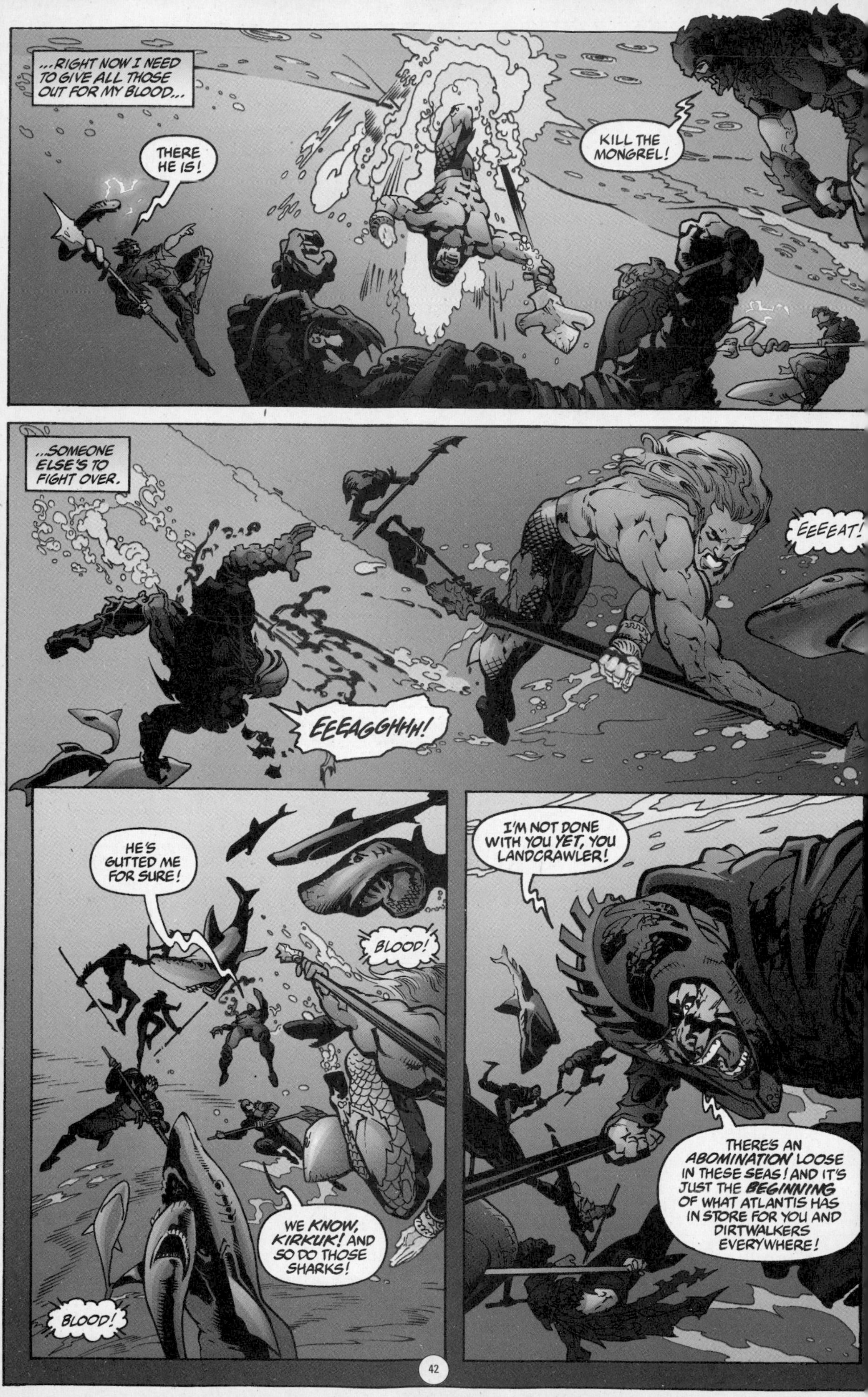
...RIGHT NOW I NEED TO GIVE ALL THOSE OUT FOR MY BLOOD...
THERE HE IS!
KILL THE MONGREL!
...SOMEONE ELSE'S TO FIGHT OVER.
EEEEAT!
EEEAGGHHH!
HE'S GUTTED ME FOR SURE!
BLOOD!
WE KNOW, KIRKUK! AND SO DO THOSE SHARKS!
BLOOD!
I'M NOT DONE WITH YOU YET, YOU LANDCRAWLER!
THERE'S AN ABOMINATION LOOSE IN THESE SEAS! AND IT'S JUST THE BEGINNING OF WHAT ATLANTIS HAS IN STORE FOR YOU AND DIRTWALKERS EVERYWHERE!

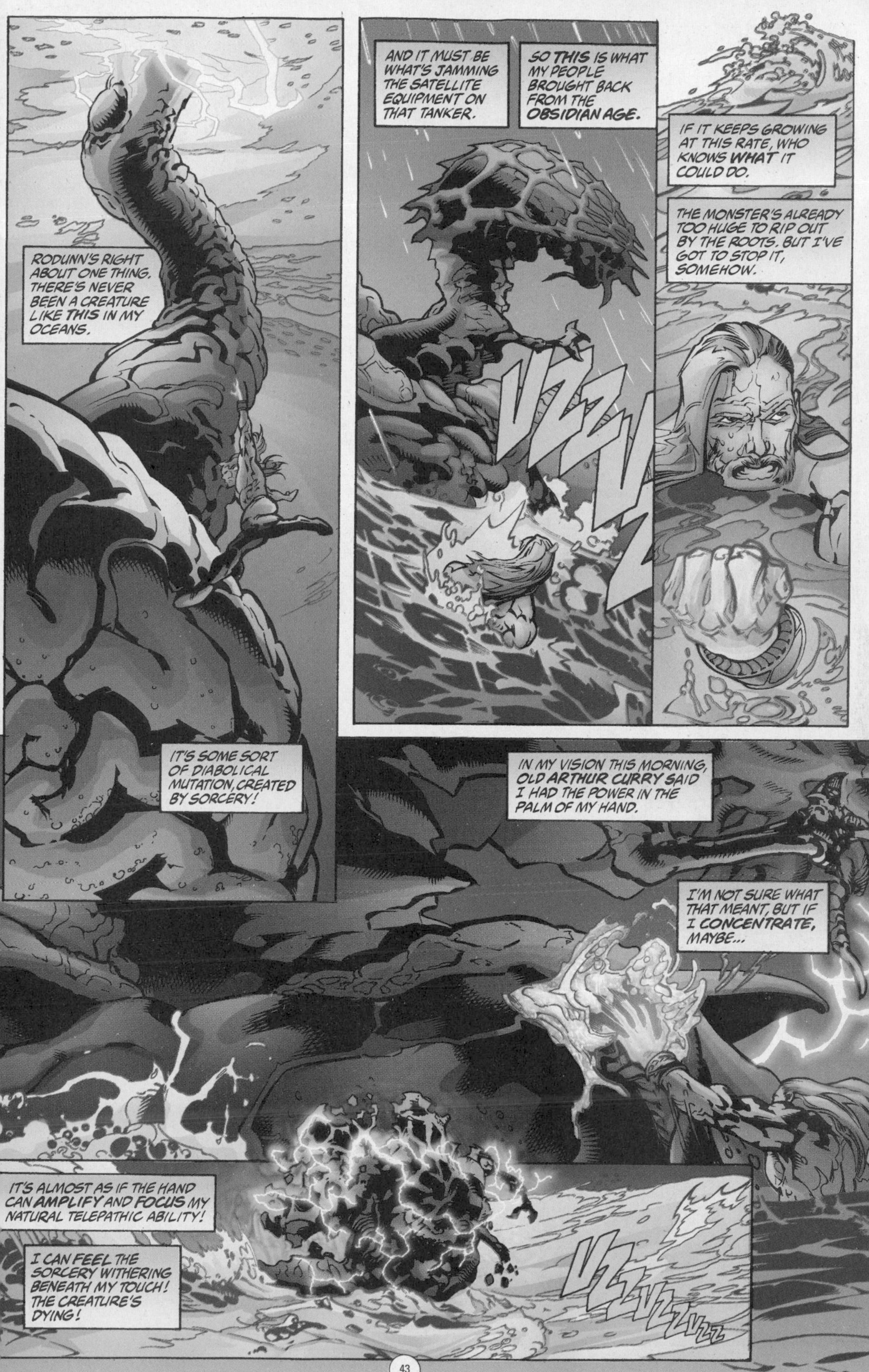
RODUNN'S RIGHT ABOUT ONE THING. THERE'S NEVER BEEN A CREATURE LIKE THIS IN MY OCEANS.
IT'S SOME SORT OF DIABOLICAL MUTATION, CREATED BY SORCERY!
AND IT MUST BE WHAT'S JAMMING THE SATELLITE EQUIPMENT ON THAT TANKER.
SO THIS IS WHAT MY PEOPLE BROUGHT BACK FROM THE OBSIDIAN AGE.
VZZZVV
IF IT KEEPS GROWING AT THIS RATE, WHO KNOWS WHAT IT COULD DO.
THE MONSTER'S ALREADY TOO HUGE TO RIP OUT BY THE ROOTS. BUT I'VE GOT TO STOP IT, SOMEHOW.
IN MY VISION THIS MORNING, OLD ARTHUR CURRY SAID I HAD THE POWER IN THE PALM OF MY HAND.
I'M NOT SURE WHAT THAT MEANT, BUT IF I CONCENTRATE, MAYBE...
IT'S ALMOST AS IF THE HAND CAN AMPLIFY AND FOCUS MY NATURAL TELEPATHIC ABILITY!
I CAN FEEL THE SORCERY WITHERING BENEATH MY TOUCH! THE CREATURE'S DYING!
VZZZVZZZVZZZ

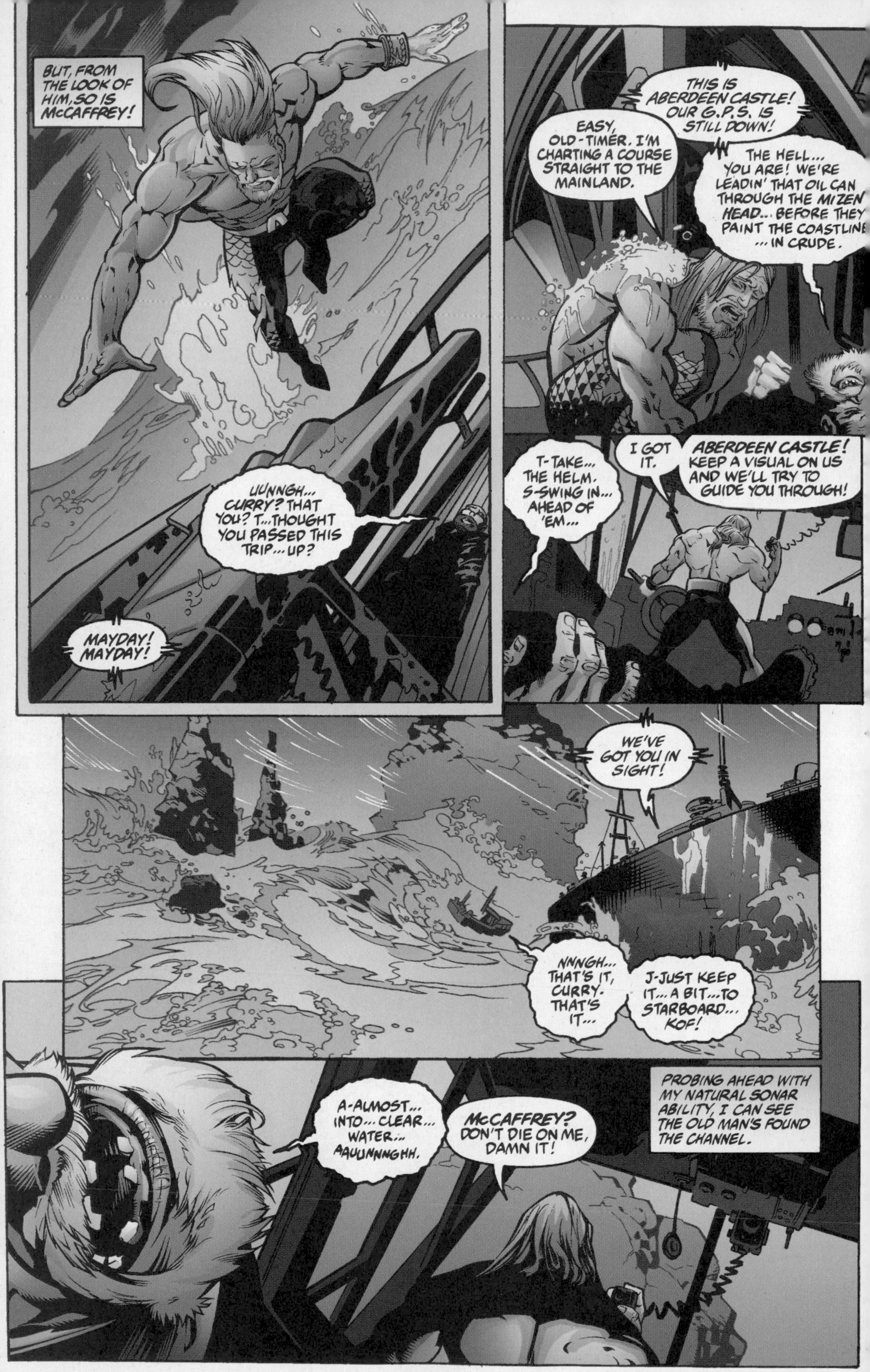
BUT, FROM THE LOOK OF HIM, SO IS McCAFFREY!
UUNNGH... CURRY? THAT YOU? T...THOUGHT YOU PASSED THIS TRIP... UP?
MAYDAY! MAYDAY!
THIS IS ABERDEEN CASTLE! OUR G.P.S. IS STILL DOWN!
EASY, OLD-TIMER. I'M CHARTING A COURSE STRAIGHT TO THE MAINLAND.
THE HELL... YOU ARE! WE'RE LEADIN' THAT OIL CAN THROUGH THE MIZEN HEAD... BEFORE THEY PAINT THE COASTLINE ... IN CRUDE.
T-TAKE... THE HELM. S-SWING IN... AHEAD OF 'EM...
I GOT IT.
ABERDEEN CASTLE! KEEP A VISUAL ON US AND WE'LL TRY TO GUIDE YOU THROUGH!
WE'VE GOT YOU IN SIGHT!
NNNGH... THAT'S IT, CURRY. THAT'S IT...
J-JUST KEEP IT... A BIT... TO STARBOARD... KOF!
PROBING AHEAD WITH MY NATURAL SONAR ABILITY, I CAN SEE THE OLD MAN'S FOUND THE CHANNEL.
A-ALMOST... INTO... CLEAR... WATER... AAUUNNNGHH.
McCAFFREY? DON'T DIE ON ME, DAMN IT!

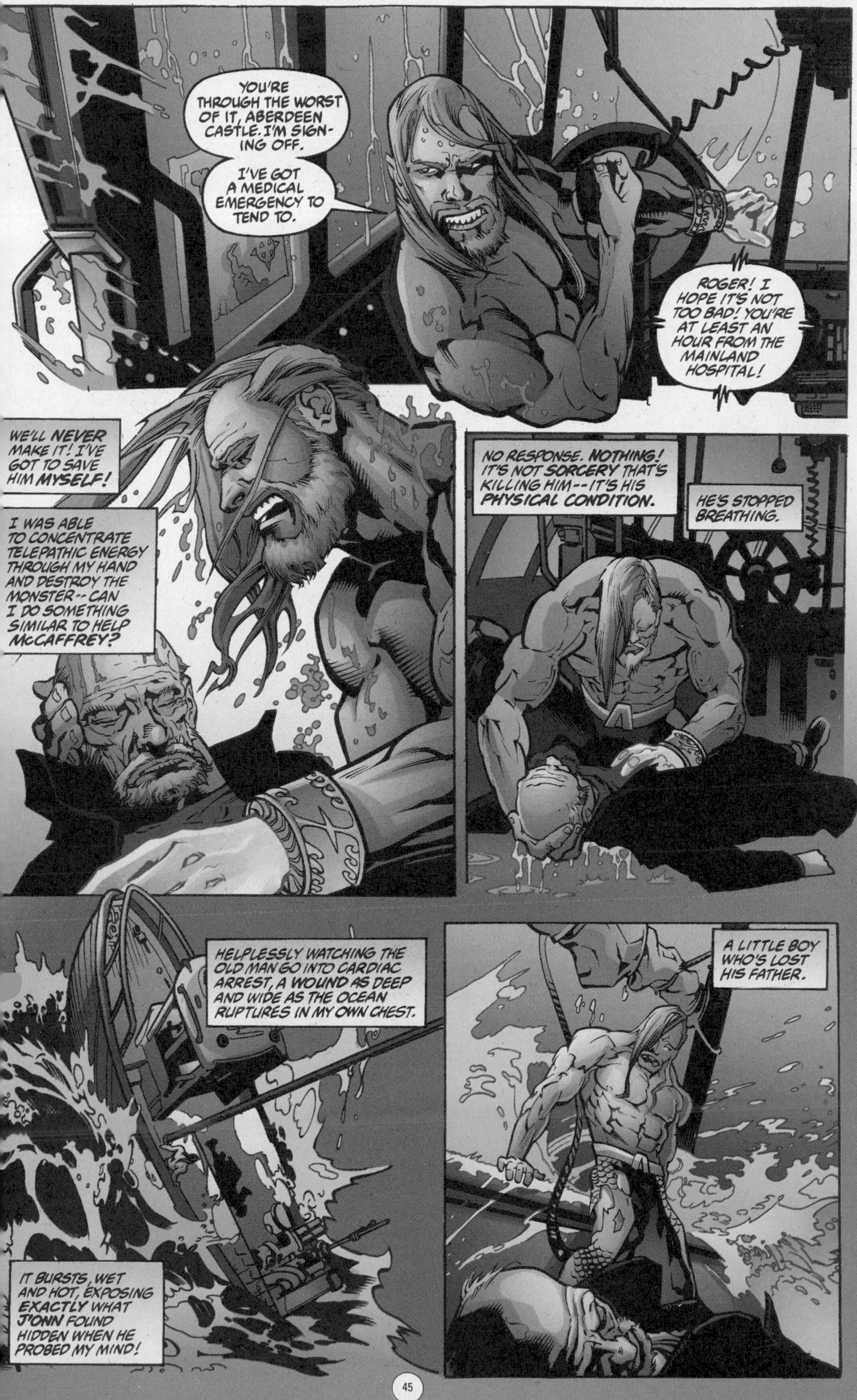
YOU'RE THROUGH THE WORST OF IT, ABERDEEN CASTLE. I'M SIGNING OFF.
I'VE GOT A MEDICAL EMERGENCY TO TEND TO.
ROGER! I HOPE IT'S NOT TOO BAD! YOU'RE AT LEAST AN HOUR FROM THE MAINLAND HOSPITAL!
WE'LL NEVER MAKE IT! I'VE GOT TO SAVE HIM MYSELF!
I WAS ABLE TO CONCENTRATE TELEPATHIC ENERGY THROUGH MY HAND AND DESTROY THE MONSTER--CAN I DO SOMETHING SIMILAR TO HELP McCAFFREY?
NO RESPONSE. NOTHING! IT'S NOT SORCERY THAT'S KILLING HIM--IT'S HIS PHYSICAL CONDITION.
HE'S STOPPED BREATHING.
HELPLESSLY WATCHING THE OLD MAN GO INTO CARDIAC ARREST, A WOUND AS DEEP AND WIDE AS THE OCEAN RUPTURES IN MY OWN CHEST.
IT BURSTS, WET AND HOT, EXPOSING EXACTLY WHAT J'ONN FOUND HIDDEN WHEN HE PROBED MY MIND!
A LITTLE BOY WHO'S LOST HIS FATHER.

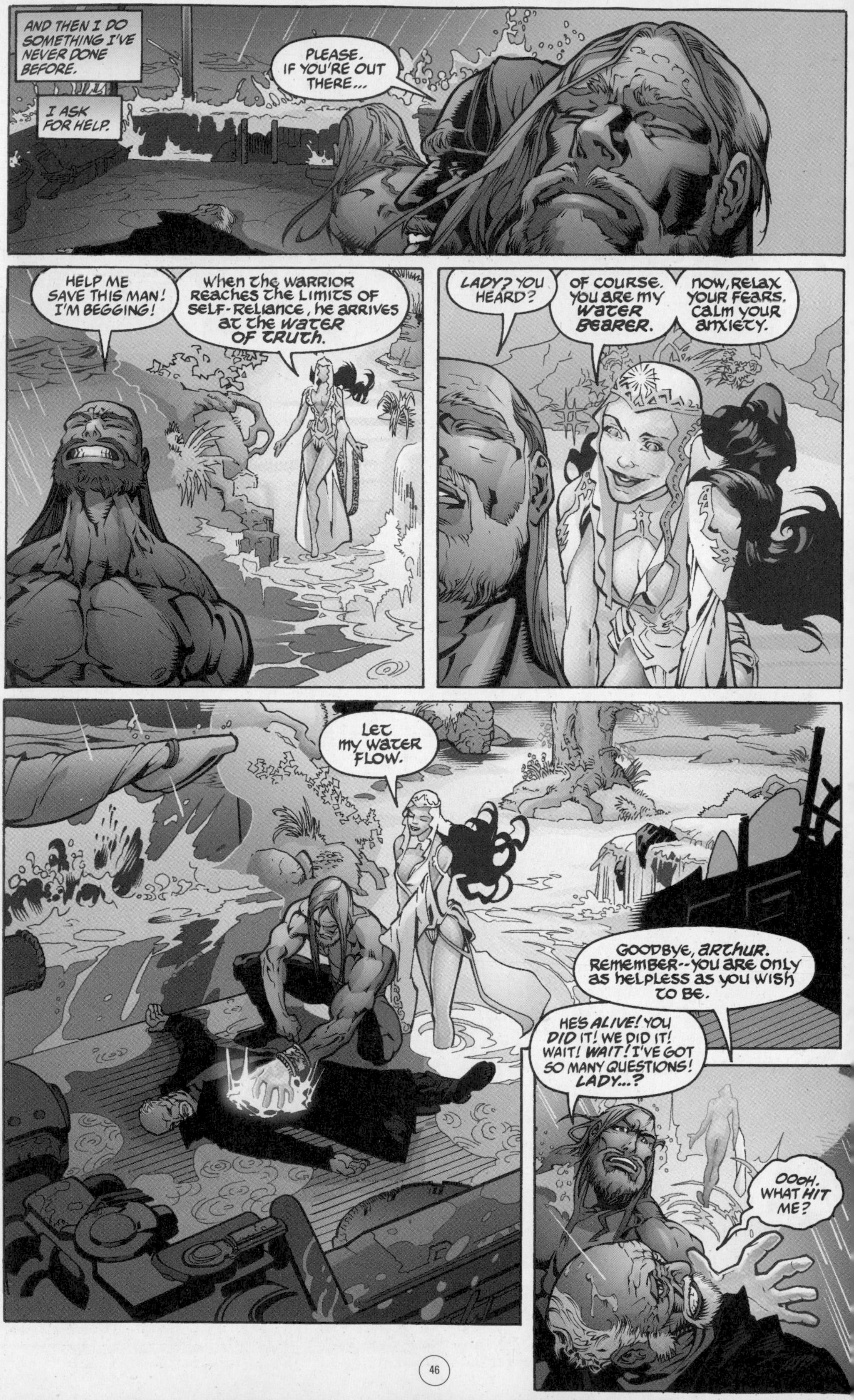
AND THEN I DO SOMETHING I'VE NEVER DONE BEFORE.
I ASK FOR HELP.
PLEASE. IF YOU'RE OUT THERE...
HELP ME SAVE THIS MAN! I'M BEGGING!
When the warrior reaches the limits of self-reliance, he arrives at the water of truth.
LADY? YOU HEARD?
OF COURSE. YOU ARE MY WATER BEARER.
NOW, RELAX YOUR FEARS. CALM YOUR ANXIETY.
LET MY WATER FLOW.
GOODBYE, ARTHUR. REMEMBER--YOU ARE ONLY AS HELPLESS AS YOU WISH TO BE.
HE'S ALIVE! YOU DID IT! WE DID IT! WAIT! WAIT! I'VE GOT SO MANY QUESTIONS! LADY...?
OOOH. WHAT HIT ME?

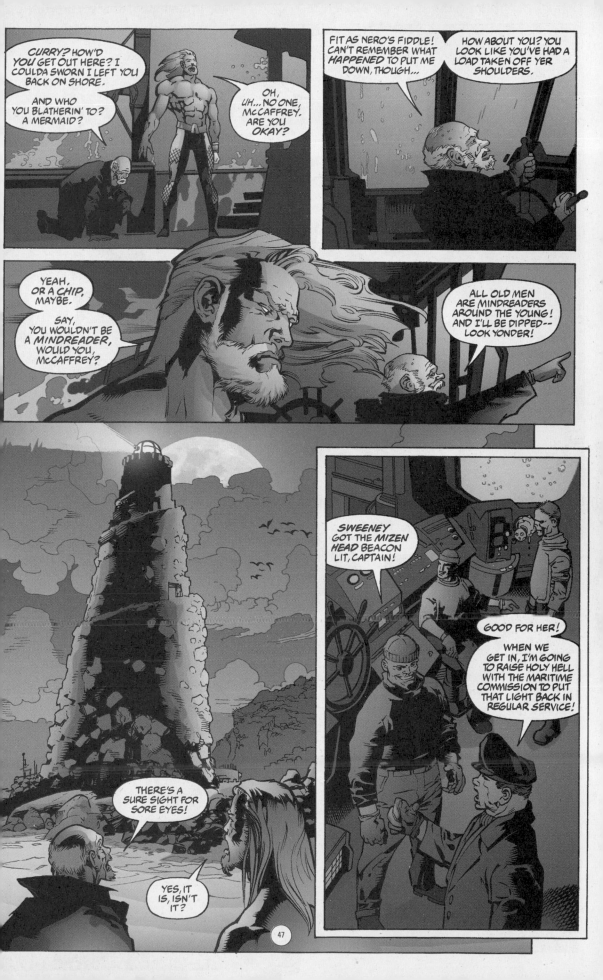

CURRY? HOW'D YOU GET OUT HERE? I COULDA SWORN I LEFT YOU BACK ON SHORE.

AND WHO YOU BLATHERIN' TO? A MERMAID?

OH, UH...NO ONE, McCAFFREY. ARE YOU OKAY?

FIT AS NERO'S FIDDLE! CAN'T REMEMBER WHAT *HAPPENED* TO PUT ME DOWN, THOUGH...

HOW ABOUT YOU? YOU LOOK LIKE YOU'VE HAD A LOAD TAKEN OFF YER SHOULDERS.

YEAH, OR A CHIP, MAYBE.

SAY, YOU WOULDN'T BE A MINDREADER, WOULD YOU, McCAFFREY?

ALL OLD MEN ARE MINDREADERS AROUND THE YOUNG! AND I'LL BE DIPPED-- LOOK YONDER!

SWEENEY GOT THE *MIZEN HEAD* BEACON LIT, CAPTAIN!

GOOD FOR HER!

WHEN WE GET IN, I'M GOING TO RAISE HOLY HELL WITH THE MARITIME COMMISSION TO PUT THAT LIGHT BACK IN REGULAR SERVICE!

THERE'S A SURE SIGHT FOR SORE EYES!

YES, IT IS, ISN'T IT?

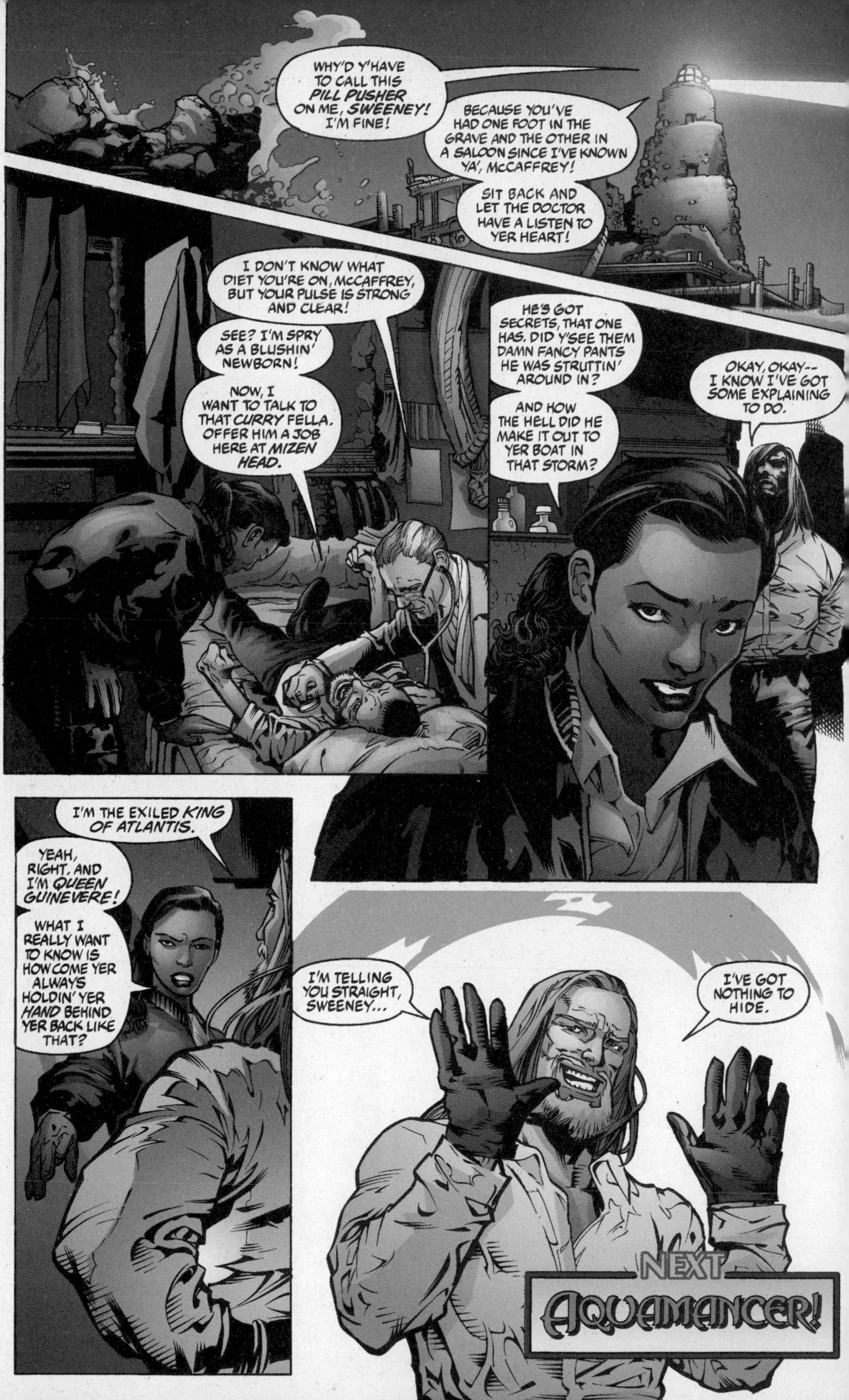
WHY'D Y'HAVE TO CALL THIS PILL PUSHER ON ME, SWEENEY! I'M FINE!
BECAUSE YOU'VE HAD ONE FOOT IN THE GRAVE AND THE OTHER IN A SALOON SINCE I'VE KNOWN YA', McCAFFREY!
SIT BACK AND LET THE DOCTOR HAVE A LISTEN TO YER HEART!
I DON'T KNOW WHAT DIET YOU'RE ON, McCAFFREY, BUT YOUR PULSE IS STRONG AND CLEAR!
SEE? I'M SPRY AS A BLUSHIN' NEWBORN!
NOW, I WANT TO TALK TO THAT CURRY FELLA. OFFER HIM A JOB HERE AT MIZEN HEAD.
HE'S GOT SECRETS, THAT ONE HAS. DID Y'SEE THEM DAMN FANCY PANTS HE WAS STRUTTIN' AROUND IN?
AND HOW THE HELL DID HE MAKE IT OUT TO YER BOAT IN THAT STORM?
OKAY, OKAY-- I KNOW I'VE GOT SOME EXPLAINING TO DO.
I'M THE EXILED KING OF ATLANTIS.
YEAH, RIGHT. AND I'M QUEEN GUINEVERE!
WHAT I REALLY WANT TO KNOW IS HOW COME YER ALWAYS HOLDIN' YER HAND BEHIND YER BACK LIKE THAT?
I'M TELLING YOU STRAIGHT, SWEENEY...
I'VE GOT NOTHING TO HIDE.
NEXT
AQUAMANCER!

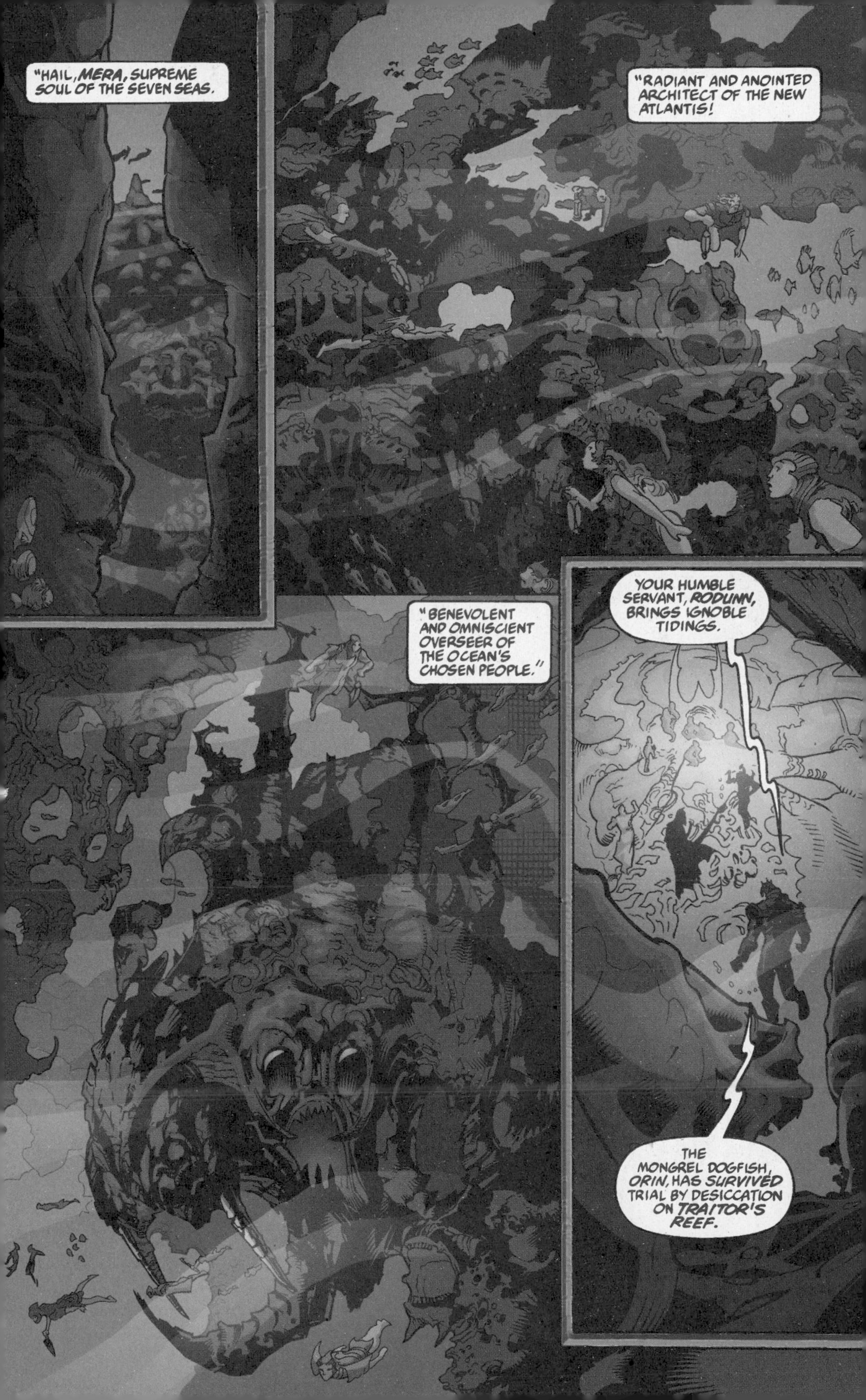
"HAIL, MERA, SUPREME SOUL OF THE SEVEN SEAS.
"RADIANT AND ANOINTED ARCHITECT OF THE NEW ATLANTIS!
"BENEVOLENT AND OMNISCIENT OVERSEER OF THE OCEAN'S CHOSEN PEOPLE."
YOUR HUMBLE SERVANT, RODUNN, BRINGS IGNOBLE TIDINGS.
THE MONGREL DOGFISH, ORIN, HAS SURVIVED TRIAL BY DESICCATION ON TRAITOR'S REEF.

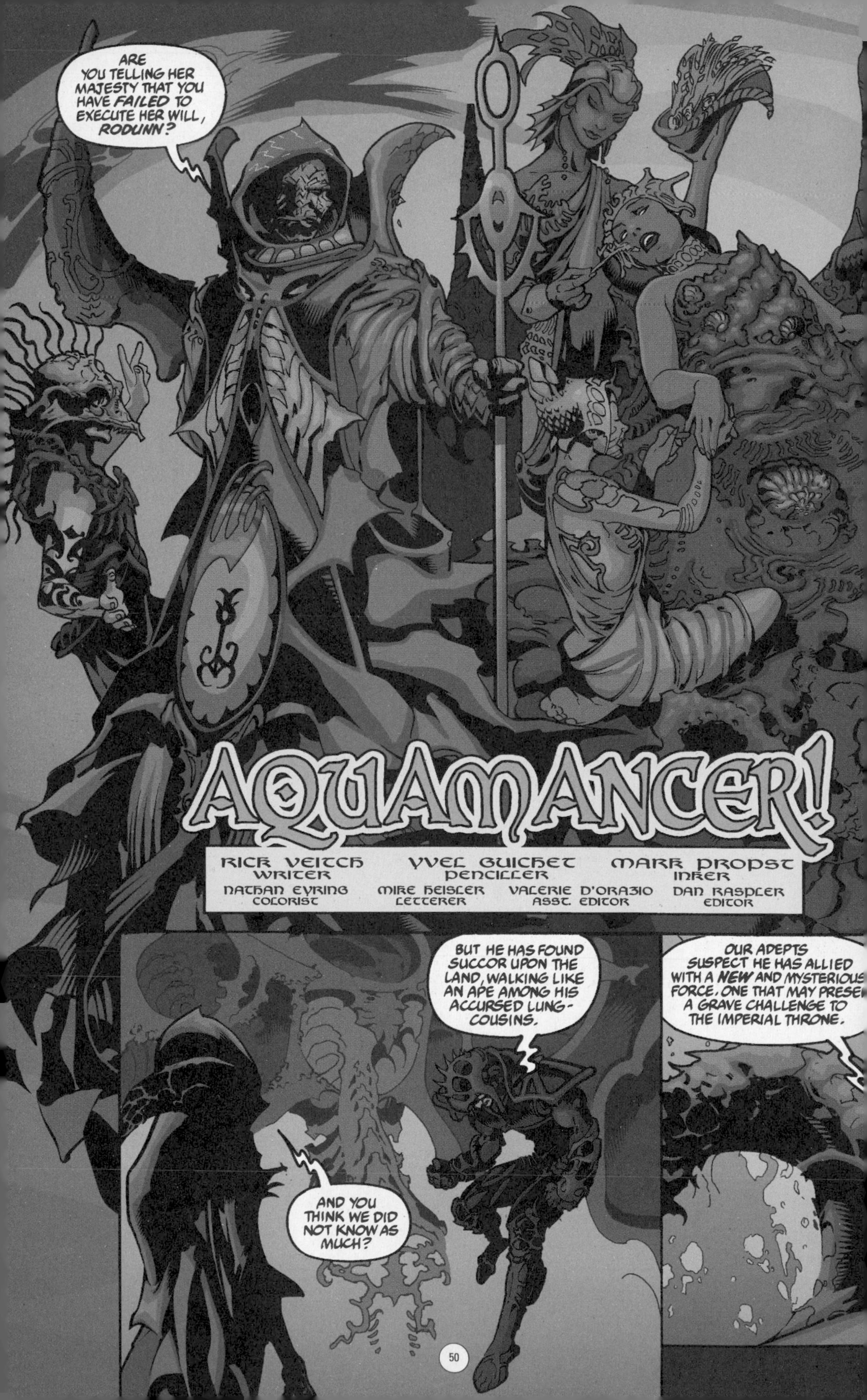
ARE YOU TELLING HER MAJESTY THAT YOU HAVE *FAILED* TO EXECUTE HER WILL, *RODUNN?*
AQUAMANCER!
RICK VEITCH WRITER
YVEL GUICHET PENCILLER
MARK PROPST INKER
NATHAN EYRING COLORIST
MIKE HEISLER LETTERER
VALERIE D'ORAZIO ASST. EDITOR
DAN RASPLER EDITOR
BUT HE HAS FOUND SUCCOR UPON THE LAND, WALKING LIKE AN APE AMONG HIS ACCURSED LUNG-COUSINS.
AND YOU THINK WE DID NOT KNOW AS MUCH?
OUR ADEPTS SUSPECT HE HAS ALLIED WITH A *NEW* AND MYSTERIOUS
FORCE. ONE THAT MAY PRESE
A GRAVE CHALLENGE TO THE IMPERIAL THRONE.

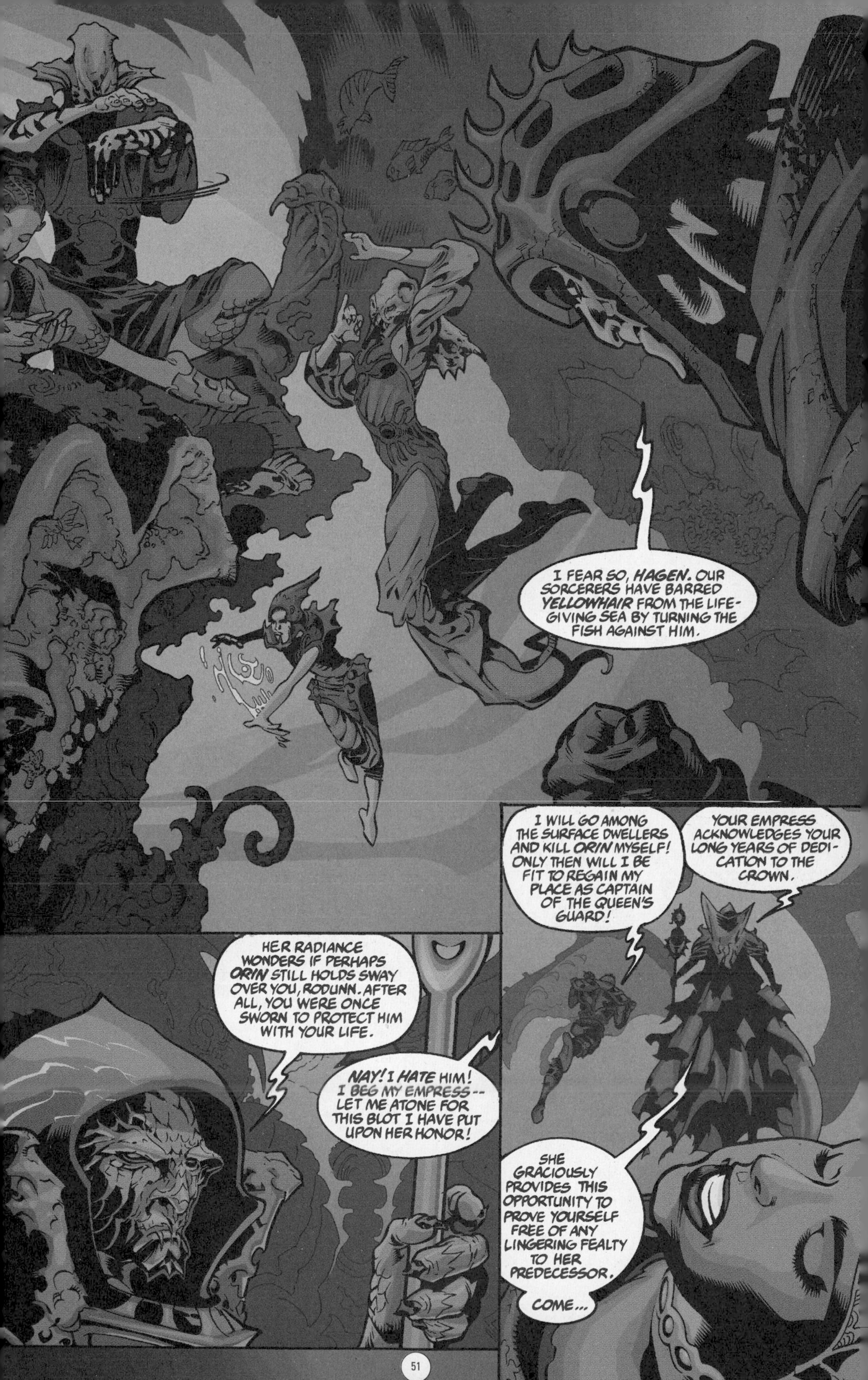
I FEAR SO, HAGEN. OUR SORCERERS HAVE BARRED YELLOWHAIR FROM THE LIFE-GIVING SEA BY TURNING THE FISH AGAINST HIM.
I WILL GO AMONG THE SURFACE DWELLERS AND KILL ORIN MYSELF! ONLY THEN WILL I BE FIT TO REGAIN MY PLACE AS CAPTAIN OF THE QUEEN'S GUARD!
YOUR EMPRESS ACKNOWLEDGES YOUR LONG YEARS OF DEDICATION TO THE CROWN.
HER RADIANCE WONDERS IF PERHAPS ORIN STILL HOLDS SWAY OVER YOU, RODUNN. AFTER ALL, YOU WERE ONCE SWORN TO PROTECT HIM WITH YOUR LIFE.
NAY! I HATE HIM! I BEG MY EMPRESS-- LET ME ATONE FOR THIS BLOT I HAVE PUT UPON HER HONOR!
SHE GRACIOUSLY PROVIDES THIS OPPORTUNITY TO PROVE YOURSELF FREE OF ANY LINGERING FEALTY TO HER PREDECESSOR.
COME...

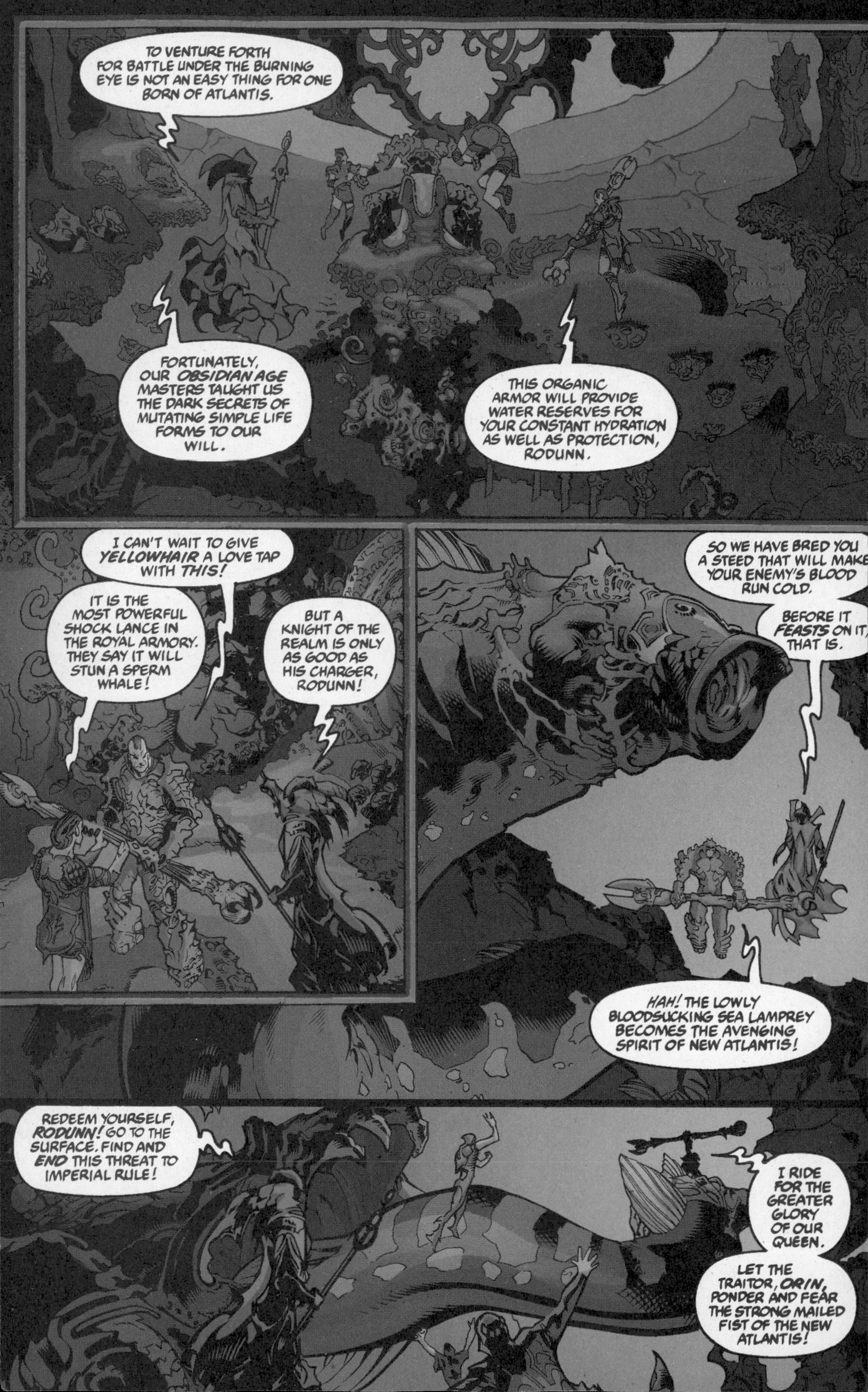
TO VENTURE FORTH FOR BATTLE UNDER THE BURNING EYE IS NOT AN EASY THING FOR ONE BORN OF ATLANTIS.
FORTUNATELY, OUR OBSIDIAN AGE MASTERS TAUGHT US THE DARK SECRETS OF MUTATING SIMPLE LIFE FORMS TO OUR WILL.
THIS ORGANIC ARMOR WILL PROVIDE WATER RESERVES FOR YOUR CONSTANT HYDRATION AS WELL AS PROTECTION, RODUNN.
I CAN'T WAIT TO GIVE YELLOWHAIR A LOVE TAP WITH THIS!
IT IS THE MOST POWERFUL SHOCK LANCE IN THE ROYAL ARMORY. THEY SAY IT WILL STUN A SPERM WHALE!
BUT A KNIGHT OF THE REALM IS ONLY AS GOOD AS HIS CHARGER, RODUNN!
SO WE HAVE BRED YOU A STEED THAT WILL MAKE YOUR ENEMY'S BLOOD RUN COLD.
BEFORE IT FEASTS ON IT, THAT IS.
HAH! THE LOWLY BLOODSUCKING SEA LAMPREY BECOMES THE AVENGING SPIRIT OF NEW ATLANTIS!
REDEEM YOURSELF, RODUNN! GO TO THE SURFACE. FIND AND END THIS THREAT TO IMPERIAL RULE!
I RIDE FOR THE GREATER GLORY OF OUR QUEEN.
LET THE TRAITOR, ORIN, PONDER AND FEAR THE STRONG MAILED FIST OF THE NEW ATLANTIS!

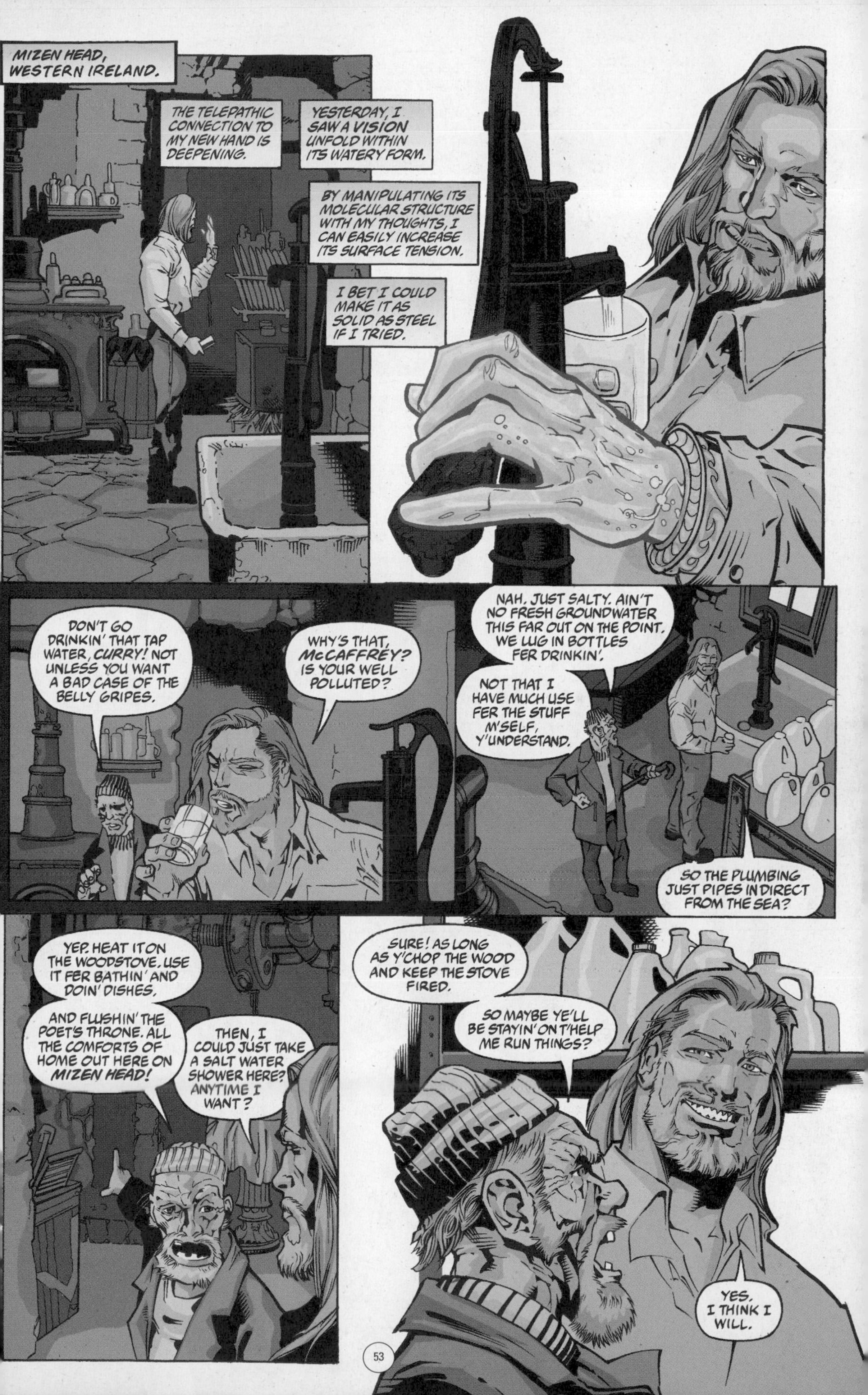
MIZEN HEAD, WESTERN IRELAND.
THE TELEPATHIC CONNECTION TO MY NEW HAND IS DEEPENING.
YESTERDAY, I SAW A VISION UNFOLD WITHIN ITS WATERY FORM.
BY MANIPULATING ITS MOLECULAR STRUCTURE WITH MY THOUGHTS, I CAN EASILY INCREASE ITS SURFACE TENSION.
I BET I COULD MAKE IT AS SOLID AS STEEL IF I TRIED.
DON'T GO DRINKIN' THAT TAP WATER, CURRY! NOT UNLESS YOU WANT A BAD CASE OF THE BELLY GRIPES.
WHY'S THAT, McCAFFREY? IS YOUR WELL POLLUTED?
NAH. JUST SALTY. AIN'T NO FRESH GROUNDWATER THIS FAR OUT ON THE POINT. WE LUG IN BOTTLES FER DRINKIN'.
NOT THAT I HAVE MUCH USE FER THE STUFF M'SELF, Y'UNDERSTAND.
SO THE PLUMBING JUST PIPES IN DIRECT FROM THE SEA?
YEP. HEAT IT ON THE WOODSTOVE. USE IT FER BATHIN' AND DOIN' DISHES.
AND FLUSHIN' THE POET'S THRONE. ALL THE COMFORTS OF HOME OUT HERE ON MIZEN HEAD!
THEN, I COULD JUST TAKE A SALT WATER SHOWER HERE? ANYTIME I WANT?
SURE! AS LONG AS Y'CHOP THE WOOD AND KEEP THE STOVE FIRED.
SO MAYBE YE'LL BE STAYIN' ON T'HELP ME RUN THINGS?
YES. I THINK I WILL.

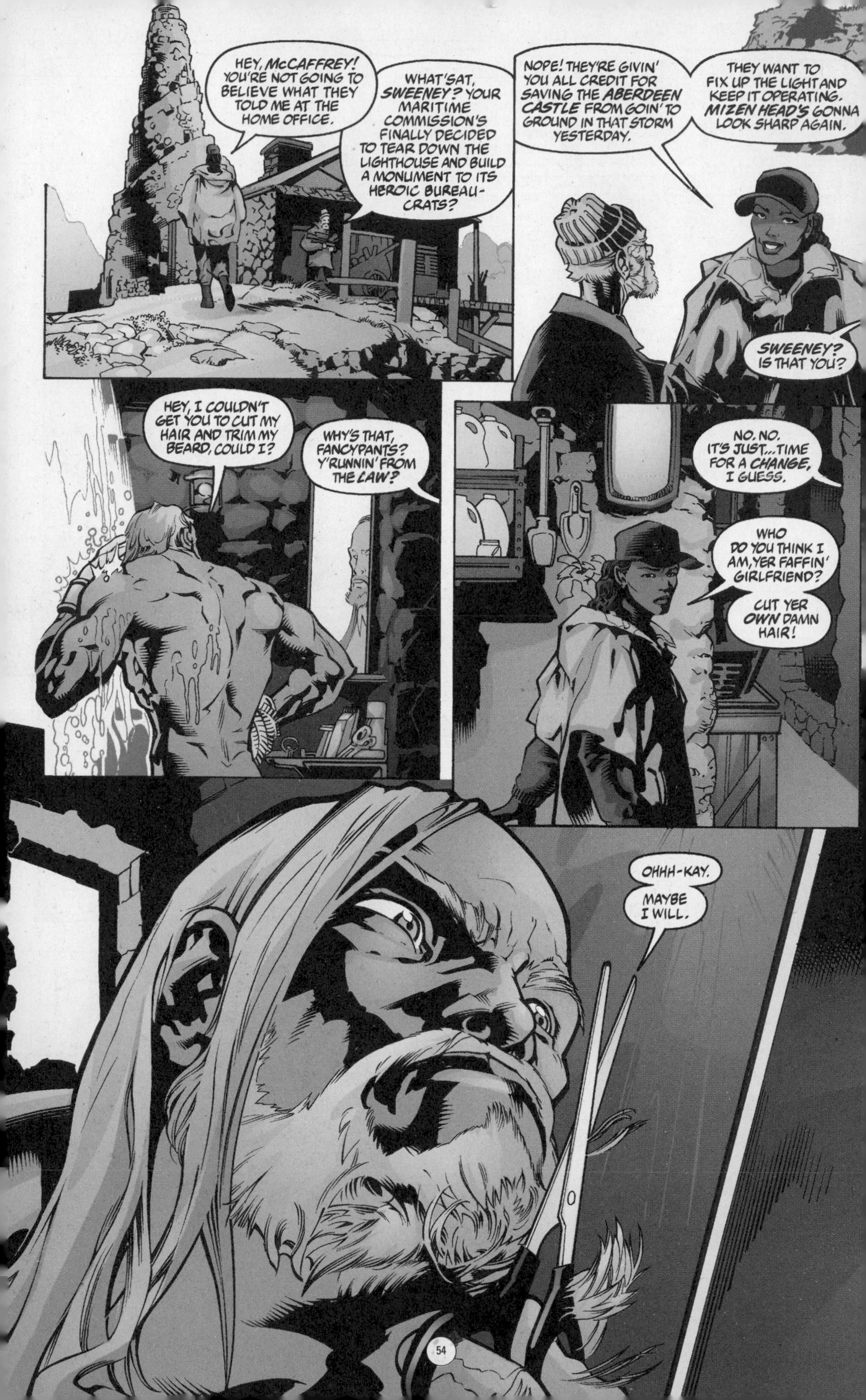
HEY, McCAFFREY! YOU'RE NOT GOING TO BELIEVE WHAT THEY TOLD ME AT THE HOME OFFICE.
WHAT'SAT, SWEENEY? YOUR MARITIME COMMISSION'S FINALLY DECIDED TO TEAR DOWN THE LIGHTHOUSE AND BUILD A MONUMENT TO ITS HEROIC BUREAU-CRATS?
NOPE! THEY'RE GIVIN' YOU ALL CREDIT FOR SAVING THE ABERDEEN CASTLE FROM GOIN' TO GROUND IN THAT STORM YESTERDAY.
THEY WANT TO FIX UP THE LIGHT AND KEEP IT OPERATING. MIZEN HEAD'S GONNA LOOK SHARP AGAIN.
SWEENEY? IS THAT YOU?
HEY, I COULDN'T GET YOU TO CUT MY HAIR AND TRIM MY BEARD, COULD I?
WHY'S THAT, FANCYPANTS? Y'RUNNIN' FROM THE LAW?
NO. NO. IT'S JUST... TIME FOR A CHANGE, I GUESS.
WHO DO YOU THINK I AM, YER FAFFIN' GIRLFRIEND?
CUT YER OWN DAMN HAIR!
OHHH-KAY.
MAYBE I WILL.

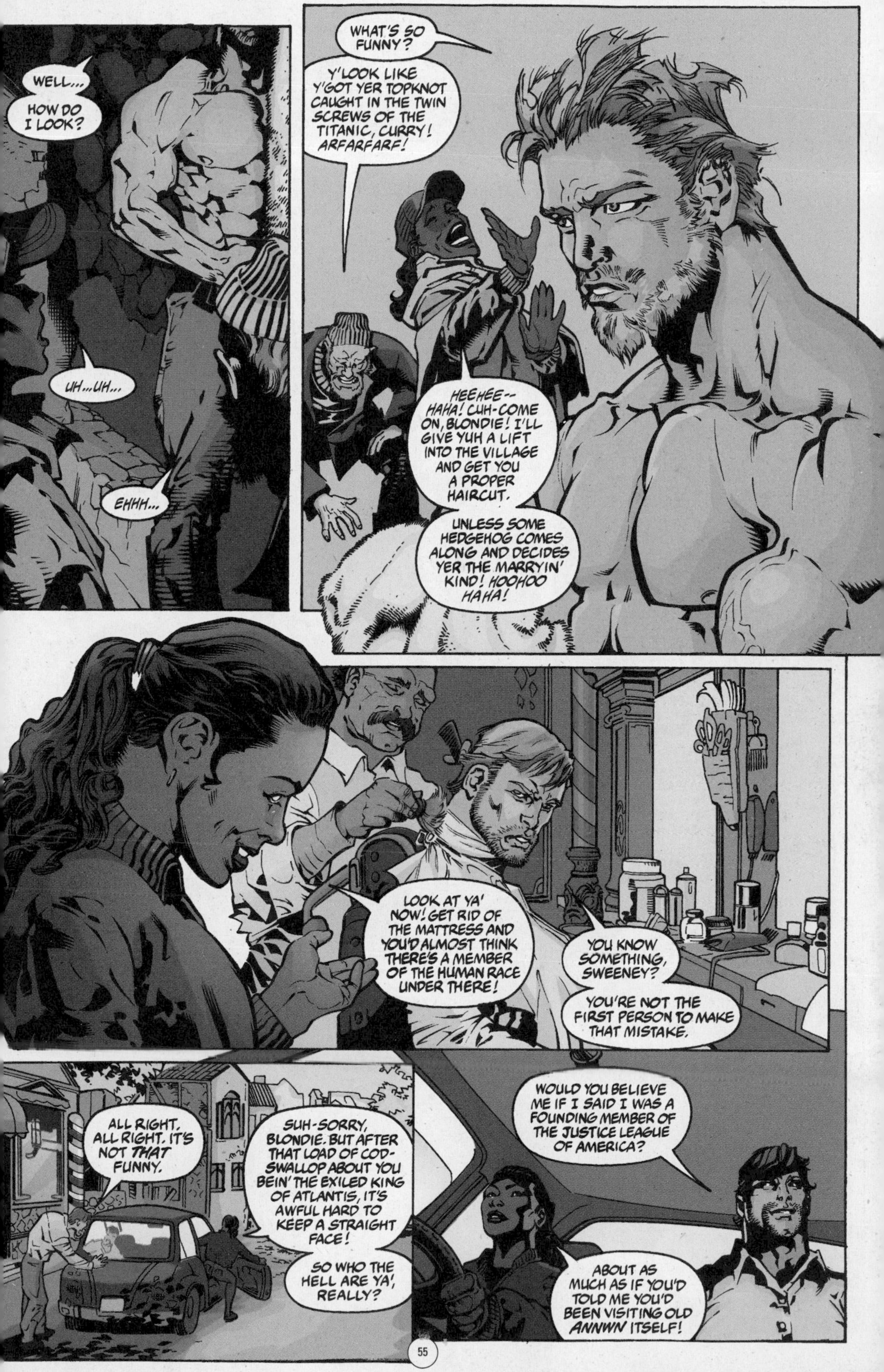
WELL... HOW DO I LOOK?
UH...UH...
EHHH...
WHAT'S SO FUNNY?
Y'LOOK LIKE Y'GOT YER TOPKNOT CAUGHT IN THE TWIN SCREWS OF THE TITANIC, CURRY! ARFARFARF!
HEEHEE--HAHA! CUH-COME ON, BLONDIE! I'LL GIVE YUH A LIFT INTO THE VILLAGE AND GET YOU A PROPER HAIRCUT.
UNLESS SOME HEDGEHOG COMES ALONG AND DECIDES YER THE MARRYIN' KIND! HOOHOO HAHA!
LOOK AT YA' NOW! GET RID OF THE MATTRESS AND YOU'D ALMOST THINK THERE'S A MEMBER OF THE HUMAN RACE UNDER THERE!
YOU KNOW SOMETHING, SWEENEY?
YOU'RE NOT THE FIRST PERSON TO MAKE THAT MISTAKE.
ALL RIGHT. ALL RIGHT. IT'S NOT THAT FUNNY.
SUH-SORRY, BLONDIE. BUT AFTER THAT LOAD OF COD-SWALLOP ABOUT YOU BEIN' THE EXILED KING OF ATLANTIS, IT'S AWFUL HARD TO KEEP A STRAIGHT FACE!
SO WHO THE HELL ARE YA', REALLY?
WOULD YOU BELIEVE ME IF I SAID I WAS A FOUNDING MEMBER OF THE JUSTICE LEAGUE OF AMERICA?
ABOUT AS MUCH AS IF YOU'D TOLD ME YOU'D BEEN VISITING OLD ANNWN ITSELF!

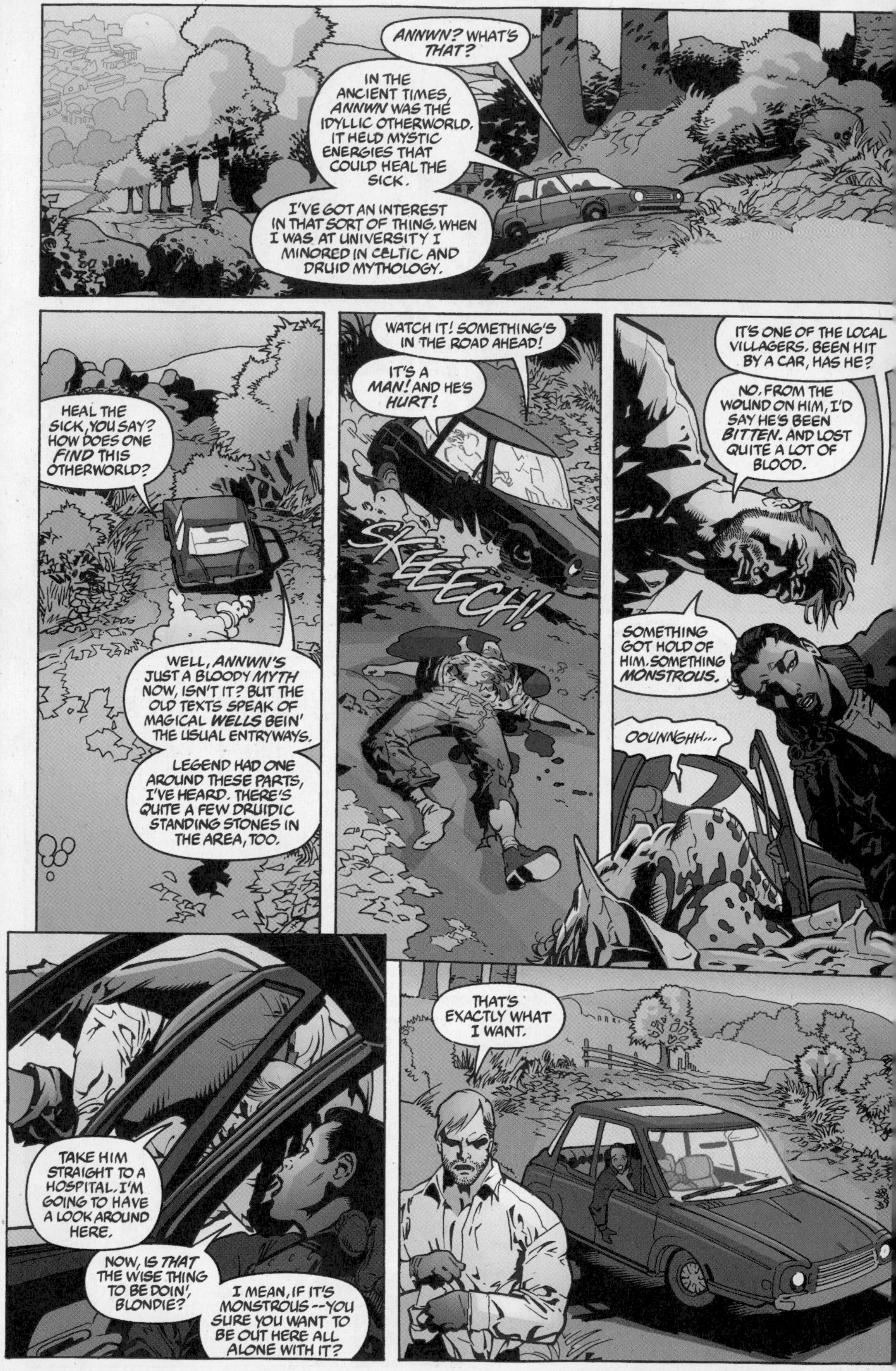
ANNWN? WHAT'S THAT?
IN THE ANCIENT TIMES, ANNWN WAS THE IDYLLIC OTHERWORLD. IT HELD MYSTIC ENERGIES THAT COULD HEAL THE SICK.
I'VE GOT AN INTEREST IN THAT SORT OF THING. WHEN I WAS AT UNIVERSITY I MINORED IN CELTIC AND DRUID MYTHOLOGY.
HEAL THE SICK, YOU SAY? HOW DOES ONE FIND THIS OTHERWORLD?
WELL, ANNWN'S JUST A BLOODY MYTH NOW, ISN'T IT? BUT THE OLD TEXTS SPEAK OF MAGICAL WELLS BEIN' THE USUAL ENTRYWAYS.
LEGEND HAD ONE AROUND THESE PARTS, I'VE HEARD. THERE'S QUITE A FEW DRUIDIC STANDING STONES IN THE AREA, TOO.
WATCH IT! SOMETHING'S IN THE ROAD AHEAD!
IT'S A MAN! AND HE'S HURT!
SKEEEECH!
IT'S ONE OF THE LOCAL VILLAGERS. BEEN HIT BY A CAR, HAS HE?
NO, FROM THE WOUND ON HIM, I'D SAY HE'S BEEN BITTEN. AND LOST QUITE A LOT OF BLOOD.
SOMETHING GOT HOLD OF HIM. SOMETHING MONSTROUS.
OOUNNGHH...
TAKE HIM STRAIGHT TO A HOSPITAL. I'M GOING TO HAVE A LOOK AROUND HERE.
NOW, IS THAT THE WISE THING TO BE DOIN', BLONDIE?
I MEAN, IF IT'S MONSTROUS--YOU SURE YOU WANT TO BE OUT HERE ALL ALONE WITH IT?
THAT'S EXACTLY WHAT I WANT.

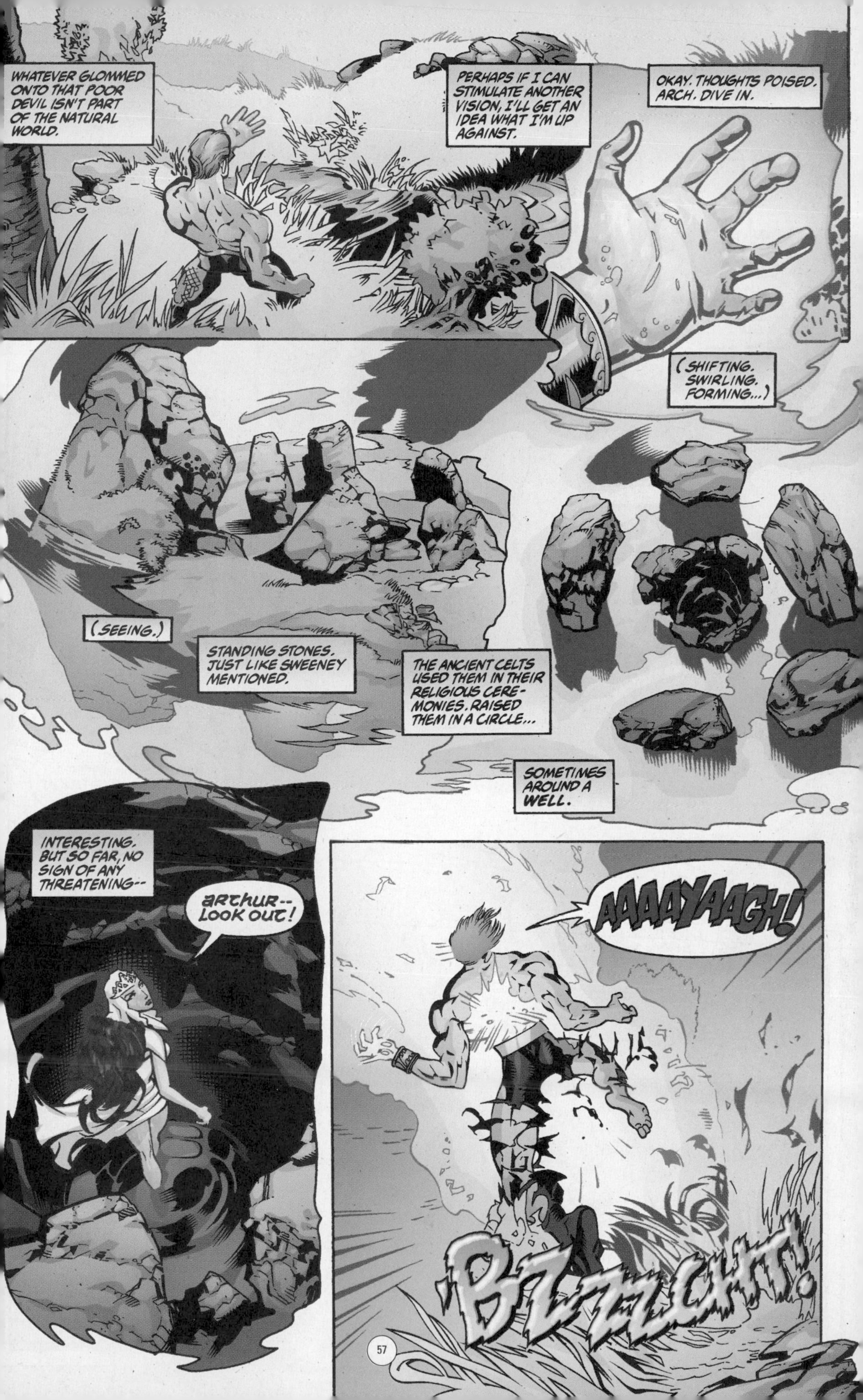

WHATEVER GLOMMED ONTO THAT POOR DEVIL ISN'T PART OF THE NATURAL WORLD.
PERHAPS IF I CAN STIMULATE ANOTHER VISION, I'LL GET AN IDEA WHAT I'M UP AGAINST.
OKAY. THOUGHTS POISED. ARCH. DIVE IN.
(SHIFTING. SWIRLING. FORMING...)
(SEEING.)
STANDING STONES. JUST LIKE SWEENEY MENTIONED.
THE ANCIENT CELTS USED THEM IN THEIR RELIGIOUS CERE-MONIES. RAISED THEM IN A CIRCLE...
SOMETIMES AROUND A WELL.
INTERESTING. BUT SO FAR, NO SIGN OF ANY THREATENING--
arthur-- look out!
AAAAYAAGH!
BZZTCHT!

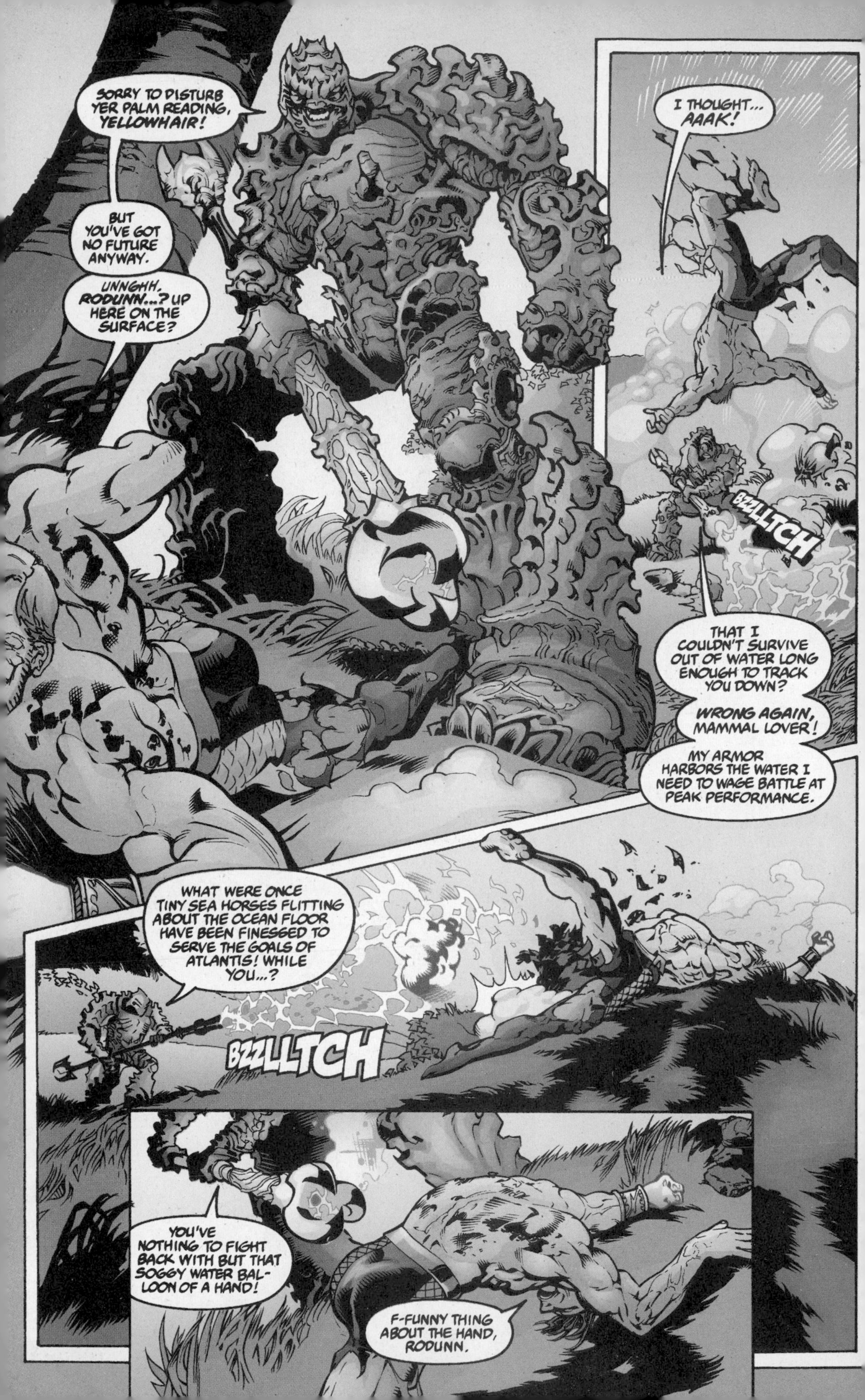
SORRY TO DISTURB YER PALM READING, YELLOWHAIR!
BUT YOU'VE GOT NO FUTURE ANYWAY.
UNNGHH. RODUNN...? UP HERE ON THE SURFACE?
I THOUGHT... AAAK!
BZZLLTCH
THAT I COULDN'T SURVIVE OUT OF WATER LONG ENOUGH TO TRACK YOU DOWN?
WRONG AGAIN, MAMMAL LOVER!
MY ARMOR HARBORS THE WATER I NEED TO WAGE BATTLE AT PEAK PERFORMANCE.
WHAT WERE ONCE TINY SEA HORSES FLITTING ABOUT THE OCEAN FLOOR HAVE BEEN FINESSED TO SERVE THE GOALS OF ATLANTIS! WHILE YOU...?
BZZLLTCH
YOU'VE NOTHING TO FIGHT BACK WITH BUT THAT SOGGY WATER BAL-LOON OF A HAND!
F-FUNNY THING ABOUT THE HAND, RODUNN.

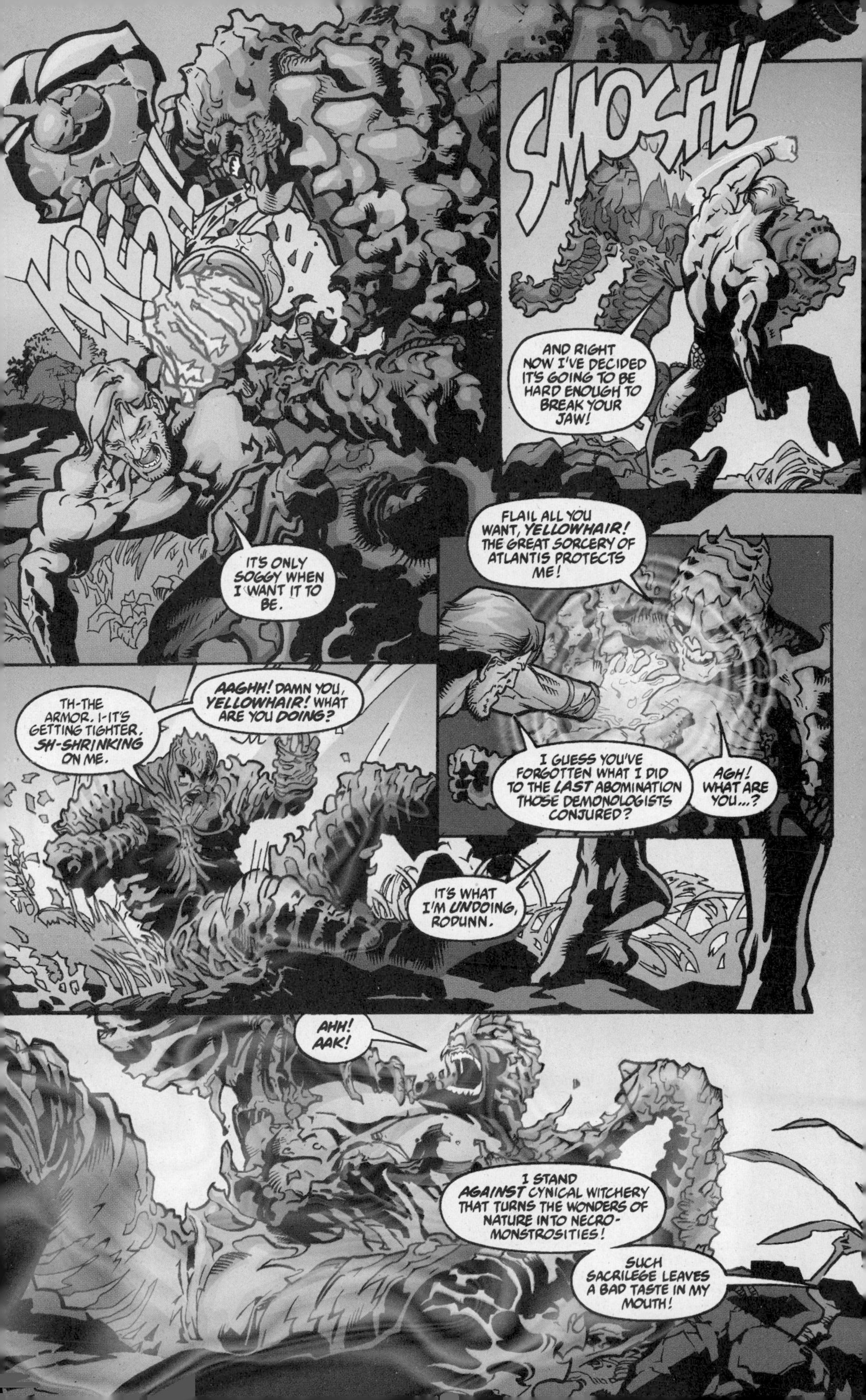
KRESH!
SHOSH!
AND RIGHT NOW I'VE DECIDED IT'S GOING TO BE HARD ENOUGH TO BREAK YOUR JAW!
IT'S ONLY SOGGY WHEN I WANT IT TO BE.
FLAIL ALL YOU WANT, YELLOWHAIR! THE GREAT SORCERY OF ATLANTIS PROTECTS ME!
I GUESS YOU'VE FORGOTTEN WHAT I DID TO THE LAST ABOMINATION THOSE DEMONOLOGISTS CONJURED?
AGH! WHAT ARE YOU...?
TH-THE ARMOR. I-IT'S GETTING TIGHTER. SH-SHRINKING ON ME.
AAGHH! DAMN YOU, YELLOWHAIR! WHAT ARE YOU DOING?
IT'S WHAT I'M UNDOING, RODUNN.
AHH! AAK!
I STAND AGAINST CYNICAL WITCHERY THAT TURNS THE WONDERS OF NATURE INTO NECRO-MONSTROSITIES!
SUCH SACRILEGE LEAVES A BAD TASTE IN MY MOUTH!

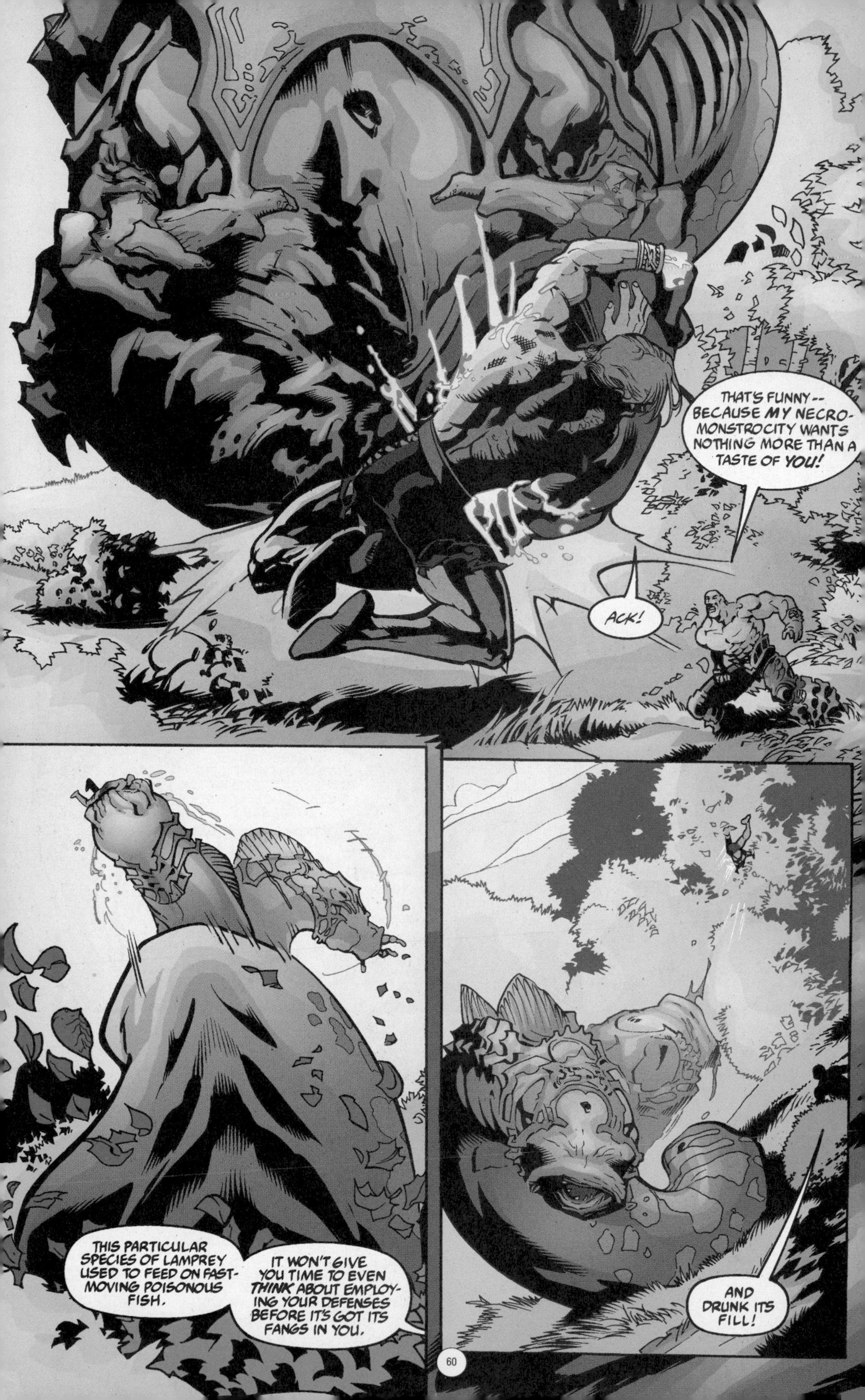
THAT'S FUNNY-- BECAUSE MY NECRO-MONSTROCITY WANTS NOTHING MORE THAN A TASTE OF YOU!
ACK!
THIS PARTICULAR SPECIES OF LAMPREY USED TO FEED ON FAST-MOVING POISONOUS FISH.
IT WON'T GIVE YOU TIME TO EVEN THINK ABOUT EMPLOYING YOUR DEFENSES BEFORE IT'S GOT ITS FANGS IN YOU.
AND DRUNK ITS FILL!

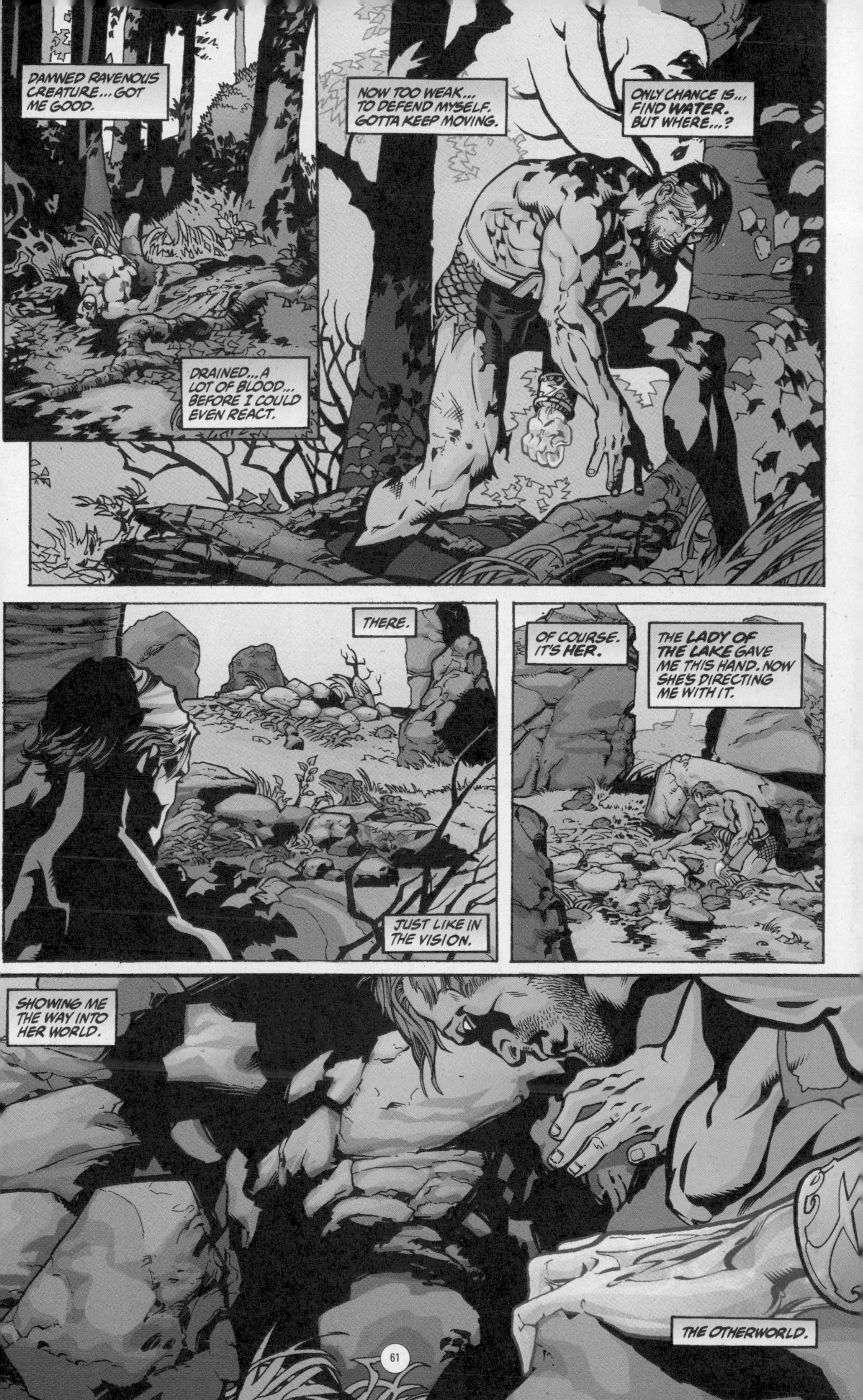
DAMNED RAVENOUS CREATURE... GOT ME GOOD.
NOW TOO WEAK... TO DEFEND MYSELF. GOTTA KEEP MOVING.
ONLY CHANCE IS... FIND WATER. BUT WHERE...?
DRAINED... A LOT OF BLOOD... BEFORE I COULD EVEN REACT.
THERE.
JUST LIKE IN THE VISION.
OF COURSE. IT'S HER.
THE LADY OF THE LAKE GAVE ME THIS HAND. NOW SHE'S DIRECTING ME WITH IT.
SHOWING ME THE WAY INTO HER WORLD.
THE OTHERWORLD.

THE COLD MOSSY BLACKNESS OF THE ANCIENT WELLHEAD SWALLOWS ME WHOLE.

ITS ENVELOPING WATER, PURE AND MERCURIAL, IS A BLESSED SALVE ON MY WOUNDS.

BUT IF I'M RIGHT, THIS WELL IS MUCH MORE THAN A SHAFT SUNK DEEP IN THE EARTH.

IT'S A PORTAL INTO A PLACE THE ANCIENT PEOPLE WHO LIVED HERE KNEW AS ANNWN.

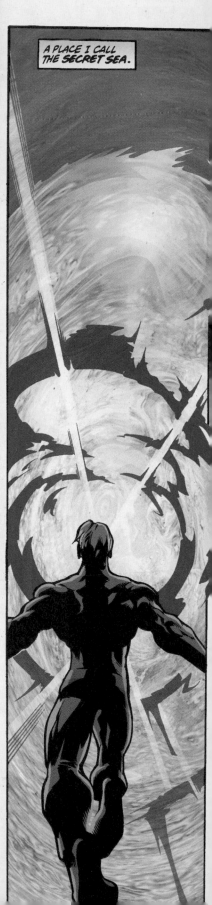

A PLACE I CALL THE SECRET SEA.

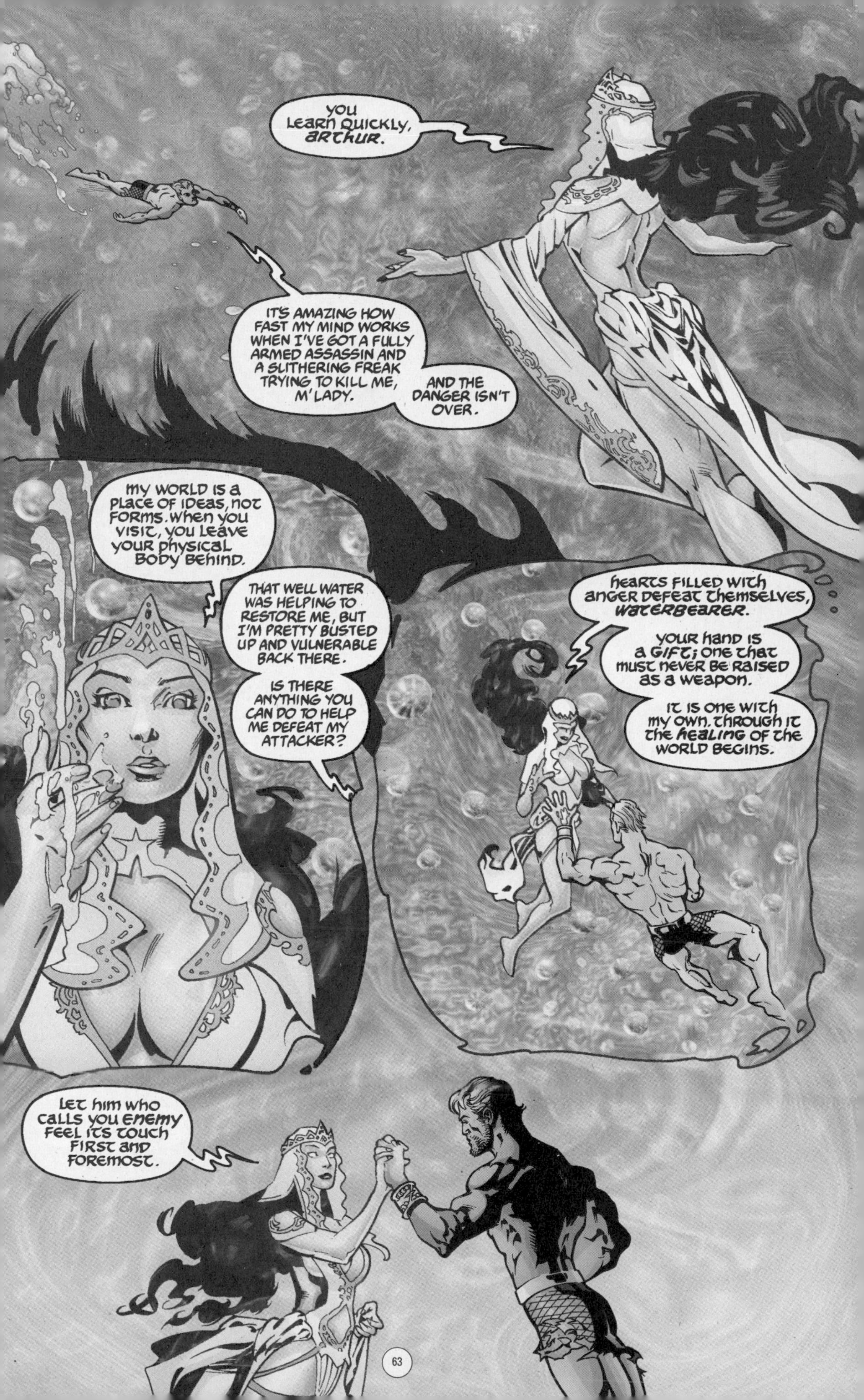

YOU LEARN QUICKLY, ARTHUR.
IT'S AMAZING HOW FAST MY MIND WORKS WHEN I'VE GOT A FULLY ARMED ASSASSIN AND A SLITHERING FREAK TRYING TO KILL ME, M'LADY.
AND THE DANGER ISN'T OVER.
MY WORLD IS A PLACE OF IDEAS, NOT FORMS. WHEN YOU VISIT, YOU LEAVE YOUR PHYSICAL BODY BEHIND.
THAT WELL WATER WAS HELPING TO RESTORE ME, BUT I'M PRETTY BUSTED UP AND VULNERABLE BACK THERE.
IS THERE ANYTHING YOU CAN DO TO HELP ME DEFEAT MY ATTACKER?
HEARTS FILLED WITH ANGER DEFEAT THEMSELVES, WATERBEARER.
YOUR HAND IS A GIFT; ONE THAT MUST NEVER BE RAISED AS A WEAPON.
IT IS ONE WITH MY OWN. THROUGH IT THE HEALING OF THE WORLD BEGINS.
LET HIM WHO CALLS YOU ENEMY FEEL ITS TOUCH FIRST AND FOREMOST.

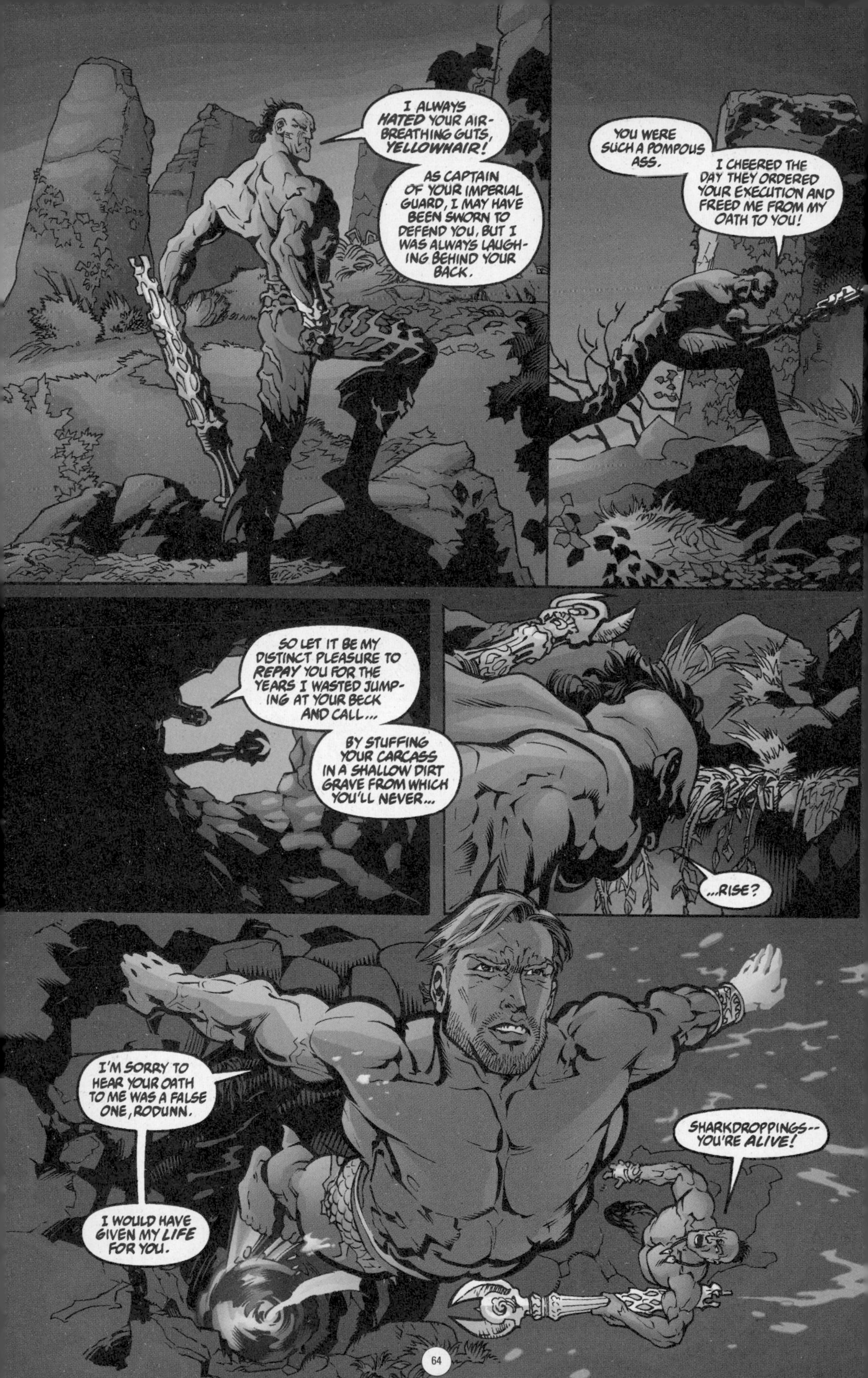

I ALWAYS HATED YOUR AIR-BREATHING GUTS, YELLOWHAIR!
AS CAPTAIN OF YOUR IMPERIAL GUARD, I MAY HAVE BEEN SWORN TO DEFEND YOU, BUT I WAS ALWAYS LAUGHING BEHIND YOUR BACK.
YOU WERE SUCH A POMPOUS ASS.
I CHEERED THE DAY THEY ORDERED YOUR EXECUTION AND FREED ME FROM MY OATH TO YOU!
SO LET IT BE MY DISTINCT PLEASURE TO REPAY YOU FOR THE YEARS I WASTED JUMPING AT YOUR BECK AND CALL...
BY STUFFING YOUR CARCASS IN A SHALLOW DIRT GRAVE FROM WHICH YOU'LL NEVER...
...RISE?
I'M SORRY TO HEAR YOUR OATH TO ME WAS A FALSE ONE, RODUNN.
I WOULD HAVE GIVEN MY LIFE FOR YOU.
SHARKDROPPINGS--YOU'RE ALIVE!

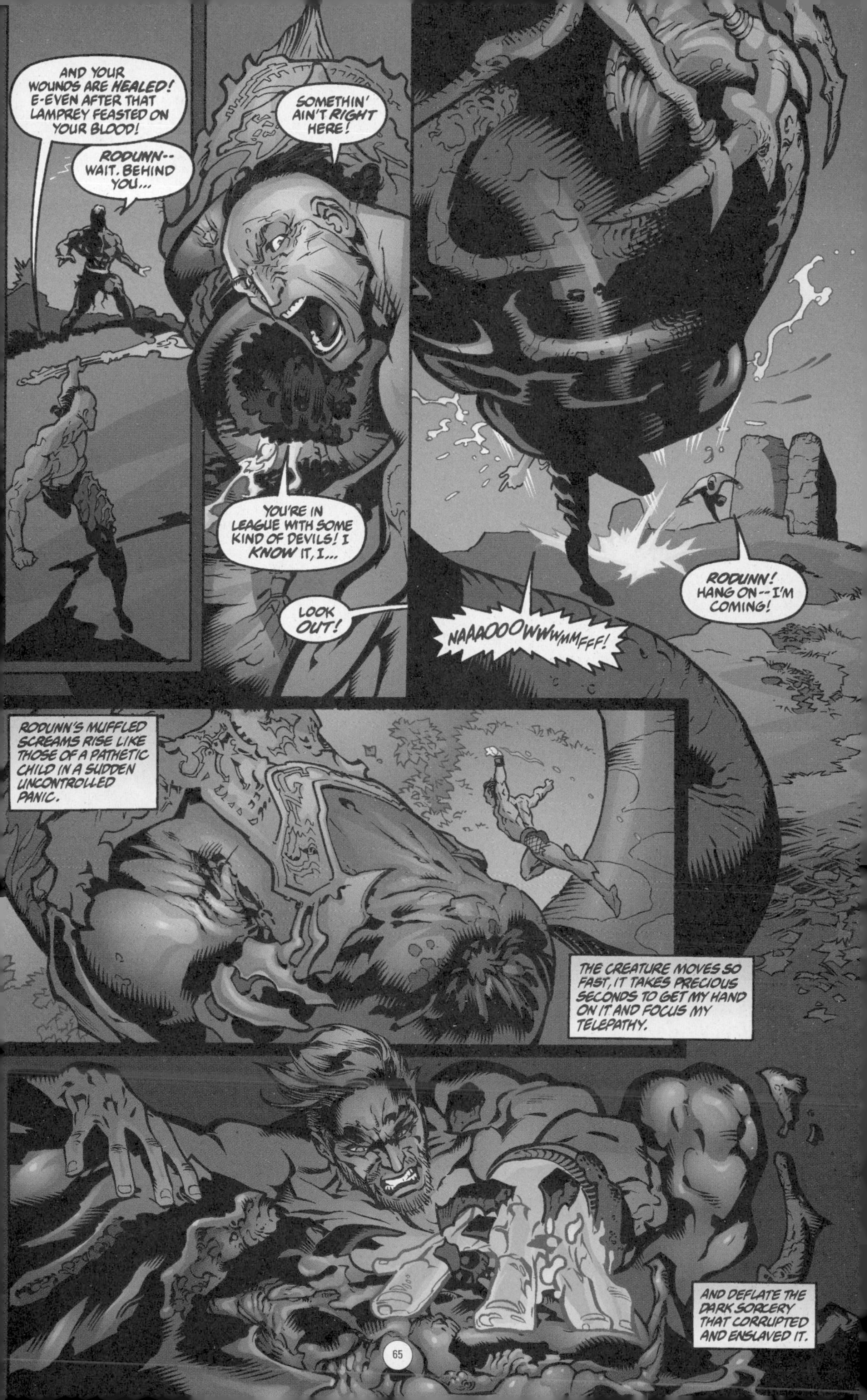

AND YOUR WOUNDS ARE HEALED! E-EVEN AFTER THAT LAMPREY FEASTED ON YOUR BLOOD!
RODUNN-- WAIT. BEHIND YOU...
SOMETHIN' AIN'T RIGHT HERE!
YOU'RE IN LEAGUE WITH SOME KIND OF DEVILS! I KNOW IT, I...
LOOK OUT!
NAAAOOOWWWMMFFF!
RODUNN! HANG ON -- I'M COMING!
RODUNN'S MUFFLED SCREAMS RISE LIKE THOSE OF A PATHETIC CHILD IN A SUDDEN UNCONTROLLED PANIC.
THE CREATURE MOVES SO FAST, IT TAKES PRECIOUS SECONDS TO GET MY HAND ON IT AND FOCUS MY TELEPATHY.
AND DEFLATE THE DARK SORCERY THAT CORRUPTED AND ENSLAVED IT.

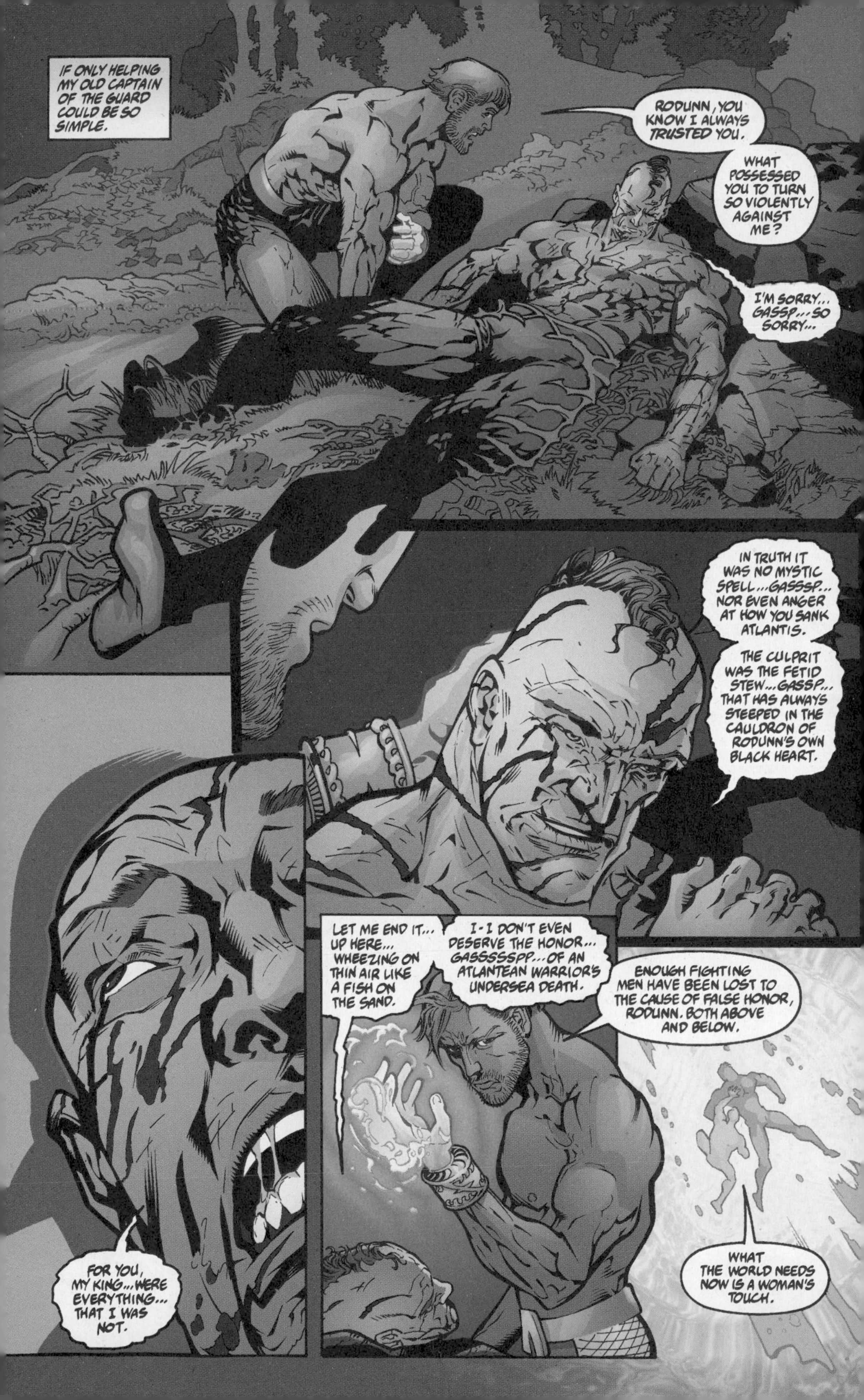
IF ONLY HELPING MY OLD CAPTAIN OF THE GUARD COULD BE SO SIMPLE.
RODUNN, YOU KNOW I ALWAYS TRUSTED YOU.
WHAT POSSESSED YOU TO TURN SO VIOLENTLY AGAINST ME?
I'M SORRY... GASSP... SO SORRY...
IN TRUTH IT WAS NO MYSTIC SPELL... GASSSP... NOR EVEN ANGER AT HOW YOU SANK ATLANTIS.
THE CULPRIT WAS THE FETID STEW... GASSP... THAT HAS ALWAYS STEEPED IN THE CAULDRON OF RODUNN'S OWN BLACK HEART.
FOR YOU, MY KING... WERE EVERYTHING... THAT I WAS NOT.
LET ME END IT... UP HERE... WHEEZING ON THIN AIR LIKE A FISH ON THE SAND.
I-I DON'T EVEN DESERVE THE HONOR... GASSSSSPP... OF AN ATLANTEAN WARRIOR'S UNDERSEA DEATH.
ENOUGH FIGHTING MEN HAVE BEEN LOST TO THE CAUSE OF FALSE HONOR, RODUNN. BOTH ABOVE AND BELOW.
WHAT THE WORLD NEEDS NOW IS A WOMAN'S TOUCH.

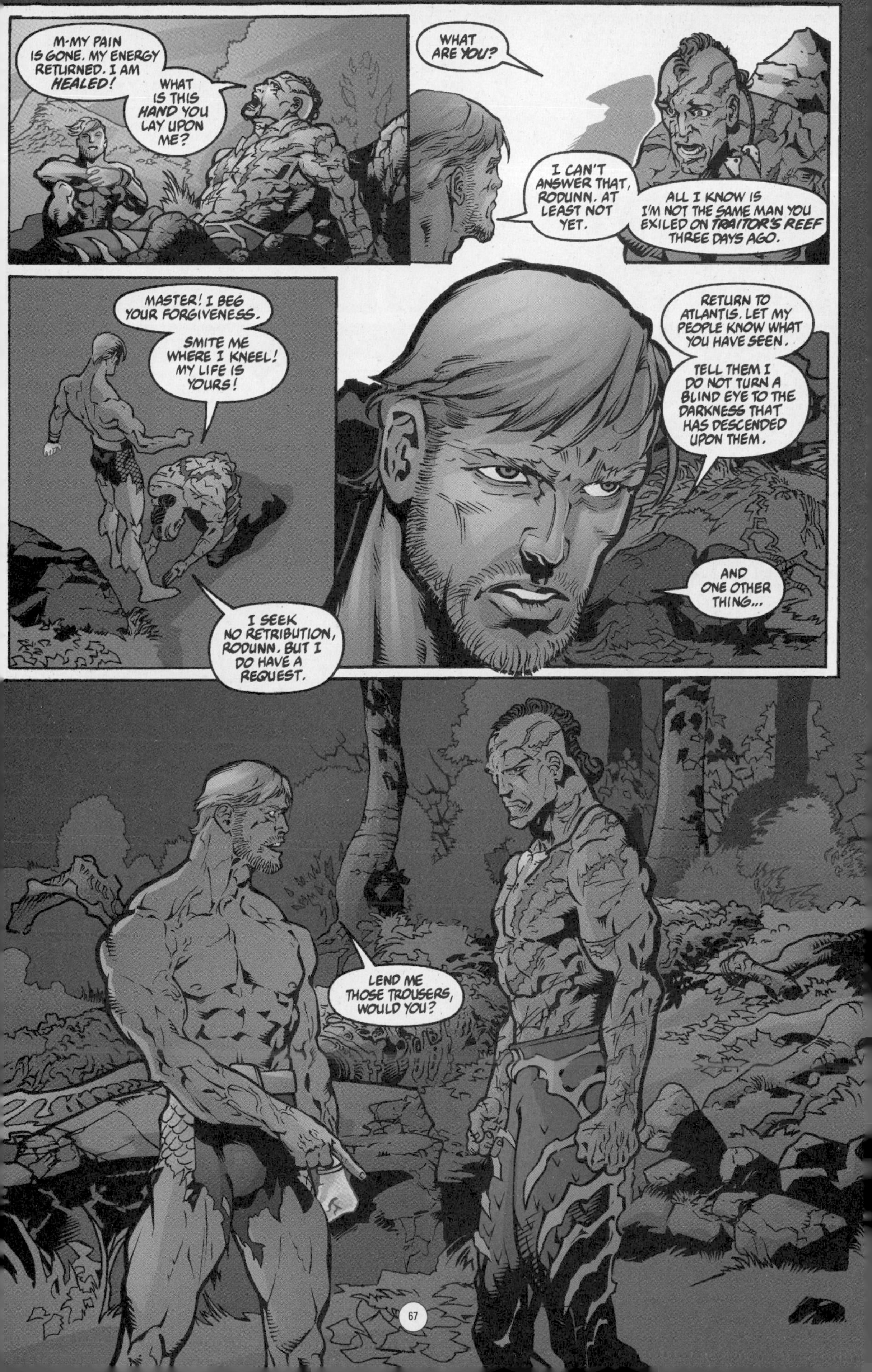
M-MY PAIN IS GONE. MY ENERGY RETURNED. I AM HEALED!
WHAT IS THIS HAND YOU LAY UPON ME?
WHAT ARE YOU?
I CAN'T ANSWER THAT, RODUNN. AT LEAST NOT YET.
ALL I KNOW IS I'M NOT THE SAME MAN YOU EXILED ON TRAITOR'S REEF THREE DAYS AGO.
MASTER! I BEG YOUR FORGIVENESS.
SMITE ME WHERE I KNEEL! MY LIFE IS YOURS!
I SEEK NO RETRIBUTION, RODUNN. BUT I DO HAVE A REQUEST.
RETURN TO ATLANTIS. LET MY PEOPLE KNOW WHAT YOU HAVE SEEN.
TELL THEM I DO NOT TURN A BLIND EYE TO THE DARKNESS THAT HAS DESCENDED UPON THEM.
AND ONE OTHER THING...
LEND ME THOSE TROUSERS, WOULD YOU?

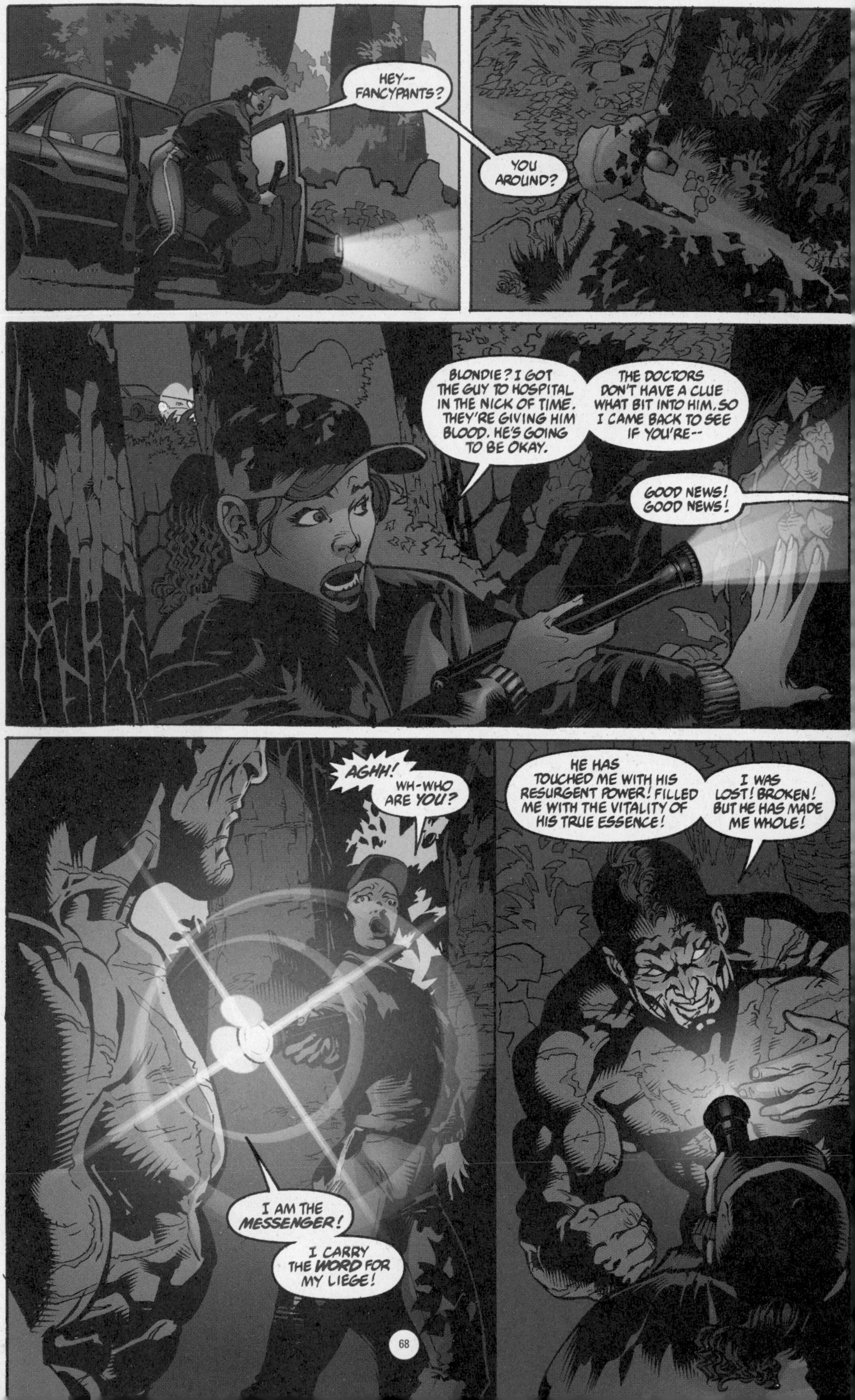
HEY--
FANCYPANTS?
YOU AROUND?
BLONDIE? I GOT THE GUY TO HOSPITAL IN THE NICK OF TIME. THEY'RE GIVING HIM BLOOD. HE'S GOING TO BE OKAY.
THE DOCTORS DON'T HAVE A CLUE WHAT BIT INTO HIM, SO I CAME BACK TO SEE IF YOU'RE--
GOOD NEWS! GOOD NEWS!
AGHH!
WH-WHO ARE YOU?
I AM THE MESSENGER!
I CARRY THE WORD FOR MY LIEGE!
HE HAS TOUCHED ME WITH HIS RESURGENT POWER! FILLED ME WITH THE VITALITY OF HIS TRUE ESSENCE!
I WAS LOST! BROKEN! BUT HE HAS MADE ME WHOLE!

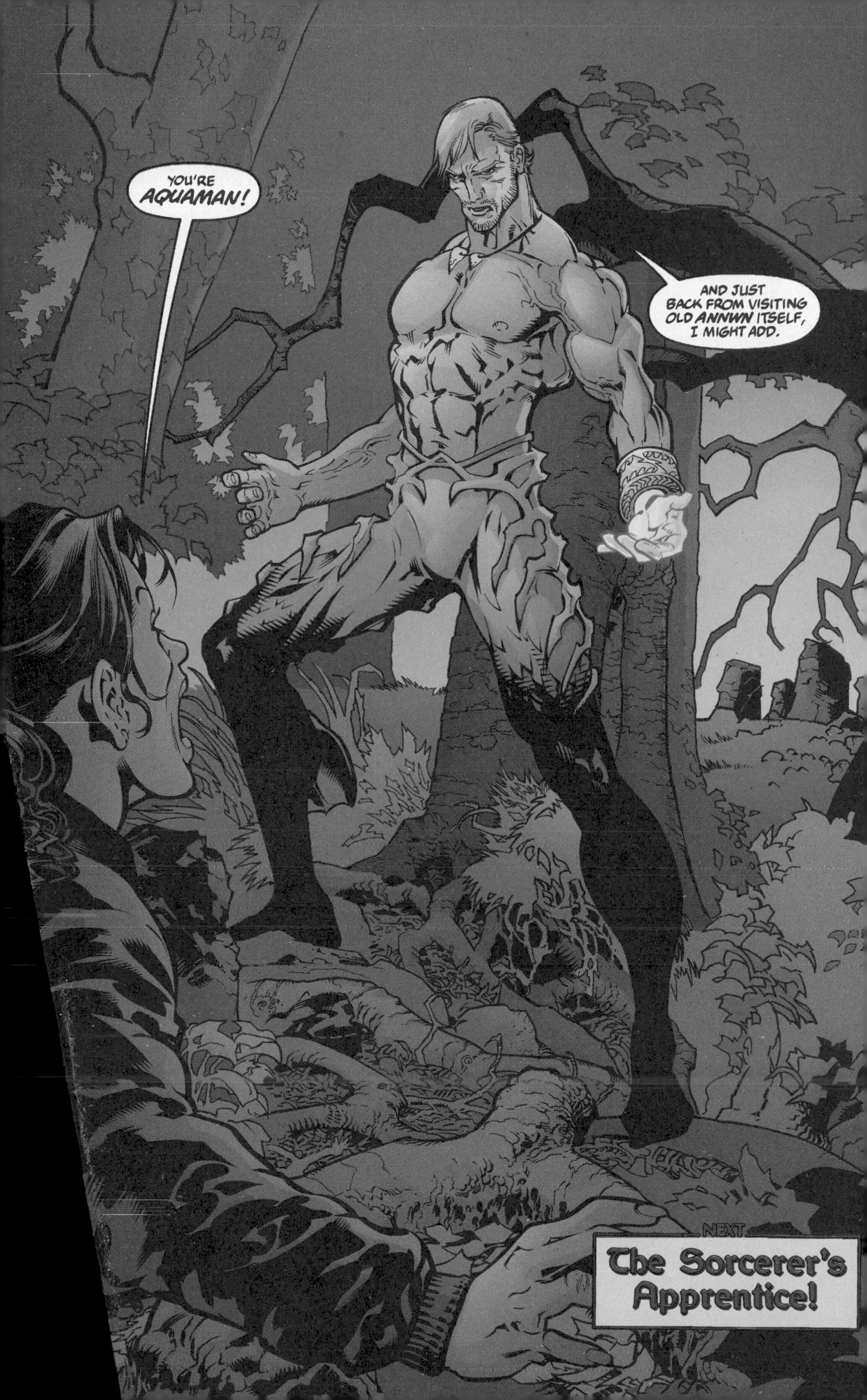
YOU'RE AQUAMAN!
AND JUST BACK FROM VISITING OLD ANNWN ITSELF, I MIGHT ADD.
NEXT
The Sorcerer's Apprentice!

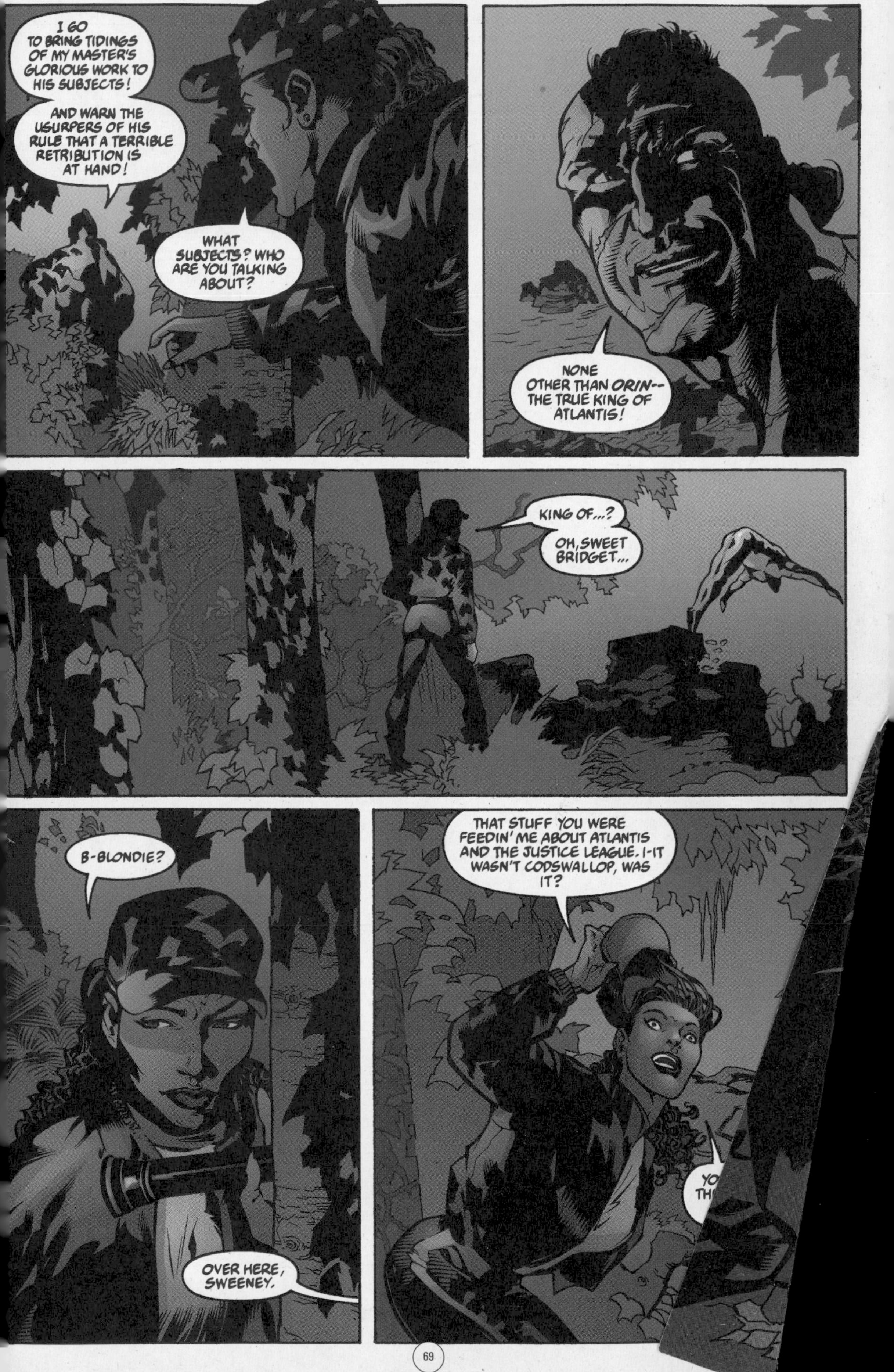
I GO TO BRING TIDINGS OF MY MASTER'S GLORIOUS WORK TO HIS SUBJECTS!
AND WARN THE USURPERS OF HIS RULE THAT A TERRIBLE RETRIBUTION IS AT HAND!
WHAT SUBJECTS? WHO ARE YOU TALKING ABOUT?
NONE OTHER THAN ORIN-- THE TRUE KING OF ATLANTIS!
KING OF...?
OH, SWEET BRIDGET...
B-BLONDIE?
OVER HERE, SWEENEY.
THAT STUFF YOU WERE FEEDIN' ME ABOUT ATLANTIS AND THE JUSTICE LEAGUE. I-IT WASN'T CODSWALLOP, WAS IT?

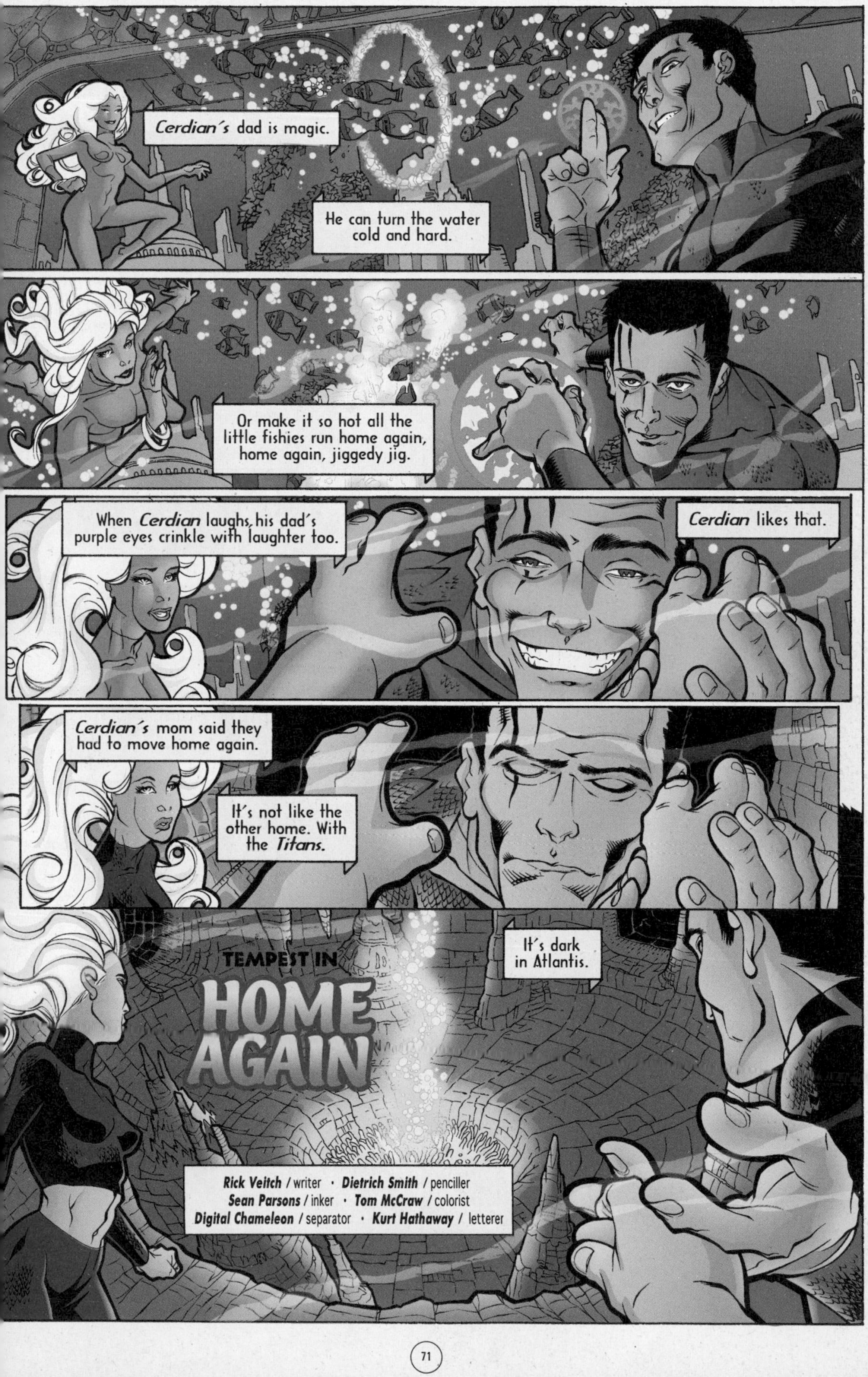
Cerdian's dad is magic.
He can turn the water cold and hard.
Or make it so hot all the little fishies run home again, home again, jiggedy jig.
When Cerdian laughs, his dad's purple eyes crinkle with laughter too.
Cerdian likes that.
Cerdian's mom said they had to move home again.
It's not like the other home. With the Titans.
It's dark in Atlantis.
TEMPEST IN
HOME AGAIN
Rick Veitch / writer · Dietrich Smith / penciller
Sean Parsons / inker · Tom McCraw / colorist
Digital Chameleon / separator · Kurt Hathaway / letterer

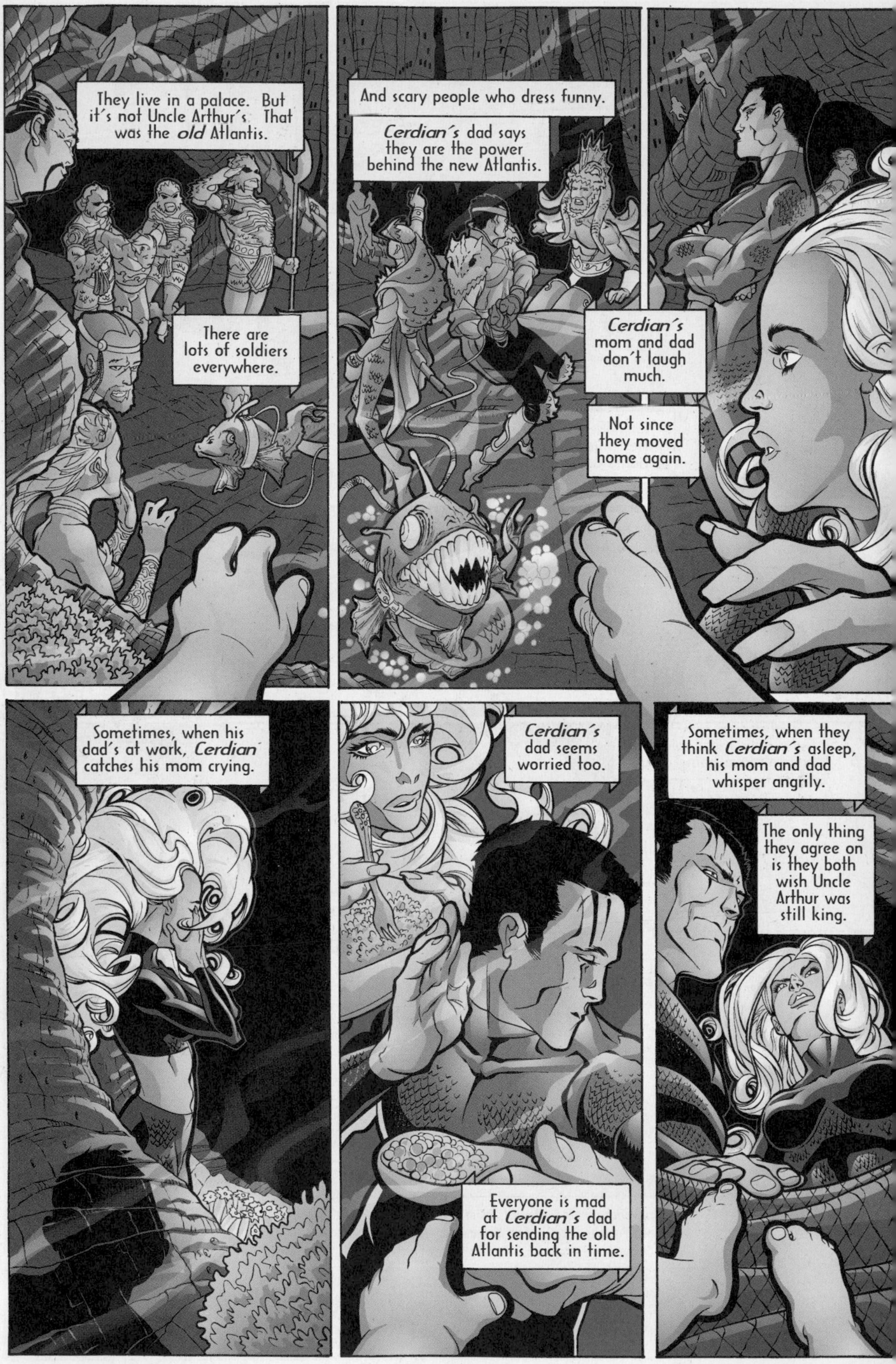
They live in a palace. But it´s not Uncle Arthur´s. That was the *old* Atlantis.
There are lots of soldiers everywhere.
And scary people who dress funny.
Cerdian´s dad says they are the power behind the new Atlantis.
Cerdian´s mom and dad don´t laugh much.
Not since they moved home again.
Sometimes, when his dad´s at work, *Cerdian* catches his mom crying.
Cerdian´s dad seems worried too.
Everyone is mad at *Cerdian´s* dad for sending the old Atlantis back in time.
Sometimes, when they think *Cerdian´s* asleep, his mom and dad whisper angrily.
The only thing they agree on is they both wish Uncle Arthur was still king.

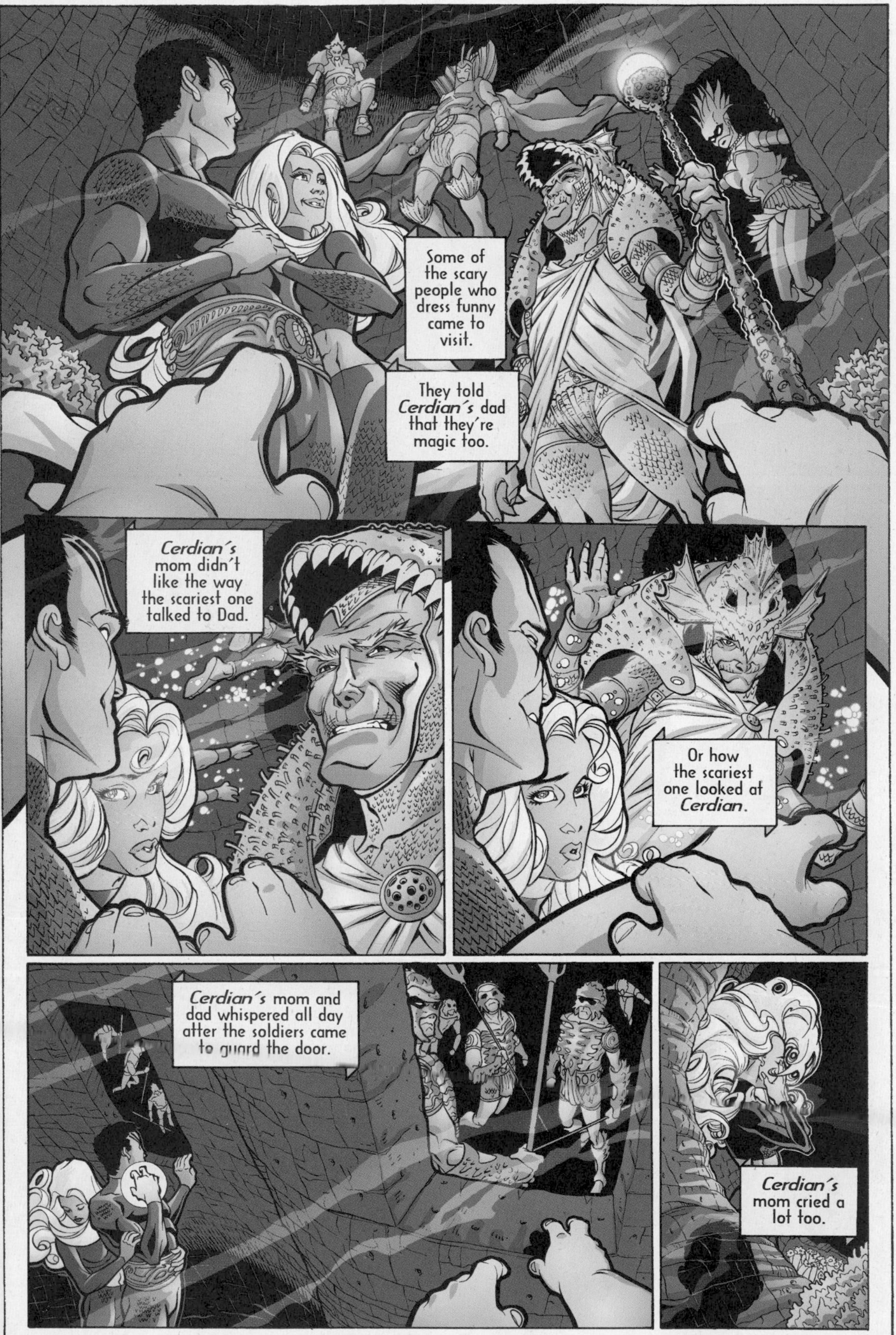
Some of the scary people who dress funny came to visit.
They told *Cerdian's* dad that they're magic too.
Cerdian's mom didn't like the way the scariest one talked to Dad.
Or how the scariest one looked at *Cerdian*.
Cerdian's mom and dad whispered all day after the soldiers came to guard the door.
Cerdian's mom cried a lot too.

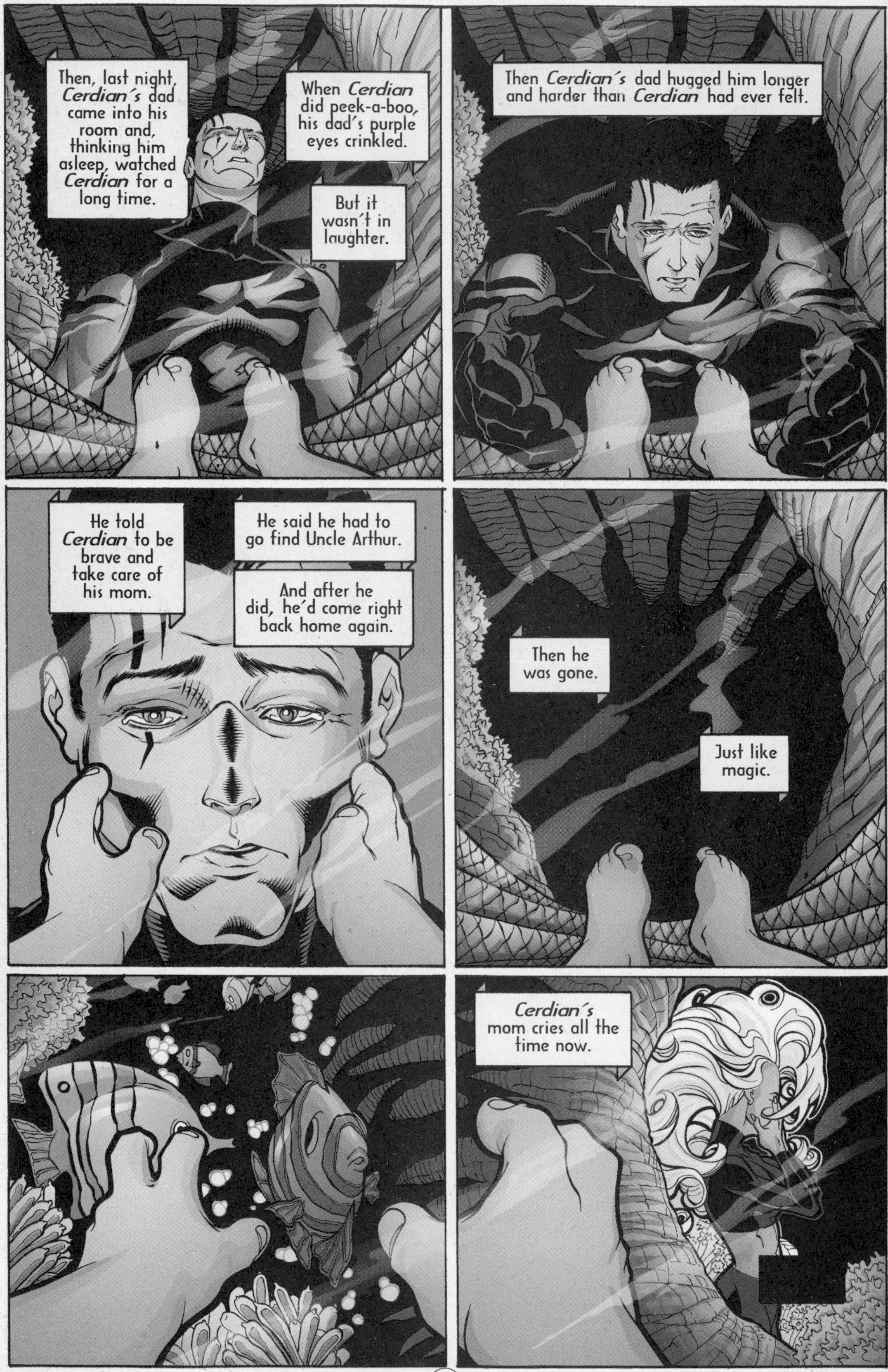

Then, last night, *Cerdian's* dad came into his room and, thinking him asleep, watched *Cerdian* for a long time.
When *Cerdian* did peek-a-boo, his dad's purple eyes crinkled.
But it wasn't in laughter.
Then *Cerdian's* dad hugged him longer and harder than *Cerdian* had ever felt.
He told *Cerdian* to be brave and take care of his mom.
He said he had to go find Uncle Arthur.
And after he did, he'd come right back home again.
Then he was gone.
Just like magic.
Cerdian's mom cries all the time now.

SO YOU WEREN'T JUST ACTIN' THE MAGGOT WITH ME, THEN?

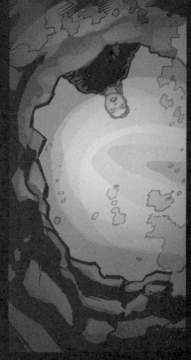

YOU REALLY *ARE* THE KING OF ATLANTIS?

I'M NOT SURE I SHOULD BE TELLING YOU THIS, *SWEENEY*...

BUT YEAH--I *USED* TO BE. BEFORE THEY EXILED ME.

UNREAL. I WAS WATCHIN' *"LOST MYSTERY"* ON THE TELLY AND IT SAID ATLANTIS DISAPPEARED IN SOME BIG SUPERHERO BATTLE.

HAS IT *RESURFACED?*

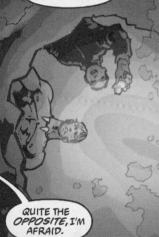

QUITE THE *OPPOSITE*, I'M AFRAID.

SO YOU'RE GOING TO, LIKE... GET YOUR THRONE BACK, RIGHT?

IF THIS WERE THE *OLD DAYS*, I'D BE RAISING AN ARMY AND STORMING THE GATES OF THE ROYAL CITY.

BUT THE OLD DAYS ARE *OVER* FOR ME.

THINGS HAVE CHANGED.

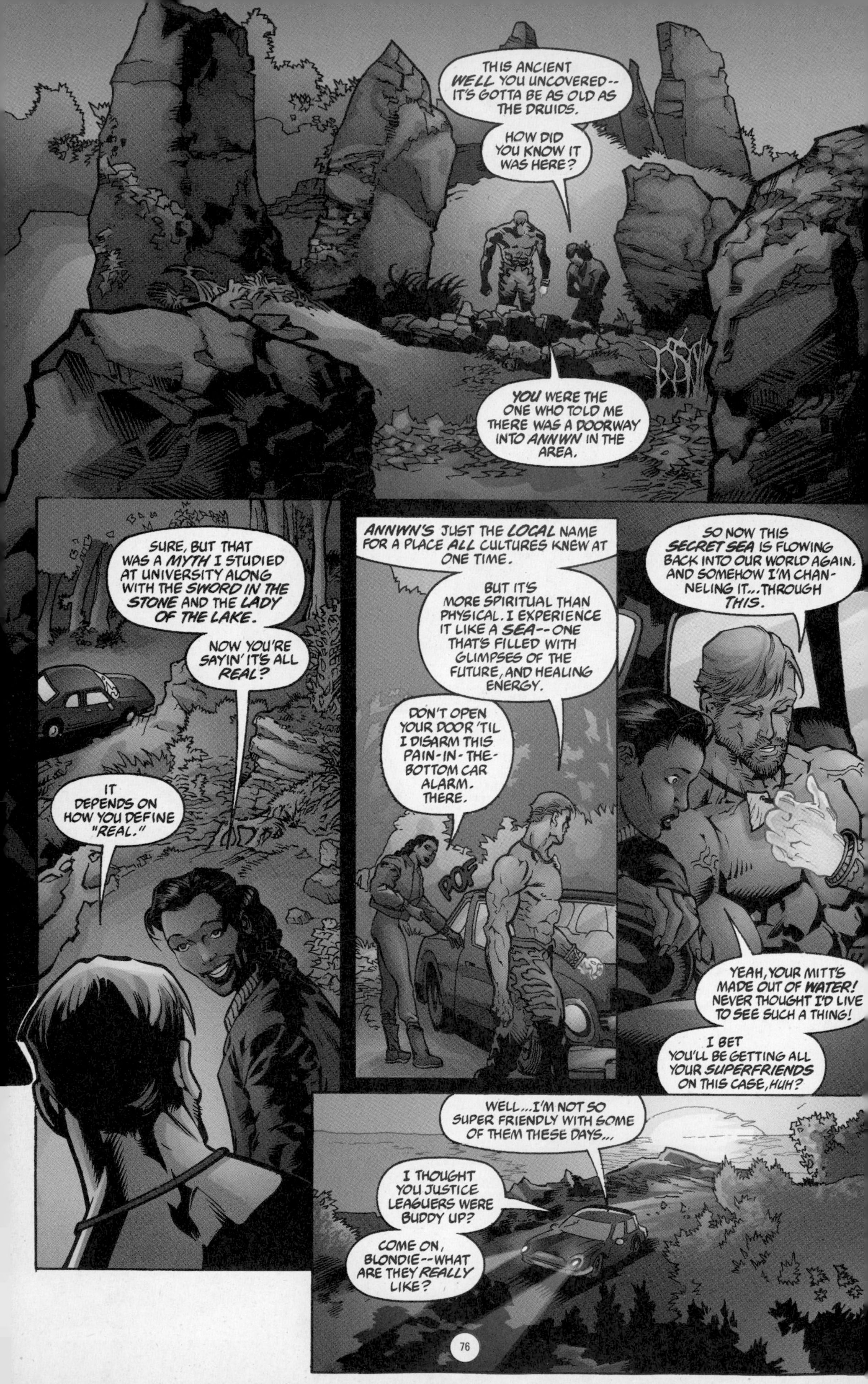
THIS ANCIENT WELL YOU UNCOVERED-- IT'S GOTTA BE AS OLD AS THE DRUIDS.
HOW DID YOU KNOW IT WAS HERE?
YOU WERE THE ONE WHO TOLD ME THERE WAS A DOORWAY INTO ANNWN IN THE AREA.
SURE, BUT THAT WAS A MYTH I STUDIED AT UNIVERSITY ALONG WITH THE SWORD IN THE STONE AND THE LADY OF THE LAKE.
NOW YOU'RE SAYIN' IT'S ALL REAL?
IT DEPENDS ON HOW YOU DEFINE "REAL."
ANNWN'S JUST THE LOCAL NAME FOR A PLACE ALL CULTURES KNEW AT ONE TIME.
BUT IT'S MORE SPIRITUAL THAN PHYSICAL. I EXPERIENCE IT LIKE A SEA--ONE THAT'S FILLED WITH GLIMPSES OF THE FUTURE, AND HEALING ENERGY.
DON'T OPEN YOUR DOOR 'TIL I DISARM THIS PAIN-IN-THE-BOTTOM CAR ALARM. THERE.
POF
SO NOW THIS SECRET SEA IS FLOWING BACK INTO OUR WORLD AGAIN, AND SOMEHOW I'M CHANNELING IT... THROUGH THIS.
YEAH, YOUR MITT'S MADE OUT OF WATER! NEVER THOUGHT I'D LIVE TO SEE SUCH A THING!
I BET YOU'LL BE GETTING ALL YOUR SUPERFRIENDS ON THIS CASE, HUH?
WELL... I'M NOT SO SUPER FRIENDLY WITH SOME OF THEM THESE DAYS...
I THOUGHT YOU JUSTICE LEAGUERS WERE BUDDY UP?
COME ON, BLONDIE--WHAT ARE THEY REALLY LIKE?

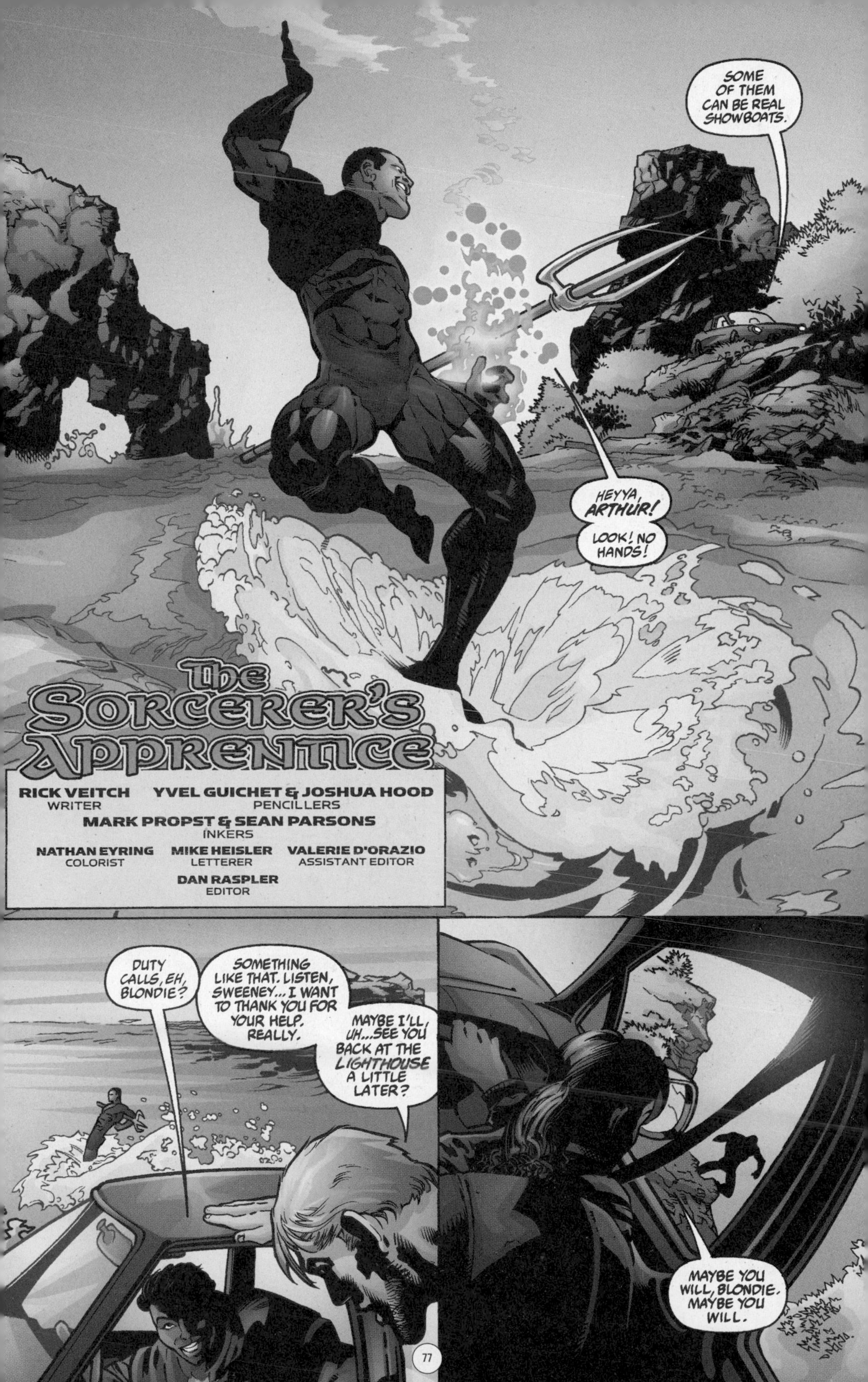
SOME OF THEM CAN BE REAL SHOWBOATS.
HEYYA, ARTHUR!
LOOK! NO HANDS!
The Sorcerer's Apprentice
RICK VEITCH WRITER
YVEL GUICHET & JOSHUA HOOD PENCILLERS
MARK PROPST & SEAN PARSONS INKERS
NATHAN EYRING COLORIST
MIKE HEISLER LETTERER
VALERIE D'ORAZIO ASSISTANT EDITOR
DAN RASPLER EDITOR
DUTY CALLS, EH, BLONDIE?
SOMETHING LIKE THAT. LISTEN, SWEENEY... I WANT TO THANK YOU FOR YOUR HELP. REALLY.
MAYBE I'LL, UH...SEE YOU BACK AT THE LIGHTHOUSE A LITTLE LATER?
MAYBE YOU WILL, BLONDIE. MAYBE YOU WILL.

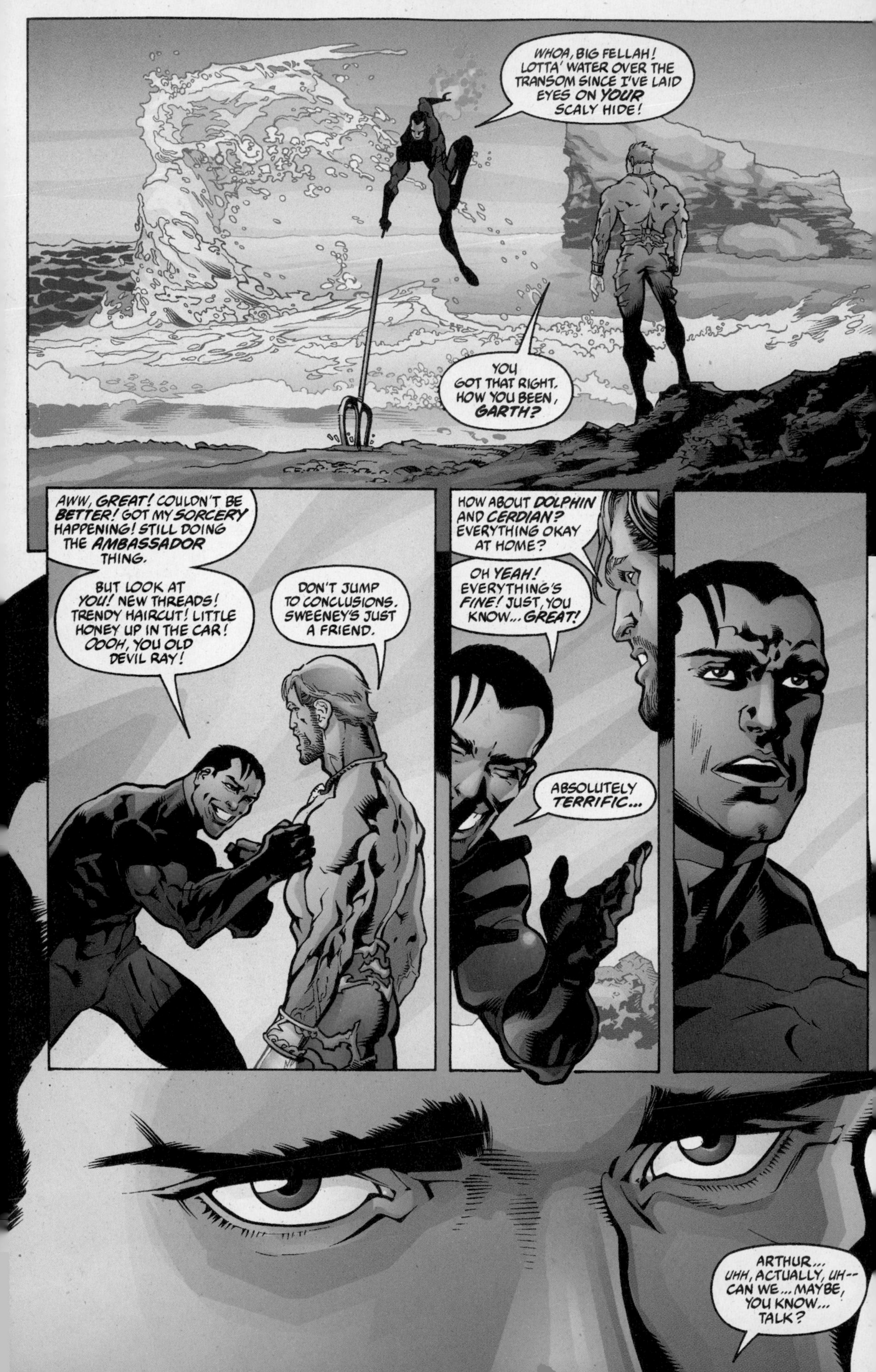
WHOA, BIG FELLAH! LOTTA' WATER OVER THE TRANSOM SINCE I'VE LAID EYES ON YOUR SCALY HIDE!
YOU GOT THAT RIGHT. HOW YOU BEEN, GARTH?
AWW, GREAT! COULDN'T BE BETTER! GOT MY SORCERY HAPPENING! STILL DOING THE AMBASSADOR THING.
BUT LOOK AT YOU! NEW THREADS! TRENDY HAIRCUT! LITTLE HONEY UP IN THE CAR! OOOH, YOU OLD DEVIL RAY!
DON'T JUMP TO CONCLUSIONS. SWEENEY'S JUST A FRIEND.
HOW ABOUT DOLPHIN AND CERDIAN? EVERYTHING OKAY AT HOME?
OH YEAH! EVERYTHING'S FINE! JUST, YOU KNOW... GREAT!
ABSOLUTELY TERRIFIC...
ARTHUR... UHH, ACTUALLY, UH-- CAN WE... MAYBE, YOU KNOW... TALK?

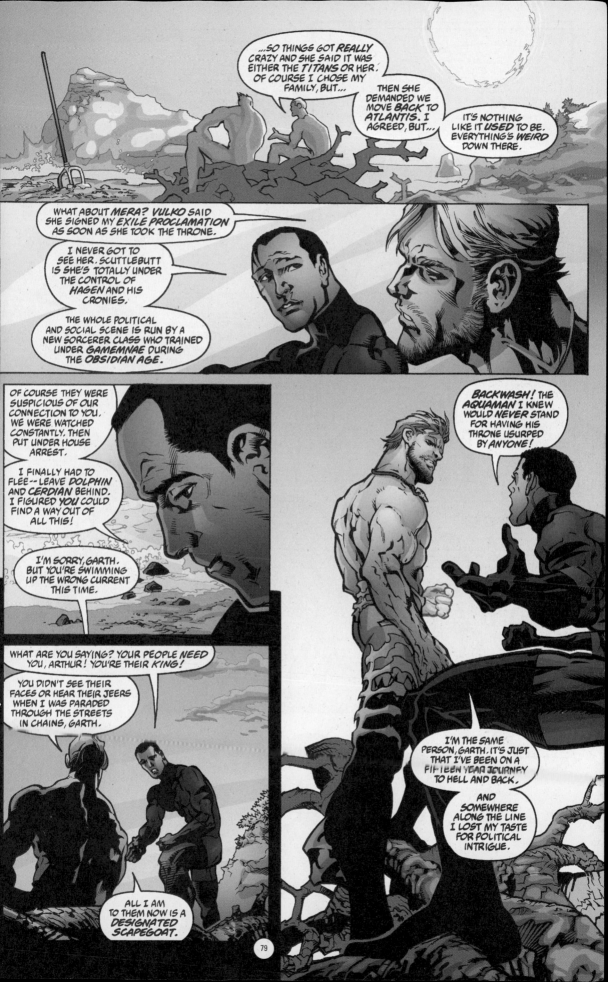

...SO THINGS GOT *REALLY* CRAZY AND SHE SAID IT WAS EITHER THE *TITANS* OR HER. OF COURSE I CHOSE MY FAMILY, BUT...

THEN SHE DEMANDED WE MOVE *BACK* TO *ATLANTIS.* I AGREED, BUT...

IT'S NOTHING LIKE IT *USED* TO BE. EVERYTHING'S *WEIRD* DOWN THERE.

WHAT ABOUT *MERA? VULKO* SAID SHE SIGNED MY *EXILE PROCLAMATION* AS SOON AS SHE TOOK THE THRONE.

I NEVER GOT TO SEE HER. *SCUTTLEBUTT* IS SHE'S TOTALLY UNDER THE CONTROL OF *HAGEN* AND HIS CRONIES.

THE WHOLE POLITICAL AND SOCIAL SCENE IS RUN BY A NEW SORCERER CLASS WHO TRAINED UNDER *GAMEMNAE* DURING THE *OBSIDIAN AGE.*

OF COURSE THEY WERE SUSPICIOUS OF OUR CONNECTION TO YOU, WE WERE WATCHED CONSTANTLY. THEN PUT UNDER HOUSE ARREST.

I FINALLY HAD TO FLEE-- LEAVE *DOLPHIN* AND *CERDIAN* BEHIND. I FIGURED *YOU* COULD FIND A WAY OUT OF ALL THIS!

I'M SORRY, GARTH. BUT YOU'RE SWIMMING UP THE WRONG CURRENT THIS TIME.

BACKWASH! THE AQUAMAN I KNEW WOULD *NEVER* STAND FOR HAVING HIS THRONE USURPED BY *ANYONE!*

WHAT ARE YOU SAYING? YOUR PEOPLE *NEED* YOU, ARTHUR! YOU'RE THEIR *KING!*

YOU DIDN'T SEE THEIR FACES OR HEAR THEIR JEERS WHEN I WAS PARADED THROUGH THE STREETS IN CHAINS, GARTH.

I'M THE SAME PERSON, GARTH. IT'S JUST THAT I'VE BEEN ON A FIFTEEN YEAR JOURNEY TO HELL AND BACK.

AND SOMEWHERE ALONG THE LINE I LOST MY TASTE FOR POLITICAL INTRIGUE.

ALL I AM TO THEM NOW IS A *DESIGNATED SCAPEGOAT.*

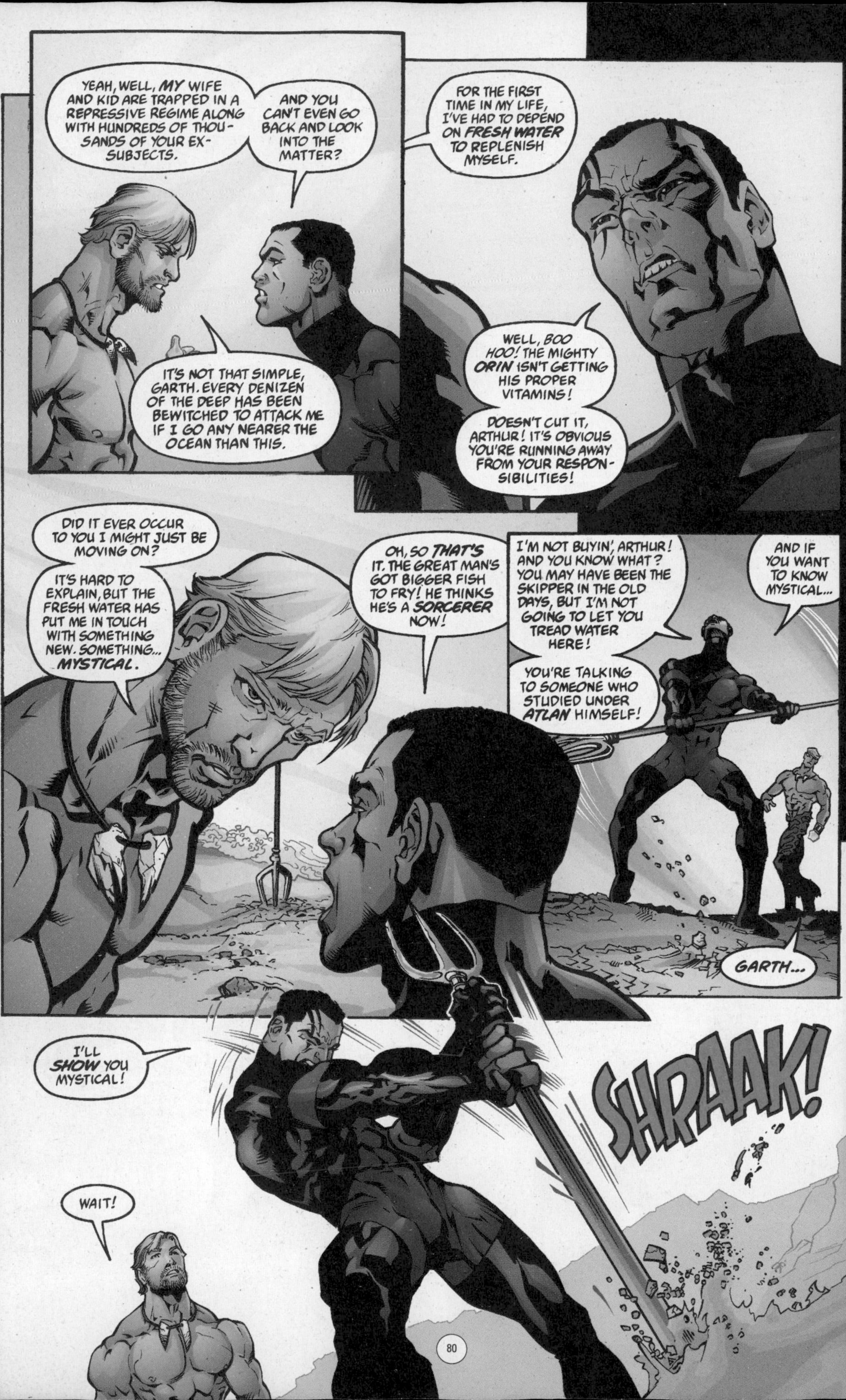
YEAH, WELL, MY WIFE AND KID ARE TRAPPED IN A REPRESSIVE REGIME ALONG WITH HUNDREDS OF THOU-SANDS OF YOUR EX-SUBJECTS.
AND YOU CAN'T EVEN GO BACK AND LOOK INTO THE MATTER?
IT'S NOT THAT SIMPLE, GARTH. EVERY DENIZEN OF THE DEEP HAS BEEN BEWITCHED TO ATTACK ME IF I GO ANY NEARER THE OCEAN THAN THIS.
FOR THE FIRST TIME IN MY LIFE, I'VE HAD TO DEPEND ON FRESH WATER TO REPLENISH MYSELF.
WELL, BOO HOO! THE MIGHTY ORIN ISN'T GETTING HIS PROPER VITAMINS!
DOESN'T CUT IT, ARTHUR! IT'S OBVIOUS YOU'RE RUNNING AWAY FROM YOUR RESPON-SIBILITIES!
DID IT EVER OCCUR TO YOU I MIGHT JUST BE MOVING ON?
IT'S HARD TO EXPLAIN, BUT THE FRESH WATER HAS PUT ME IN TOUCH WITH SOMETHING NEW. SOMETHING... MYSTICAL.
OH, SO THAT'S IT. THE GREAT MAN'S GOT BIGGER FISH TO FRY! HE THINKS HE'S A SORCERER NOW!
I'M NOT BUYIN', ARTHUR! AND YOU KNOW WHAT? YOU MAY HAVE BEEN THE SKIPPER IN THE OLD DAYS, BUT I'M NOT GOING TO LET YOU TREAD WATER HERE!
YOU'RE TALKING TO SOMEONE WHO STUDIED UNDER ATLAN HIMSELF!
AND IF YOU WANT TO KNOW MYSTICAL...
GARTH...
I'LL SHOW YOU MYSTICAL!
SHRAAK!
WAIT!

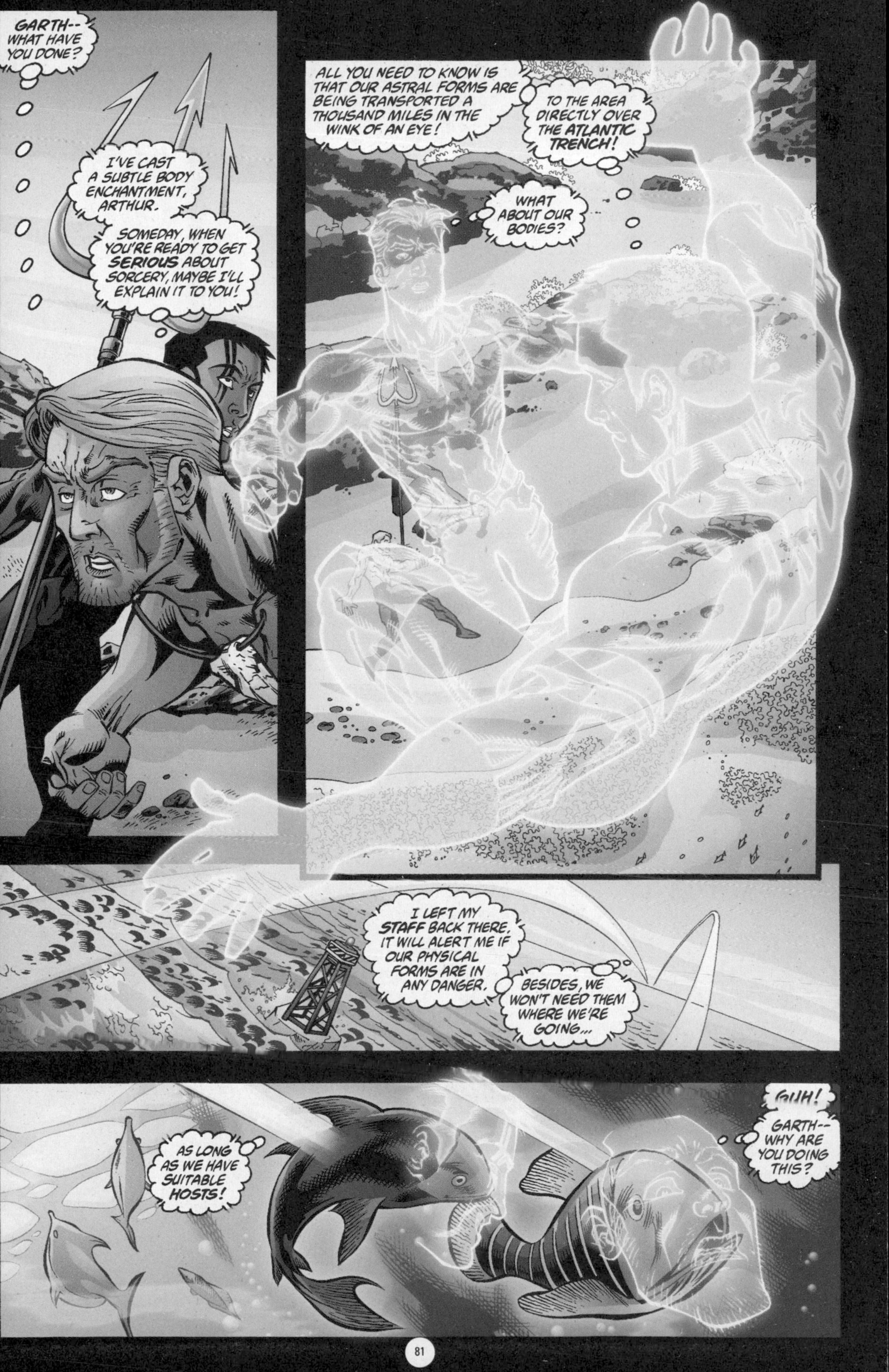
GARTH-- WHAT HAVE YOU DONE?
I'VE CAST A SUBTLE BODY ENCHANTMENT, ARTHUR.
SOMEDAY, WHEN YOU'RE READY TO GET SERIOUS ABOUT SORCERY, MAYBE I'LL EXPLAIN IT TO YOU!
ALL YOU NEED TO KNOW IS THAT OUR ASTRAL FORMS ARE BEING TRANSPORTED A THOUSAND MILES IN THE WINK OF AN EYE!
TO THE AREA DIRECTLY OVER THE ATLANTIC TRENCH!
WHAT ABOUT OUR BODIES?
I LEFT MY STAFF BACK THERE. IT WILL ALERT ME IF OUR PHYSICAL FORMS ARE IN ANY DANGER.
BESIDES, WE WON'T NEED THEM WHERE WE'RE GOING...
AS LONG AS WE HAVE SUITABLE HOSTS!
GUH!
GARTH-- WHY ARE YOU DOING THIS?

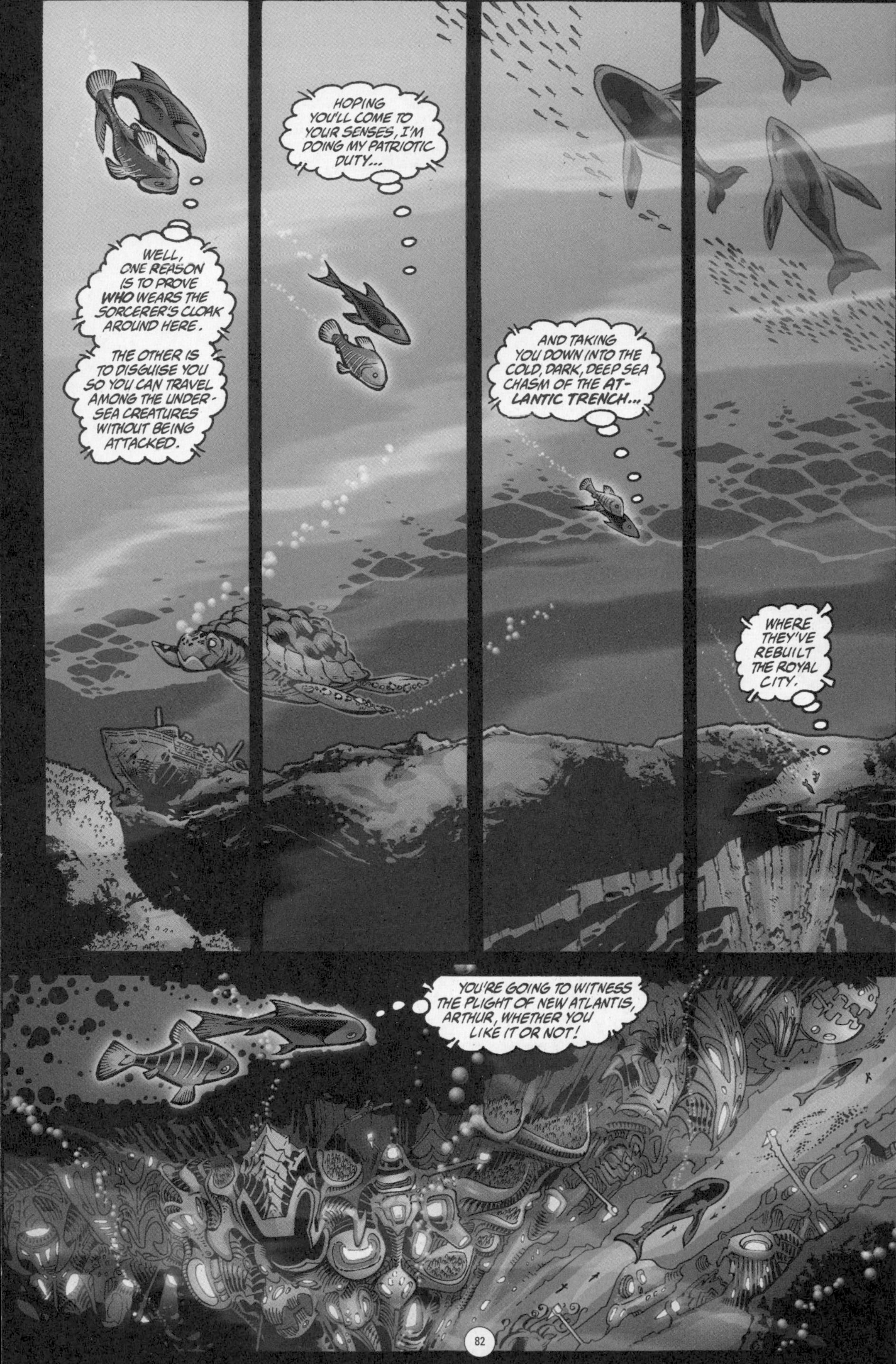
WELL, ONE REASON IS TO PROVE WHO WEARS THE SORCERER'S CLOAK AROUND HERE.
THE OTHER IS TO DISGUISE YOU SO YOU CAN TRAVEL AMONG THE UNDER-SEA CREATURES WITHOUT BEING ATTACKED.
HOPING YOU'LL COME TO YOUR SENSES, I'M DOING MY PATRIOTIC DUTY...
AND TAKING YOU DOWN INTO THE COLD, DARK, DEEP SEA CHASM OF THE AT-LANTIC TRENCH...
WHERE THEY'VE REBUILT THE ROYAL CITY.
YOU'RE GOING TO WITNESS THE PLIGHT OF NEW ATLANTIS, ARTHUR, WHETHER YOU LIKE IT OR NOT!

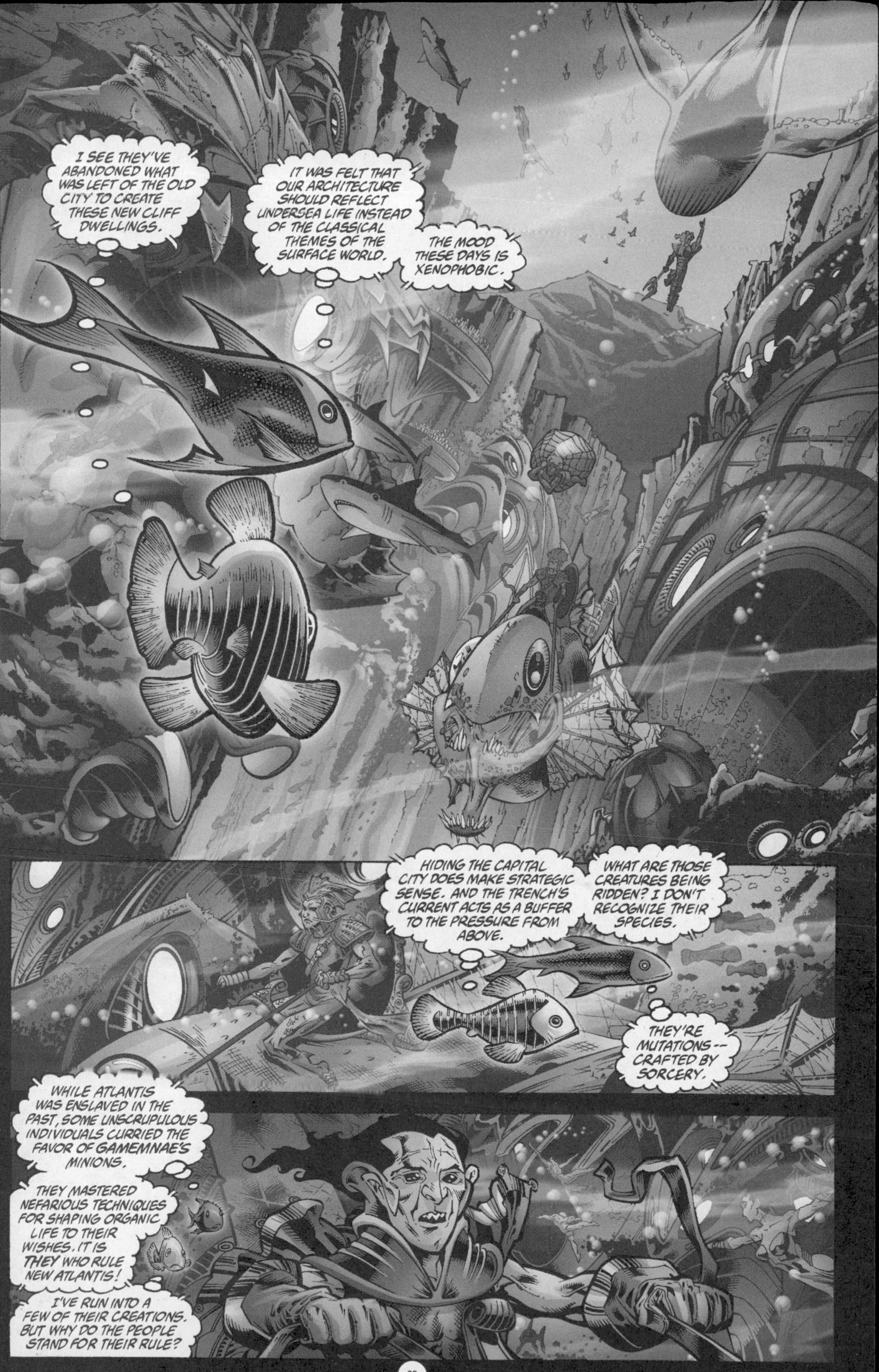
I SEE THEY'VE ABANDONED WHAT WAS LEFT OF THE OLD CITY TO CREATE THESE NEW CLIFF DWELLINGS.
IT WAS FELT THAT OUR ARCHITECTURE SHOULD REFLECT UNDERSEA LIFE INSTEAD OF THE CLASSICAL THEMES OF THE SURFACE WORLD.
THE MOOD THESE DAYS IS XENOPHOBIC.
HIDING THE CAPITAL CITY DOES MAKE STRATEGIC SENSE. AND THE TRENCH'S CURRENT ACTS AS A BUFFER TO THE PRESSURE FROM ABOVE.
WHAT ARE THOSE CREATURES BEING RIDDEN? I DON'T RECOGNIZE THEIR SPECIES.
THEY'RE MUTATIONS-- CRAFTED BY SORCERY.
WHILE ATLANTIS WAS ENSLAVED IN THE PAST, SOME UNSCRUPULOUS INDIVIDUALS CURRIED THE FAVOR OF GAMEMNAE'S MINIONS.
THEY MASTERED NEFARIOUS TECHNIQUES FOR SHAPING ORGANIC LIFE TO THEIR WISHES. IT IS THEY WHO RULE NEW ATLANTIS!
I'VE RUN INTO A FEW OF THEIR CREATIONS. BUT WHY DO THE PEOPLE STAND FOR THEIR RULE?

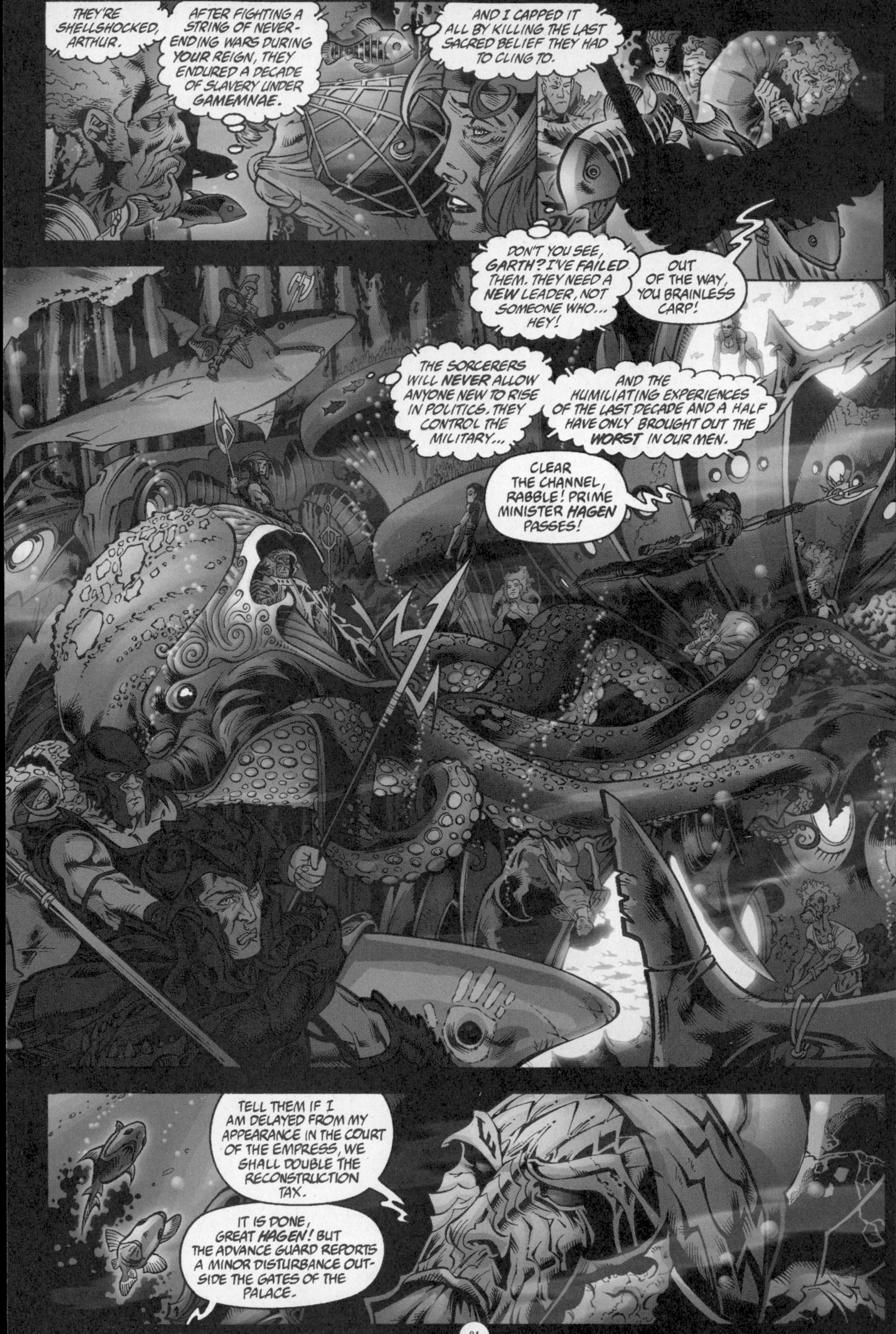
THEY'RE SHELLSHOCKED, ARTHUR.
AFTER FIGHTING A STRING OF NEVER-ENDING WARS DURING YOUR REIGN, THEY ENDURED A DECADE OF SLAVERY UNDER GAMEMNAE.
AND I CAPPED IT ALL BY KILLING THE LAST SACRED BELIEF THEY HAD TO CLING TO.
DON'T YOU SEE, GARTH? I'VE FAILED THEM. THEY NEED A NEW LEADER, NOT SOMEONE WHO... HEY!
OUT OF THE WAY, YOU BRAINLESS CARP!
THE SORCERERS WILL NEVER ALLOW ANYONE NEW TO RISE IN POLITICS. THEY CONTROL THE MILITARY...
AND THE HUMILIATING EXPERIENCES OF THE LAST DECADE AND A HALF HAVE ONLY BROUGHT OUT THE WORST IN OUR MEN.
CLEAR THE CHANNEL, RABBLE! PRIME MINISTER HAGEN PASSES!
TELL THEM IF I AM DELAYED FROM MY APPEARANCE IN THE COURT OF THE EMPRESS, WE SHALL DOUBLE THE RECONSTRUCTION TAX.
IT IS DONE, GREAT HAGEN! BUT THE ADVANCE GUARD REPORTS A MINOR DISTURBANCE OUTSIDE THE GATES OF THE PALACE.

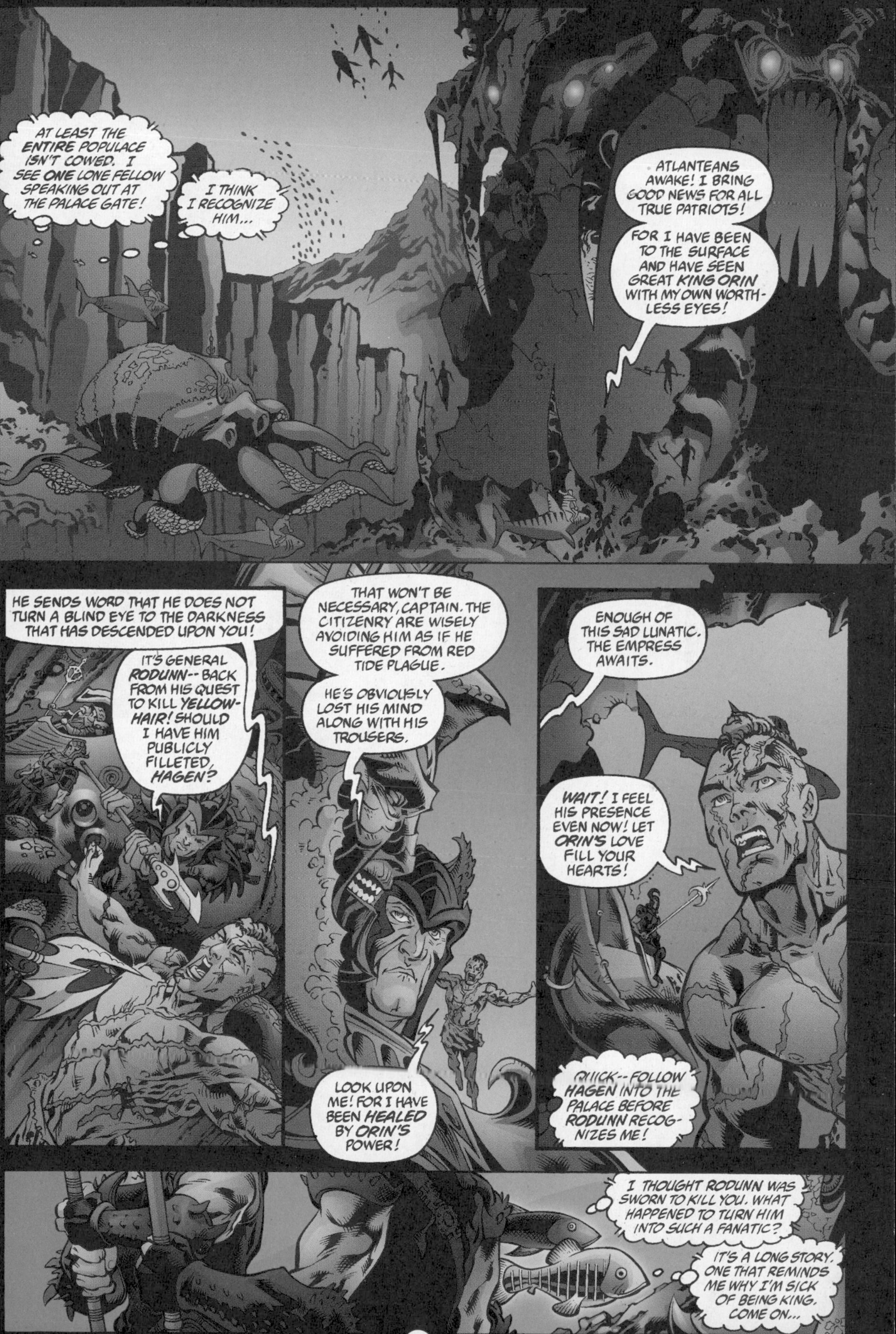

AT LEAST THE ENTIRE POPULACE ISN'T COWED. I SEE ONE LONE FELLOW SPEAKING OUT AT THE PALACE GATE!
I THINK I RECOGNIZE HIM...
ATLANTEANS AWAKE! I BRING GOOD NEWS FOR ALL TRUE PATRIOTS!
FOR I HAVE BEEN TO THE SURFACE AND HAVE SEEN GREAT KING ORIN WITH MY OWN WORTHLESS EYES!
HE SENDS WORD THAT HE DOES NOT TURN A BLIND EYE TO THE DARKNESS THAT HAS DESCENDED UPON YOU!
IT'S GENERAL RODUNN-- BACK FROM HIS QUEST TO KILL YELLOW-HAIR! SHOULD I HAVE HIM PUBLICLY FILLETED, HAGEN?
THAT WON'T BE NECESSARY, CAPTAIN. THE CITIZENRY ARE WISELY AVOIDING HIM AS IF HE SUFFERED FROM RED TIDE PLAGUE.
HE'S OBVIOUSLY LOST HIS MIND ALONG WITH HIS TROUSERS.
LOOK UPON ME! FOR I HAVE BEEN HEALED BY ORIN'S POWER!
ENOUGH OF THIS SAD LUNATIC. THE EMPRESS AWAITS.
WAIT! I FEEL HIS PRESENCE EVEN NOW! LET ORIN'S LOVE FILL YOUR HEARTS!
QUICK-- FOLLOW HAGEN INTO THE PALACE BEFORE RODUNN RECOGNIZES ME!
I THOUGHT RODUNN WAS SWORN TO KILL YOU. WHAT HAPPENED TO TURN HIM INTO SUCH A FANATIC?
IT'S A LONG STORY. ONE THAT REMINDS ME WHY I'M SICK OF BEING KING. COME ON...

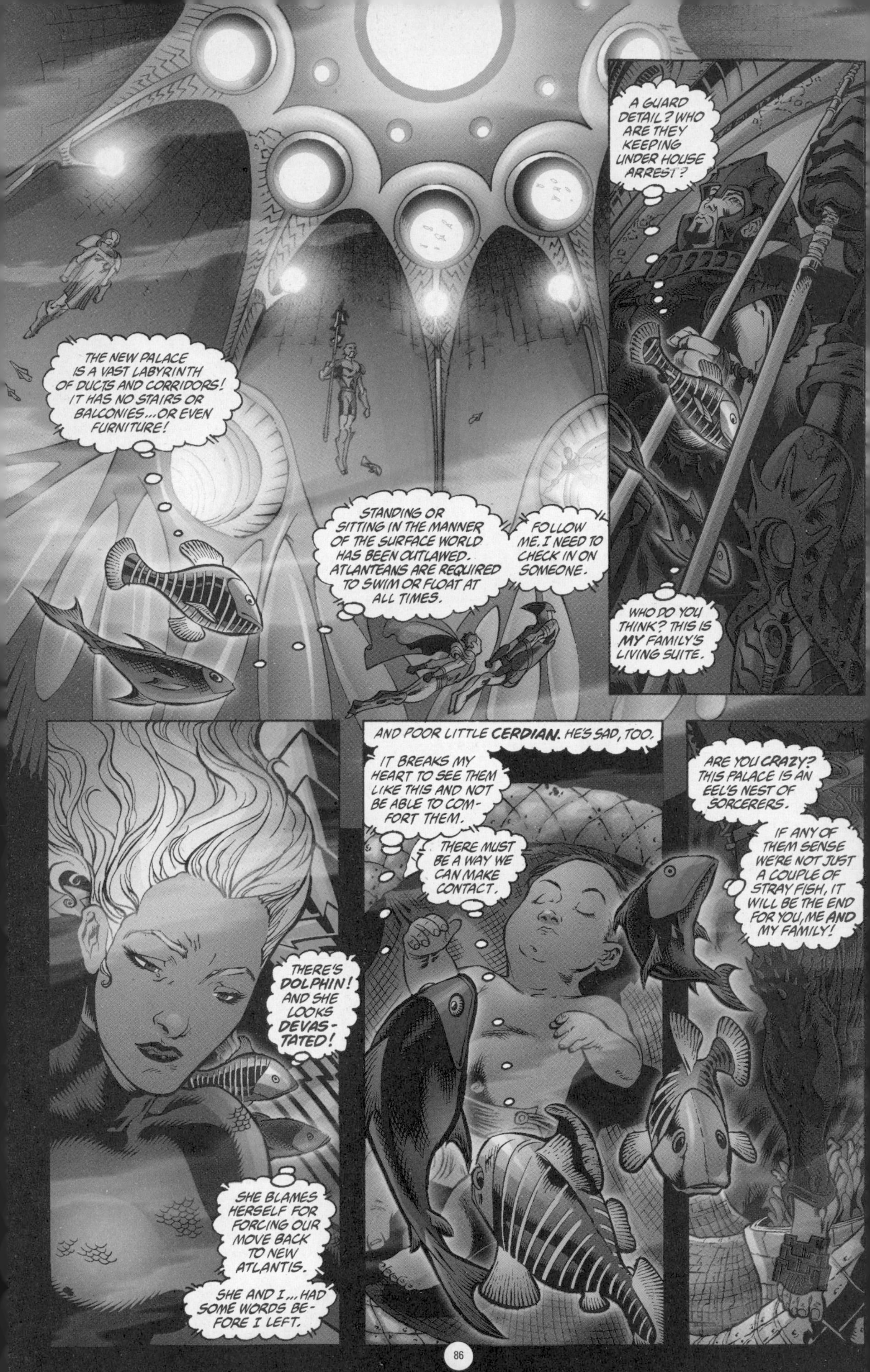
THE NEW PALACE IS A VAST LABYRINTH OF DUCTS AND CORRIDORS! IT HAS NO STAIRS OR BALCONIES... OR EVEN FURNITURE!
STANDING OR SITTING IN THE MANNER OF THE SURFACE WORLD HAS BEEN OUTLAWED. ATLANTEANS ARE REQUIRED TO SWIM OR FLOAT AT ALL TIMES.
FOLLOW ME. I NEED TO CHECK IN ON SOMEONE.
A GUARD DETAIL? WHO ARE THEY KEEPING UNDER HOUSE ARREST?
WHO DO YOU THINK? THIS IS MY FAMILY'S LIVING SUITE.
THERE'S DOLPHIN! AND SHE LOOKS DEVASTATED!
SHE BLAMES HERSELF FOR FORCING OUR MOVE BACK TO NEW ATLANTIS.
SHE AND I... HAD SOME WORDS BEFORE I LEFT.
AND POOR LITTLE CERDIAN. HE'S SAD, TOO.
IT BREAKS MY HEART TO SEE THEM LIKE THIS AND NOT BE ABLE TO COMFORT THEM.
THERE MUST BE A WAY WE CAN MAKE CONTACT.
ARE YOU CRAZY? THIS PALACE IS AN EEL'S NEST OF SORCERERS.
IF ANY OF THEM SENSE WE'RE NOT JUST A COUPLE OF STRAY FISH, IT WILL BE THE END FOR YOU, ME AND MY FAMILY!

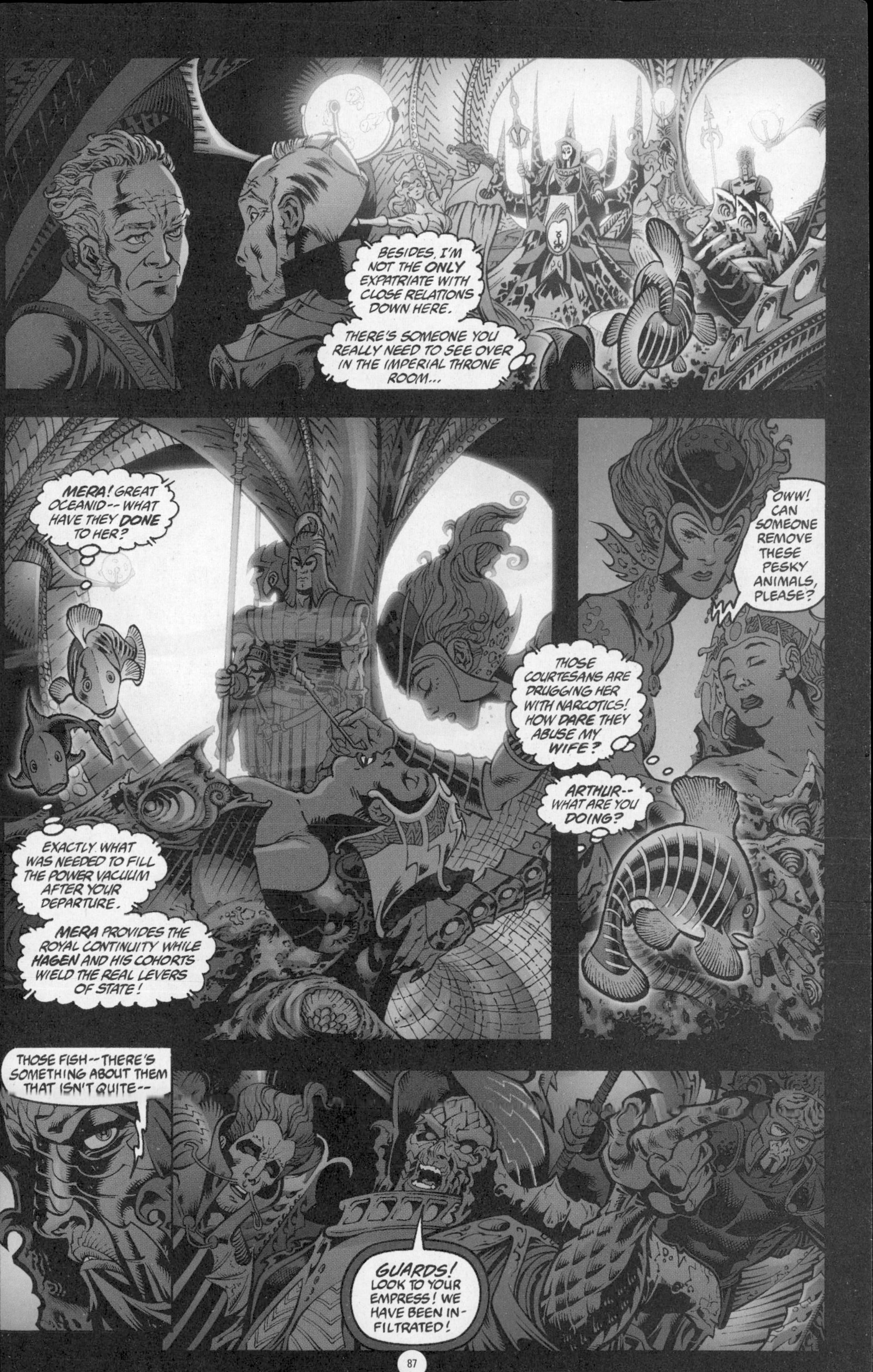
BESIDES, I'M NOT THE ONLY EXPATRIATE WITH CLOSE RELATIONS DOWN HERE.
THERE'S SOMEONE YOU REALLY NEED TO SEE OVER IN THE IMPERIAL THRONE ROOM...
MERA! GREAT OCEANID-- WHAT HAVE THEY DONE TO HER?
EXACTLY WHAT WAS NEEDED TO FILL THE POWER VACUUM AFTER YOUR DEPARTURE.
MERA PROVIDES THE ROYAL CONTINUITY WHILE HAGEN AND HIS COHORTS WIELD THE REAL LEVERS OF STATE!
OWW! CAN SOMEONE REMOVE THESE PESKY ANIMALS, PLEASE?
THOSE COURTESANS ARE DRUGGING HER WITH NARCOTICS! HOW DARE THEY ABUSE MY WIFE?
ARTHUR-- WHAT ARE YOU DOING?
THOSE FISH-- THERE'S SOMETHING ABOUT THEM THAT ISN'T QUITE--
GUARDS! LOOK TO YOUR EMPRESS! WE HAVE BEEN IN-FILTRATED!

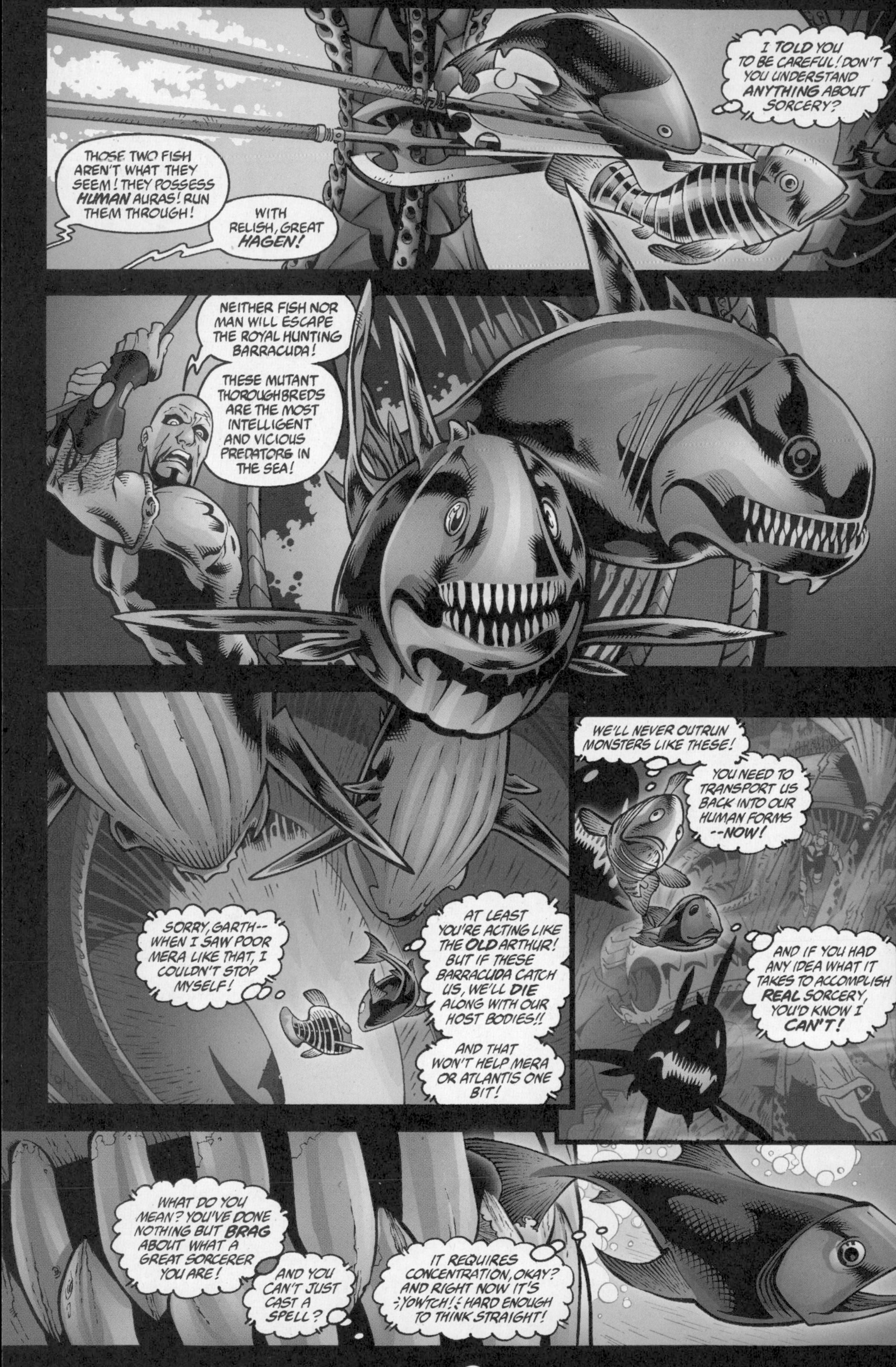
I TOLD YOU TO BE CAREFUL! DON'T YOU UNDERSTAND ANYTHING ABOUT SORCERY?
THOSE TWO FISH AREN'T WHAT THEY SEEM! THEY POSSESS HUMAN AURAS! RUN THEM THROUGH!
WITH RELISH, GREAT HAGEN!
NEITHER FISH NOR MAN WILL ESCAPE THE ROYAL HUNTING BARRACUDA!
THESE MUTANT THOROUGHBREDS ARE THE MOST INTELLIGENT AND VICIOUS PREDATORS IN THE SEA!
SORRY, GARTH-- WHEN I SAW POOR MERA LIKE THAT, I COULDN'T STOP MYSELF!
AT LEAST YOU'RE ACTING LIKE THE OLD ARTHUR! BUT IF THESE BARRACUDA CATCH US, WE'LL DIE ALONG WITH OUR HOST BODIES!!
AND THAT WON'T HELP MERA OR ATLANTIS ONE BIT!
WE'LL NEVER OUTRUN MONSTERS LIKE THESE!
YOU NEED TO TRANSPORT US BACK INTO OUR HUMAN FORMS --NOW!
AND IF YOU HAD ANY IDEA WHAT IT TAKES TO ACCOMPLISH REAL SORCERY, YOU'D KNOW I CAN'T!
WHAT DO YOU MEAN? YOU'VE DONE NOTHING BUT BRAG ABOUT WHAT A GREAT SORCERER YOU ARE!
AND YOU CAN'T JUST CAST A SPELL?
IT REQUIRES CONCENTRATION, OKAY? AND RIGHT NOW IT'S -YOWTCH!- HARD ENOUGH TO THINK STRAIGHT!

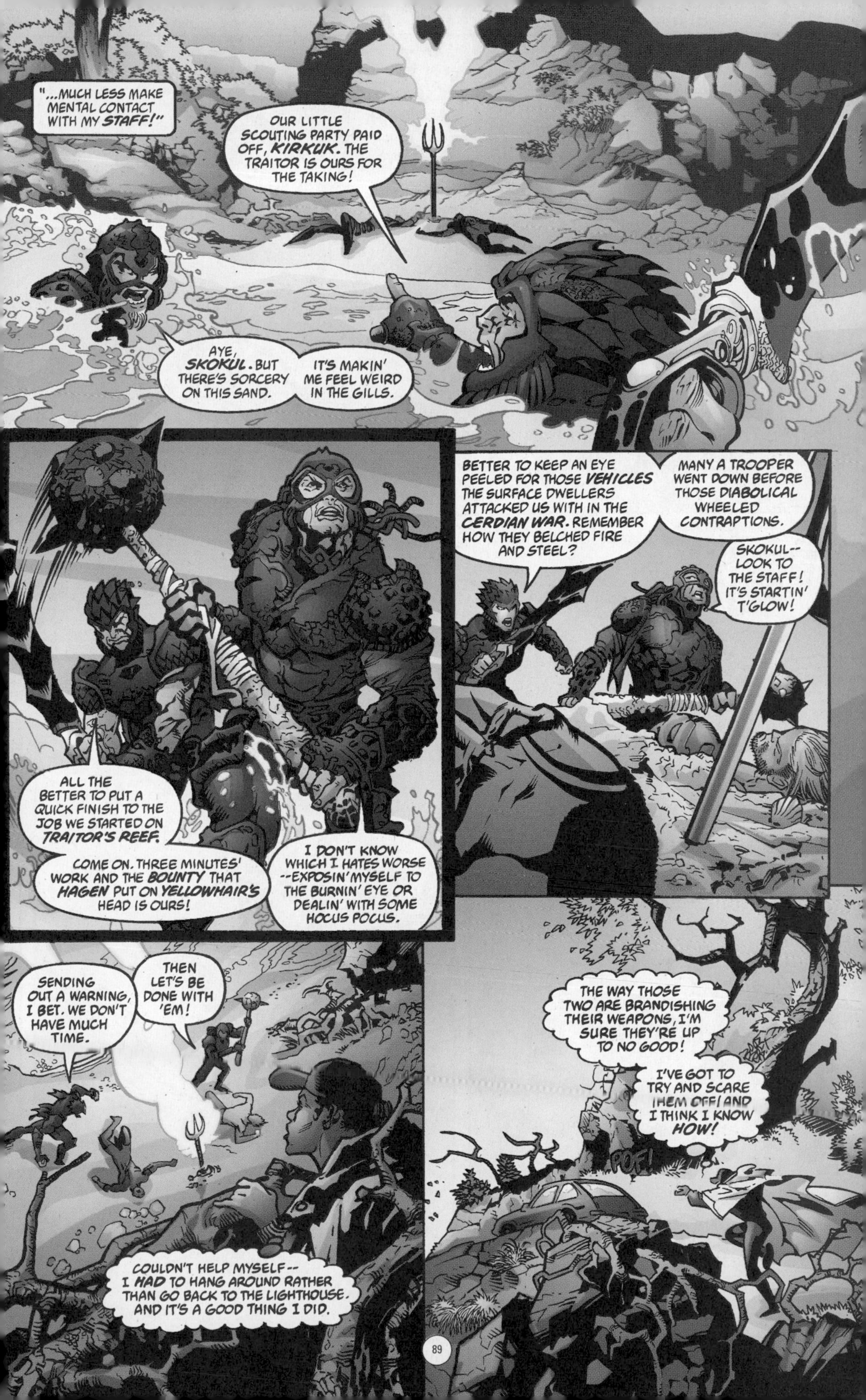
"...MUCH LESS MAKE MENTAL CONTACT WITH MY STAFF!"
OUR LITTLE SCOUTING PARTY PAID OFF, KIRKUK. THE TRAITOR IS OURS FOR THE TAKING!
AYE, SKOKUL. BUT THERE'S SORCERY ON THIS SAND.
IT'S MAKIN' ME FEEL WEIRD IN THE GILLS.
ALL THE BETTER TO PUT A QUICK FINISH TO THE JOB WE STARTED ON TRAITOR'S REEF.
COME ON. THREE MINUTES' WORK AND THE BOUNTY THAT HAGEN PUT ON YELLOWHAIR'S HEAD IS OURS!
I DON'T KNOW WHICH I HATES WORSE --EXPOSIN' MYSELF TO THE BURNIN' EYE OR DEALIN' WITH SOME HOCUS POCUS.
BETTER TO KEEP AN EYE PEELED FOR THOSE VEHICLES THE SURFACE DWELLERS ATTACKED US WITH IN THE CERDIAN WAR. REMEMBER HOW THEY BELCHED FIRE AND STEEL?
MANY A TROOPER WENT DOWN BEFORE THOSE DIABOLICAL WHEELED CONTRAPTIONS.
SKOKUL-- LOOK TO THE STAFF! IT'S STARTIN' T'GLOW!
SENDING OUT A WARNING, I BET. WE DON'T HAVE MUCH TIME.
THEN LET'S BE DONE WITH 'EM!
COULDN'T HELP MYSELF-- I HAD TO HANG AROUND RATHER THAN GO BACK TO THE LIGHTHOUSE. AND IT'S A GOOD THING I DID.
THE WAY THOSE TWO ARE BRANDISHING THEIR WEAPONS, I'M SURE THEY'RE UP TO NO GOOD!
I'VE GOT TO TRY AND SCARE THEM OFF! AND I THINK I KNOW HOW!
POF!

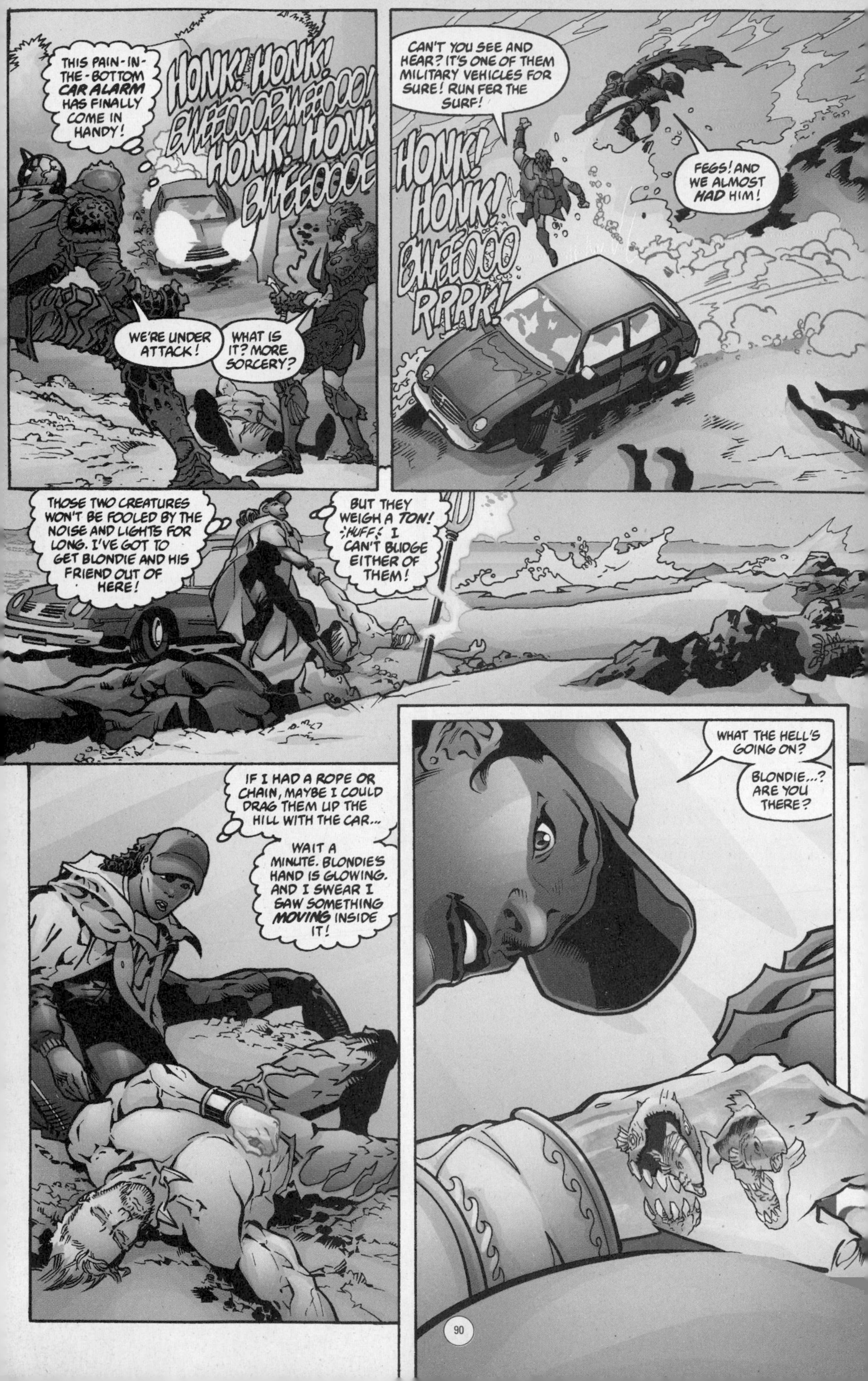
THIS PAIN-IN-THE-BOTTOM CAR ALARM HAS FINALLY COME IN HANDY!
HONK! HONK! BWEEOOOBWEEOOO! HONK! HONK BWEEOOOE
WE'RE UNDER ATTACK!
WHAT IS IT? MORE SORCERY?
CAN'T YOU SEE AND HEAR? IT'S ONE OF THEM MILITARY VEHICLES FOR SURE! RUN FER THE SURF!
FEGS! AND WE ALMOST HAD HIM!
HONK! HONK! BWEEOOO RRRK!
THOSE TWO CREATURES WON'T BE FOOLED BY THE NOISE AND LIGHTS FOR LONG. I'VE GOT TO GET BLONDIE AND HIS FRIEND OUT OF HERE!
BUT THEY WEIGH A TON! HUFF I CAN'T BUDGE EITHER OF THEM!
IF I HAD A ROPE OR CHAIN, MAYBE I COULD DRAG THEM UP THE HILL WITH THE CAR...
WAIT A MINUTE. BLONDIE'S HAND IS GLOWING. AND I SWEAR I SAW SOMETHING MOVING INSIDE IT!
WHAT THE HELL'S GOING ON?
BLONDIE...? ARE YOU THERE?

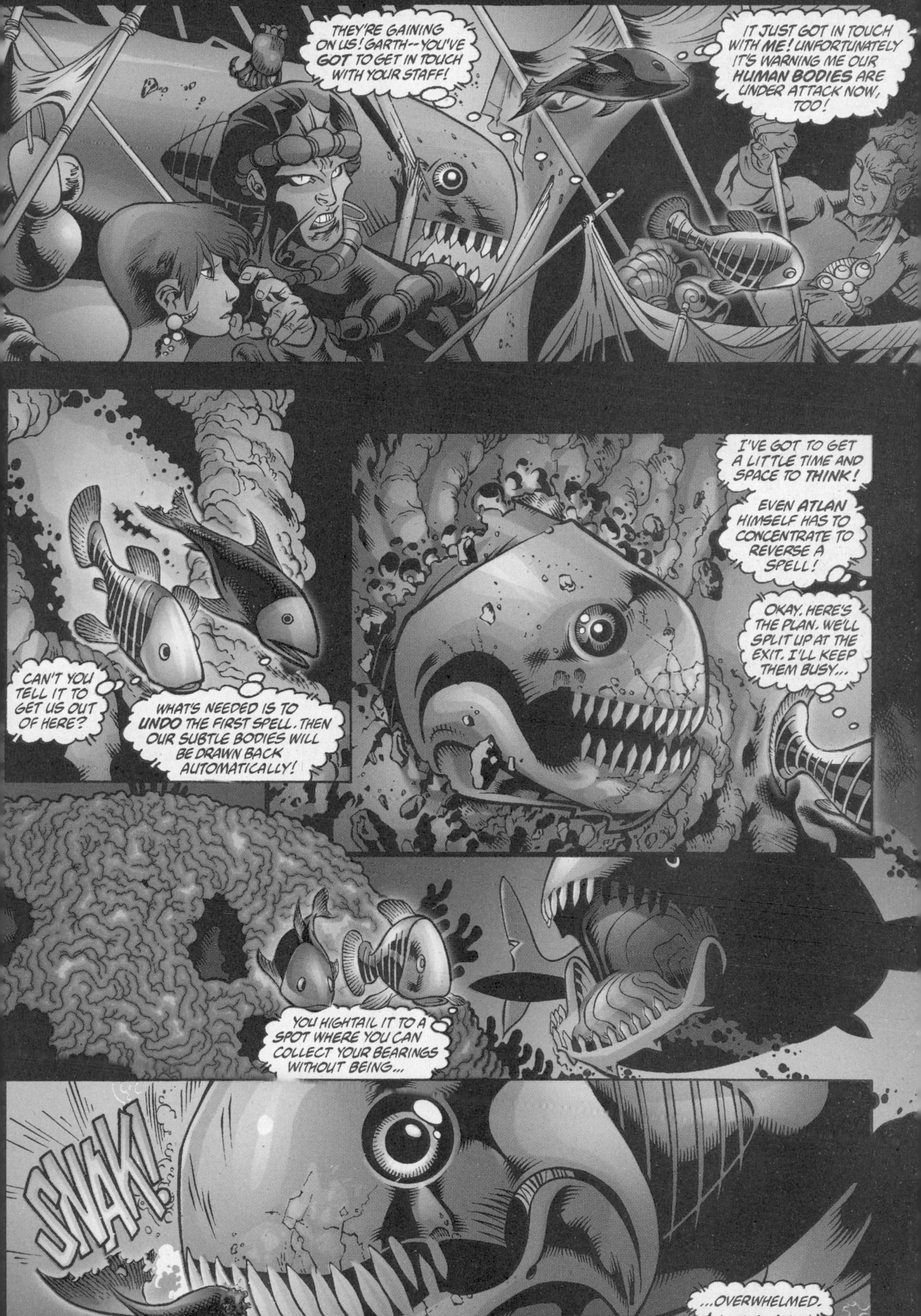
THEY'RE GAINING ON US! GARTH--YOU'VE GOT TO GET IN TOUCH WITH YOUR STAFF!
IT JUST GOT IN TOUCH WITH ME! UNFORTUNATELY IT'S WARNING ME OUR HUMAN BODIES ARE UNDER ATTACK NOW, TOO!
CAN'T YOU TELL IT TO GET US OUT OF HERE?
WHAT'S NEEDED IS TO UNDO THE FIRST SPELL. THEN OUR SUBTLE BODIES WILL BE DRAWN BACK AUTOMATICALLY!
I'VE GOT TO GET A LITTLE TIME AND SPACE TO THINK!
EVEN ATLAN HIMSELF HAS TO CONCENTRATE TO REVERSE A SPELL!
OKAY. HERE'S THE PLAN. WE'LL SPLIT UP AT THE EXIT. I'LL KEEP THEM BUSY...
YOU HIGHTAIL IT TO A SPOT WHERE YOU CAN COLLECT YOUR BEARINGS WITHOUT BEING...
SNAK!
...OVERWHELMED.

GARTH--I THINK WE'VE BEEN EATEN BY ONE OF THOSE BARRACUDA. ARE YOU OKAY?

A-ARRGHH! I'M CAUGHT IN ITS TEETH! IT'S CHEWING ME... TO PIECES! AAOOWWGHH!

DAMN! NOW THE BRUTE IS SWALLOWING. FORCING US BACK INTO ITS STOMACH...

A FEW MOMENTS IN THAT ACID POOL AND WE'RE DONE FOR.

ACRID BILE...SO CAUSTIC...IT'S BURNING RIGHT THROUGH US! GARTH'S HOST BODY IS ALREADY IN SHOCK!

AND HE SAID IF THESE FISH DIE, THEN SO DO WE!

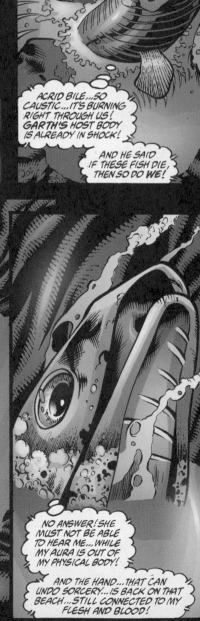

ONLY ONE HOPE LEFT...THE LADY OF THE LAKE!

LADY--ARE YOU THERE? PLEASE--I NEED YOUR HELP! LADY?

NO ANSWER! SHE MUST NOT BE ABLE TO HEAR ME...WHILE MY AURA IS OUT OF MY PHYSICAL BODY!

AND THE HAND...THAT CAN UNDO SORCERY...IS BACK ON THAT BEACH...STILL CONNECTED TO MY FLESH AND BLOOD!

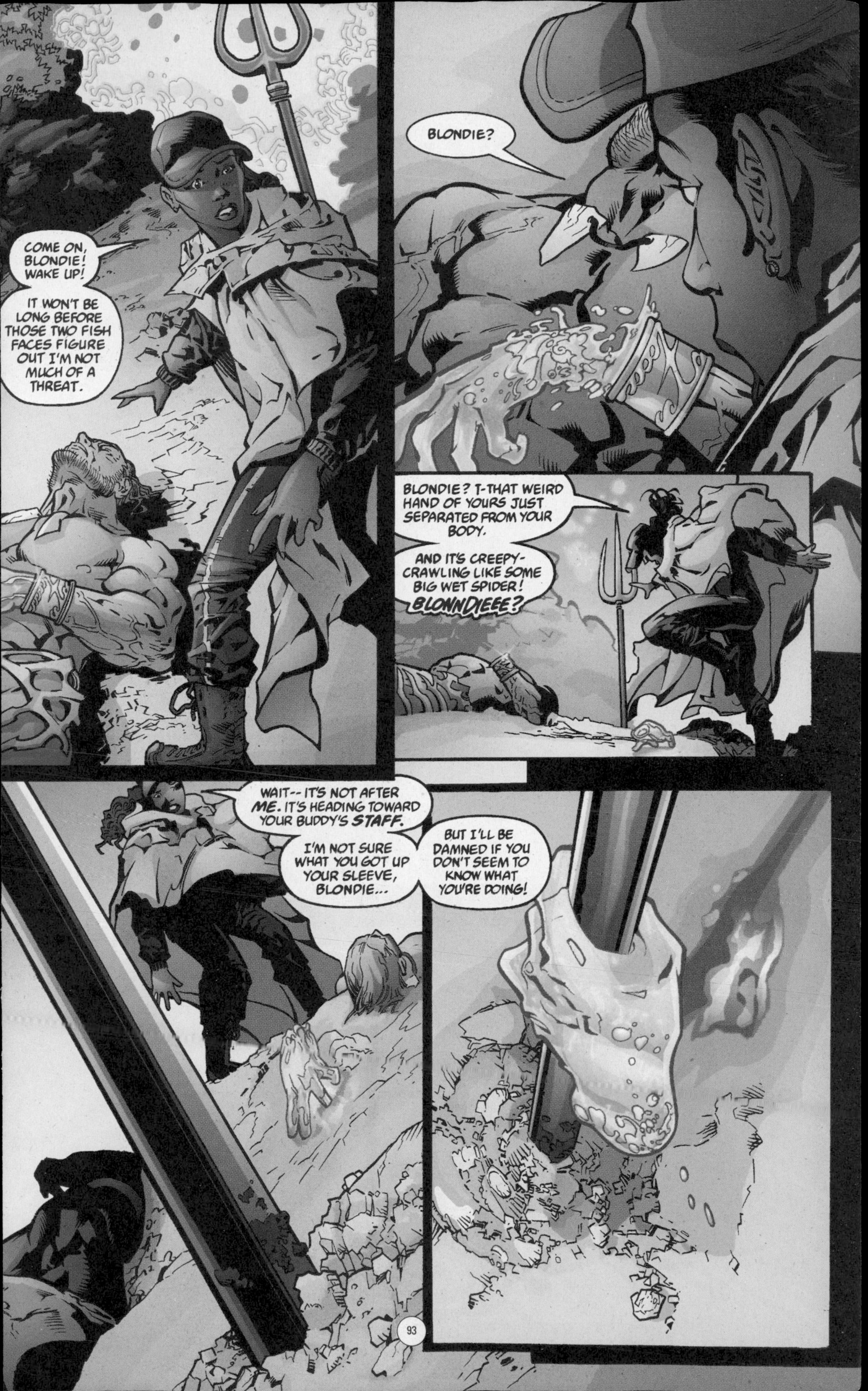
COME ON, BLONDIE! WAKE UP!
IT WON'T BE LONG BEFORE THOSE TWO FISH FACES FIGURE OUT I'M NOT MUCH OF A THREAT.
BLONDIE?
BLONDIE? T-THAT WEIRD HAND OF YOURS JUST SEPARATED FROM YOUR BODY.
AND IT'S CREEPY-CRAWLING LIKE SOME BIG WET SPIDER! BLONNDIEEE?
WAIT-- IT'S NOT AFTER ME. IT'S HEADING TOWARD YOUR BUDDY'S STAFF.
I'M NOT SURE WHAT YOU GOT UP YOUR SLEEVE, BLONDIE...
BUT I'LL BE DAMNED IF YOU DON'T SEEM TO KNOW WHAT YOU'RE DOING!

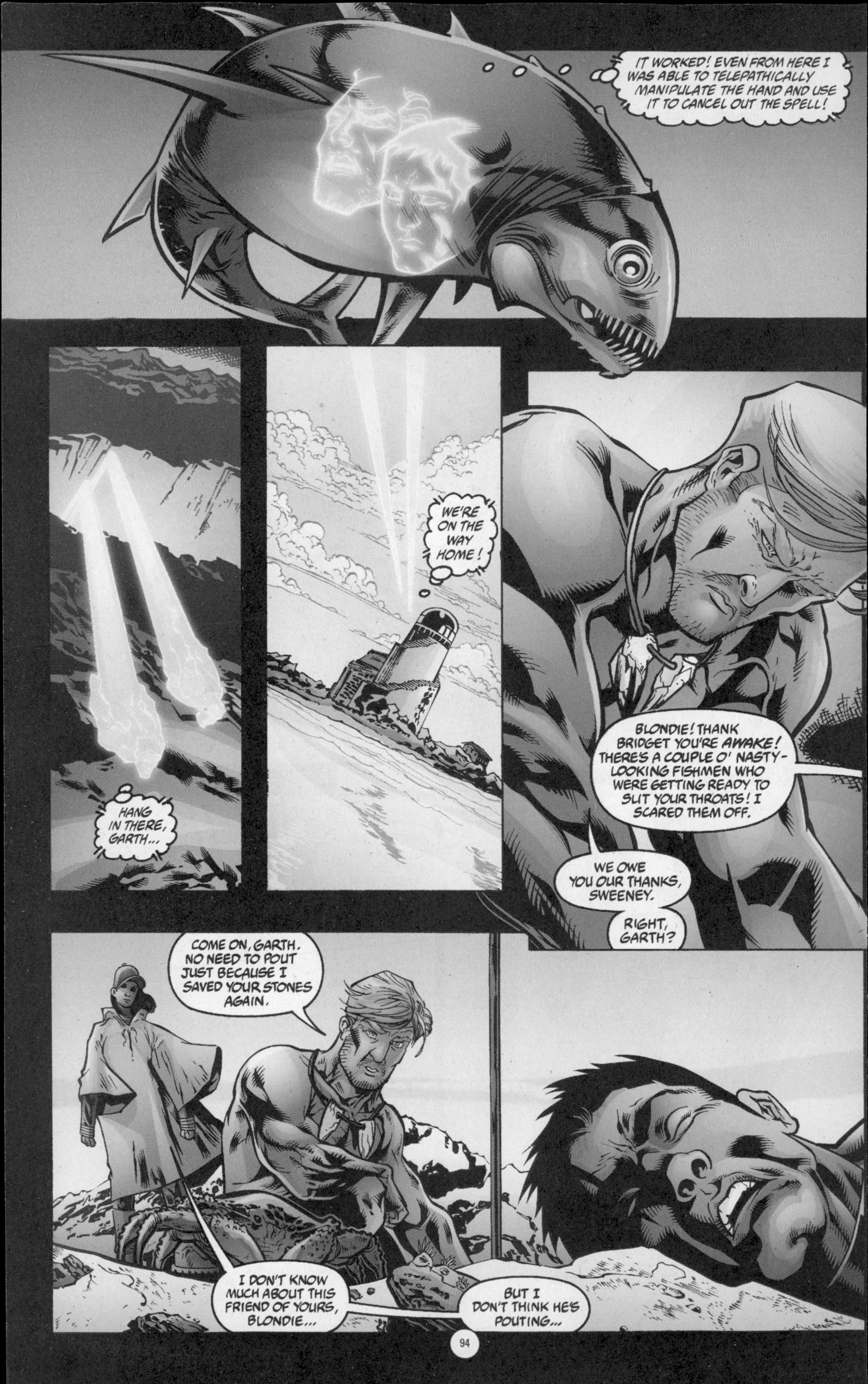

IT WORKED! EVEN FROM HERE I WAS ABLE TO TELEPATHICALLY MANIPULATE THE HAND AND USE IT TO CANCEL OUT THE SPELL!
HANG IN THERE, GARTH...
WE'RE ON THE WAY HOME!
BLONDIE! THANK BRIDGET YOU'RE AWAKE! THERE'S A COUPLE O' NASTY-LOOKING FISHMEN WHO WERE GETTING READY TO SLIT YOUR THROATS! I SCARED THEM OFF.
WE OWE YOU OUR THANKS, SWEENEY.
RIGHT, GARTH?
COME ON, GARTH. NO NEED TO POUT JUST BECAUSE I SAVED YOUR STONES AGAIN.
I DON'T KNOW MUCH ABOUT THIS FRIEND OF YOURS, BLONDIE...
BUT I DON'T THINK HE'S POUTING...

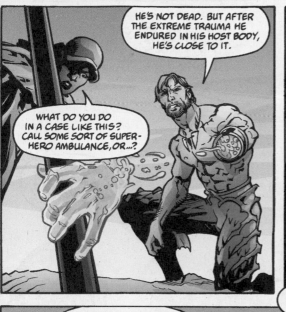

HE'S NOT DEAD. BUT AFTER THE EXTREME TRAUMA HE ENDURED IN HIS HOST BODY, HE'S CLOSE TO IT.

WHAT DO YOU DO IN A CASE LIKE THIS? CALL SOME SORT OF SUPER-HERO AMBULANCE, OR...?

NO-- WHAT I DO IS CHANNEL THE HEALING ENERGY OF THE SECRET SEA INTO HIM. I ONLY PRAY I'M NOT TOO LATE.

Y'MEAN THE ANNWN MYTH? JUST LIKE THAT?

YEAH. JUST LIKE THAT.

WHOOEE. WHAT HAPPENED? LAST THING I REMEMBER WAS A HUNGRY BARRACUDA MISTAKING ME FOR A HAPPY MEAL.

HOW DID I GET US BACK HERE?

YOU DIDN'T. I DID-- WITH THIS. IT HAS THE ABILITY TO UNDO SORCERY.

AHH. SO YOU LET ME GO ON ABOUT WHAT A GREAT SORCERER I AM, WHILE ALL THE TIME YOU CAN NULLIFY MY POWER. PERFECT.

ARTHUR-- WHY DO I ALWAYS END UP FEELING LIKE A HOPELESS DWEEB AROUND YOU?

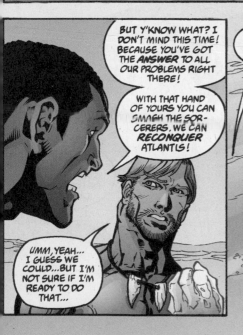

BUT Y'KNOW WHAT? I DON'T MIND THIS TIME! BECAUSE YOU'VE GOT THE ANSWER TO ALL OUR PROBLEMS RIGHT THERE!

WITH THAT HAND OF YOURS YOU CAN SMASH THE SORCERERS. WE CAN RECONQUER ATLANTIS!

UMM, YEAH... I GUESS WE COULD...BUT I'M NOT SURE IF I'M READY TO DO THAT...

WHAT DO YOU MEAN, "NOT READY"? YOU SAW WHAT'S GOING ON! YOU'RE THE KING, ARTHUR!

YOU'VE GOT THE POWER--NOW YOU'VE GOT TO USE IT TO TAKE BACK YOUR RIGHTFUL THRONE! IF NOT FOR YOU OR ME, THEN THINK OF MERA!

WHAT WAS I THINKING? DAMMIT, GARTH--YOU'RE RIGHT!

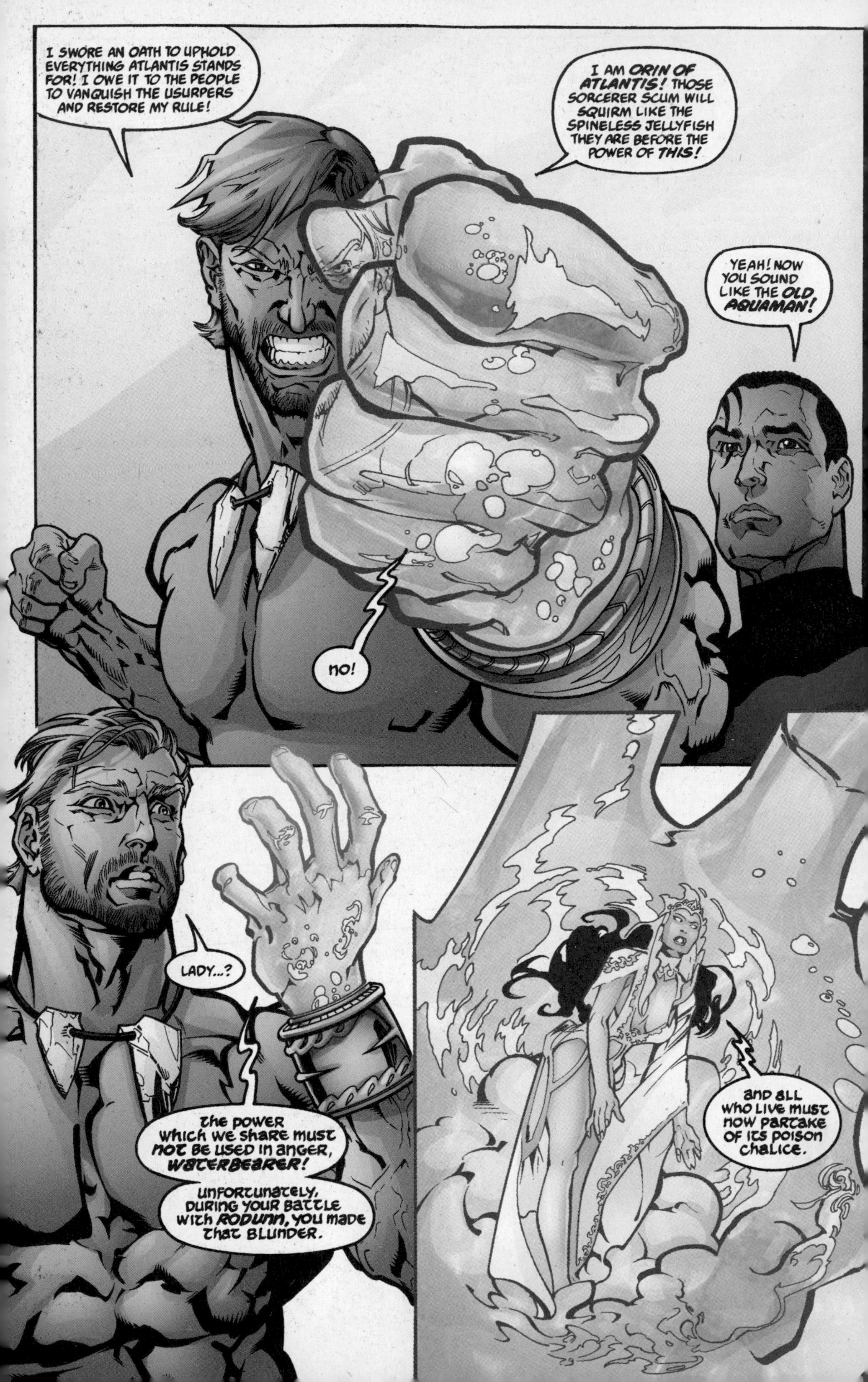
I SWORE AN OATH TO UPHOLD EVERYTHING ATLANTIS STANDS FOR! I OWE IT TO THE PEOPLE TO VANQUISH THE USURPERS AND RESTORE MY RULE!
I AM ORIN OF ATLANTIS! THOSE SORCERER SCUM WILL SQUIRM LIKE THE SPINELESS JELLYFISH THEY ARE BEFORE THE POWER OF THIS!
YEAH! NOW YOU SOUND LIKE THE OLD AQUAMAN!
no!
LADY...?
the power which we share must not be used in anger, WATERBEARER!
unfortunately, during your battle with RODUNN, you made that blunder.
and all who live must now partake of its poison chalice.

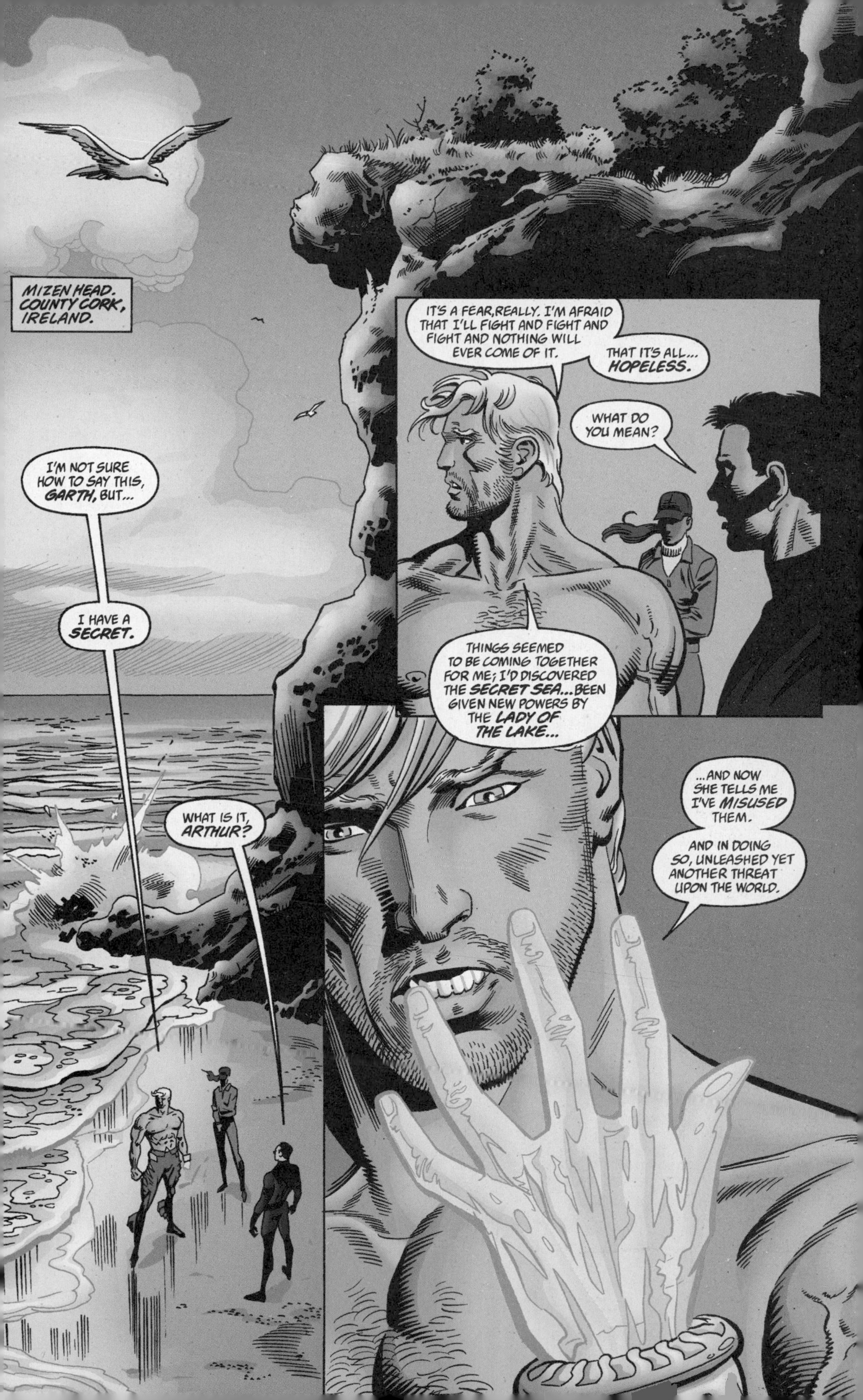

MIZEN HEAD. COUNTY CORK, IRELAND.
I'M NOT SURE HOW TO SAY THIS, GARTH, BUT...
I HAVE A SECRET.
WHAT IS IT, ARTHUR?
IT'S A FEAR, REALLY. I'M AFRAID THAT I'LL FIGHT AND FIGHT AND FIGHT AND NOTHING WILL EVER COME OF IT.
THAT IT'S ALL... HOPELESS.
WHAT DO YOU MEAN?
THINGS SEEMED TO BE COMING TOGETHER FOR ME; I'D DISCOVERED THE SECRET SEA...BEEN GIVEN NEW POWERS BY THE LADY OF THE LAKE...
...AND NOW SHE TELLS ME I'VE MISUSED THEM.
AND IN DOING SO, UNLEASHED YET ANOTHER THREAT UPON THE WORLD.

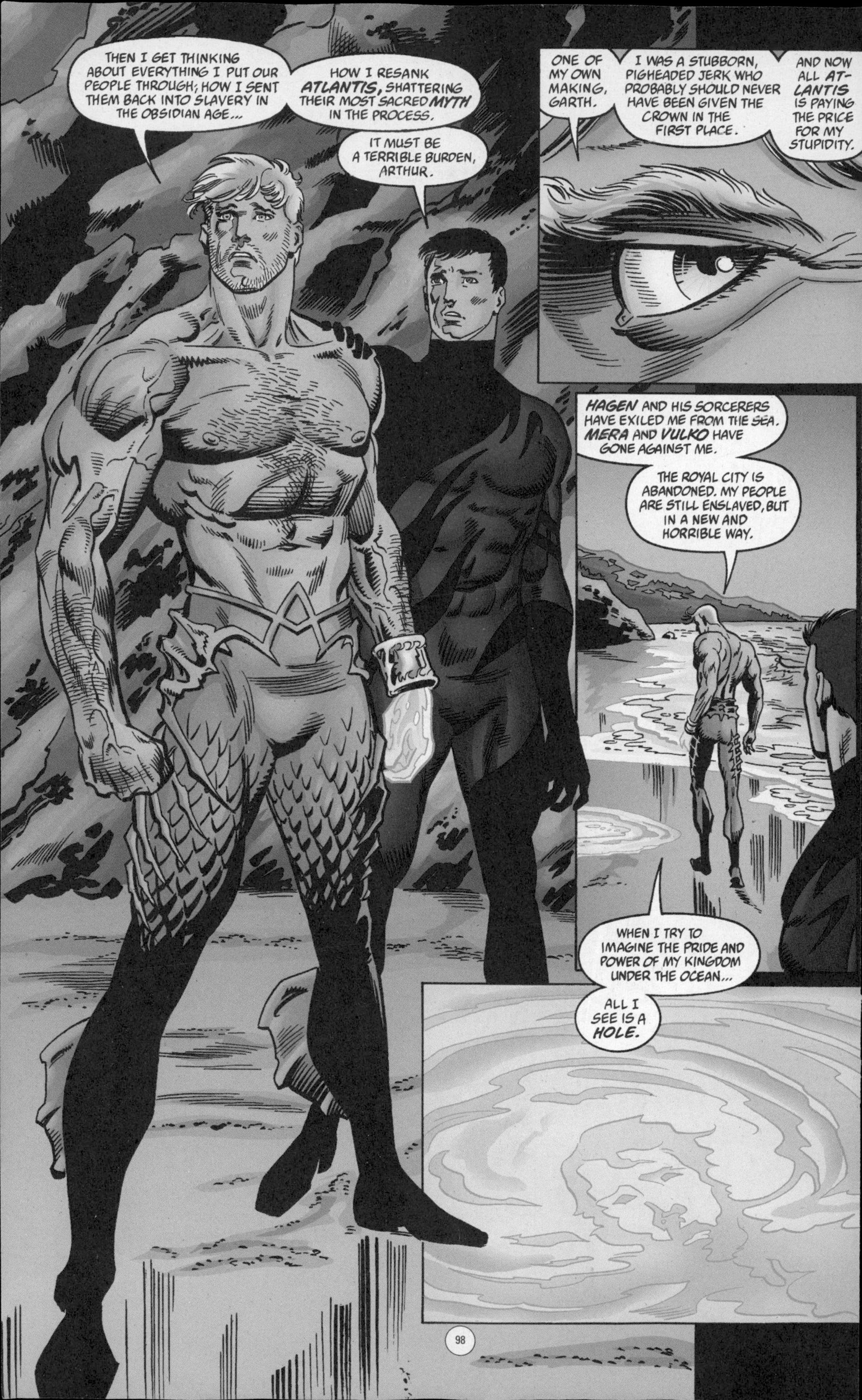
THEN I GET THINKING ABOUT EVERYTHING I PUT OUR PEOPLE THROUGH; HOW I SENT THEM BACK INTO SLAVERY IN THE OBSIDIAN AGE...
HOW I RESANK ATLANTIS, SHATTERING THEIR MOST SACRED MYTH IN THE PROCESS.
IT MUST BE A TERRIBLE BURDEN, ARTHUR.
ONE OF MY OWN MAKING, GARTH.
I WAS A STUBBORN, PIGHEADED JERK WHO PROBABLY SHOULD NEVER HAVE BEEN GIVEN THE CROWN IN THE FIRST PLACE.
AND NOW ALL ATLANTIS IS PAYING THE PRICE FOR MY STUPIDITY.
HAGEN AND HIS SORCERERS HAVE EXILED ME FROM THE SEA. MERA AND VULKO HAVE GONE AGAINST ME.
THE ROYAL CITY IS ABANDONED. MY PEOPLE ARE STILL ENSLAVED, BUT IN A NEW AND HORRIBLE WAY.
WHEN I TRY TO IMAGINE THE PRIDE AND POWER OF MY KINGDOM UNDER THE OCEAN...
ALL I SEE IS A HOLE.

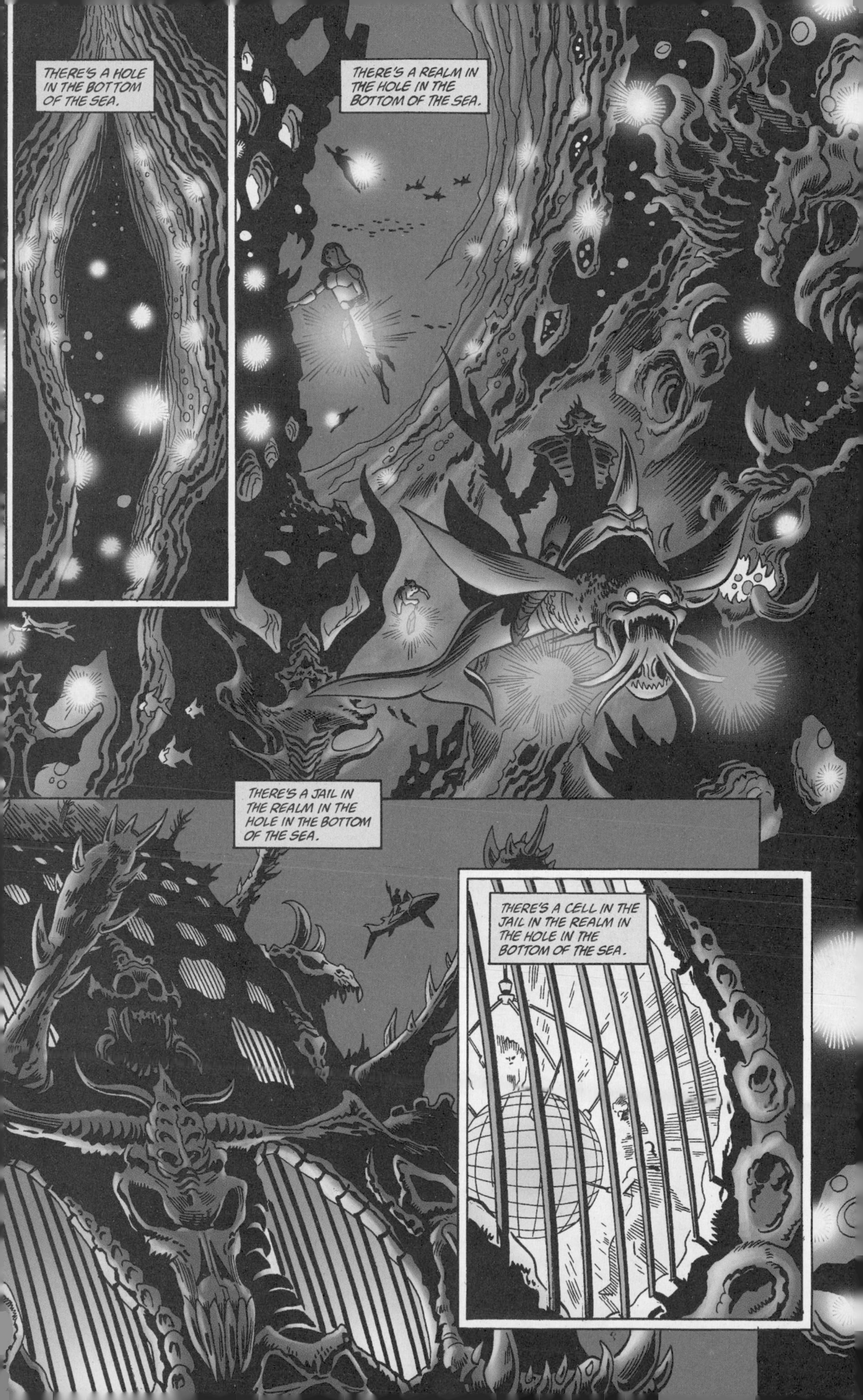
THERE'S A HOLE IN THE BOTTOM OF THE SEA.
THERE'S A REALM IN THE HOLE IN THE BOTTOM OF THE SEA.
THERE'S A JAIL IN THE REALM IN THE HOLE IN THE BOTTOM OF THE SEA.
THERE'S A CELL IN THE JAIL IN THE REALM IN THE HOLE IN THE BOTTOM OF THE SEA.

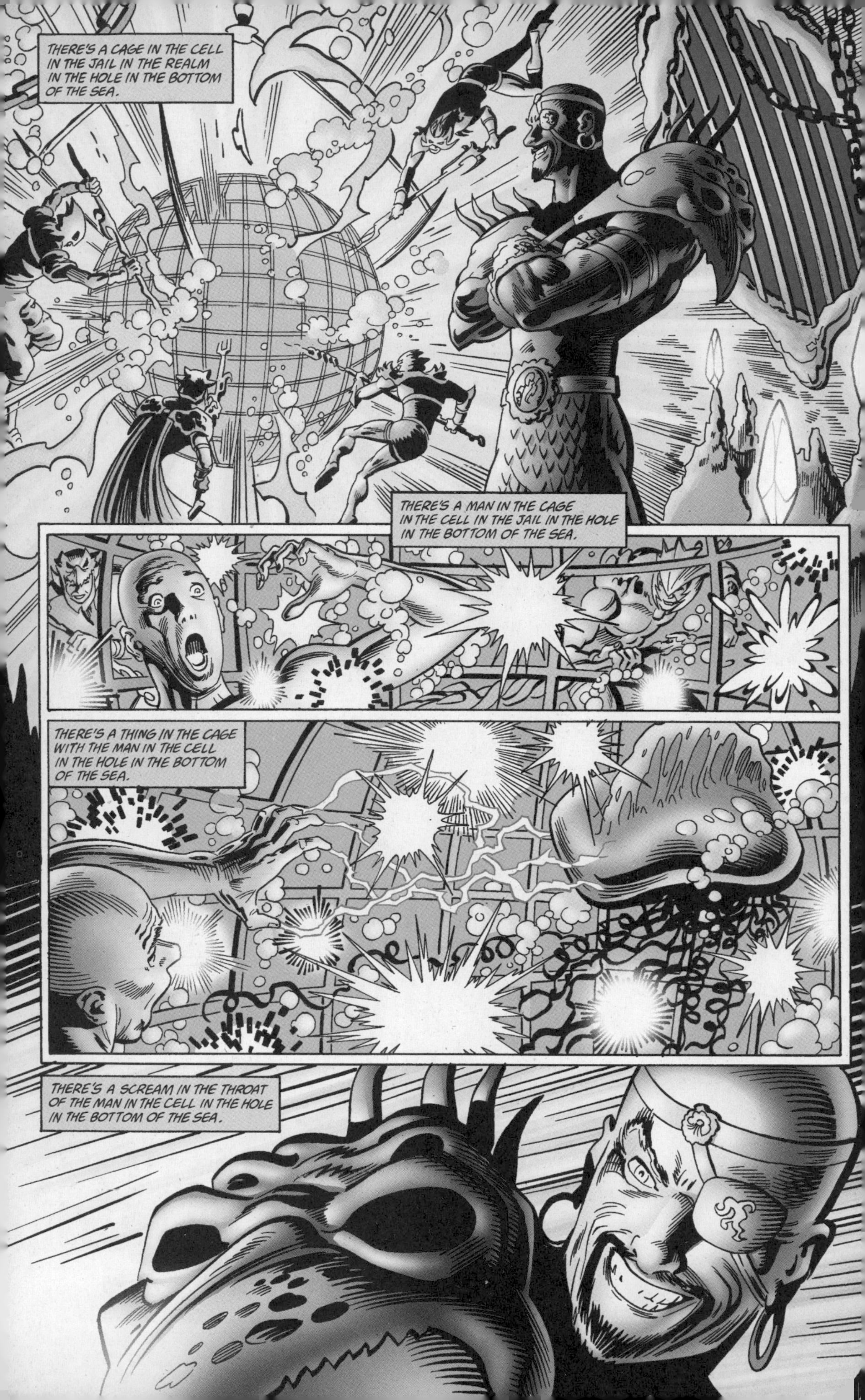
THERE'S A CAGE IN THE CELL IN THE JAIL IN THE REALM IN THE HOLE IN THE BOTTOM OF THE SEA.
THERE'S A MAN IN THE CAGE IN THE CELL IN THE JAIL IN THE HOLE IN THE BOTTOM OF THE SEA.
THERE'S A THING IN THE CAGE WITH THE MAN IN THE CELL IN THE HOLE IN THE BOTTOM OF THE SEA.
THERE'S A SCREAM IN THE THROAT OF THE MAN IN THE CELL IN THE HOLE IN THE BOTTOM OF THE SEA.

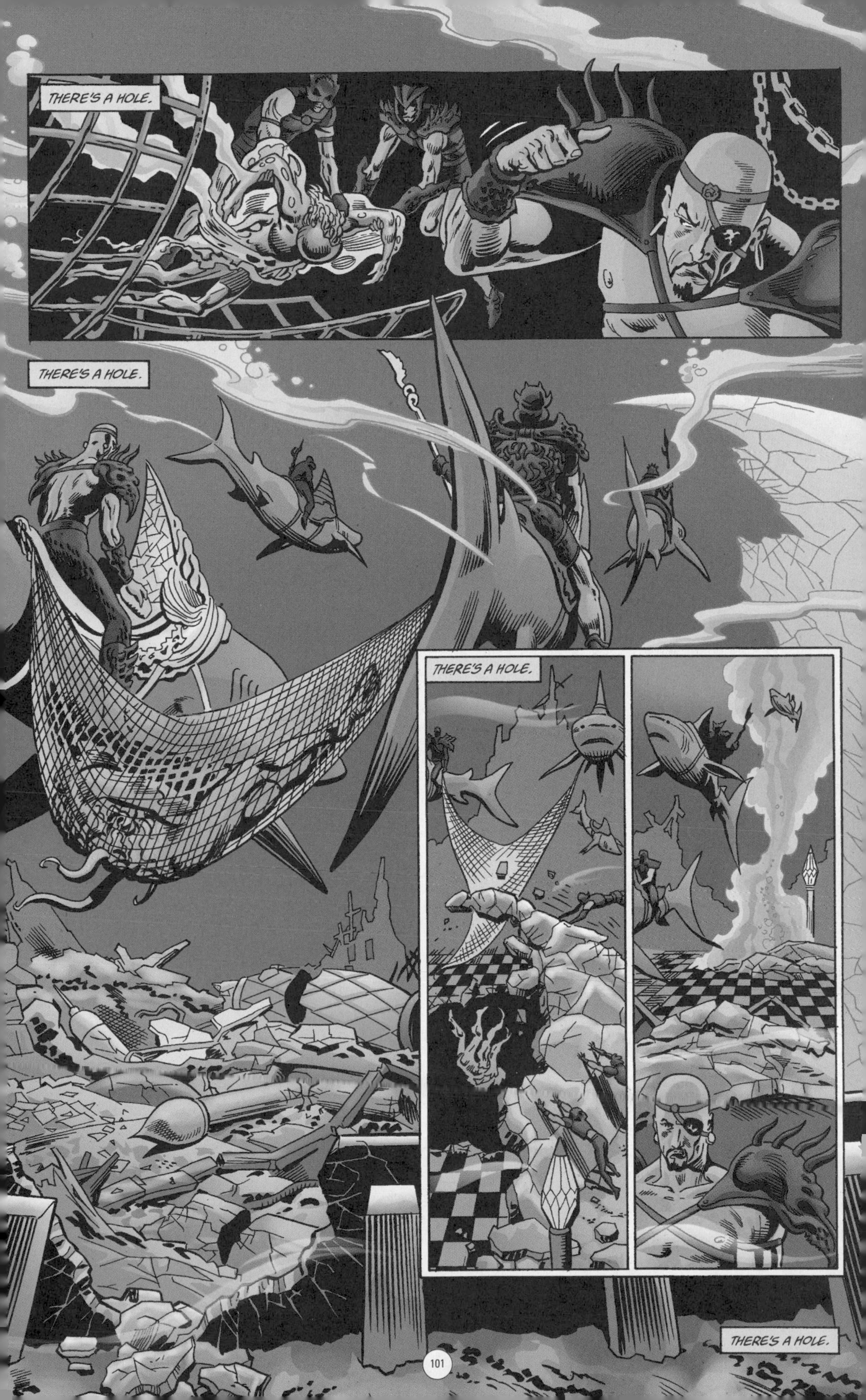
THERE'S A HOLE.
THERE'S A HOLE.
THERE'S A HOLE.
THERE'S A HOLE.

THERE'S A HOLE IN THE BOTTOM OF THE SEA

RICK VEITCH WRITER
NORM BREYFOGLE PENCILLER
DENNIS JANKE INKER
TOM McCRAW & DIGITAL CHAMELEON COLORISTS
MIKE HEISLE LETTERER

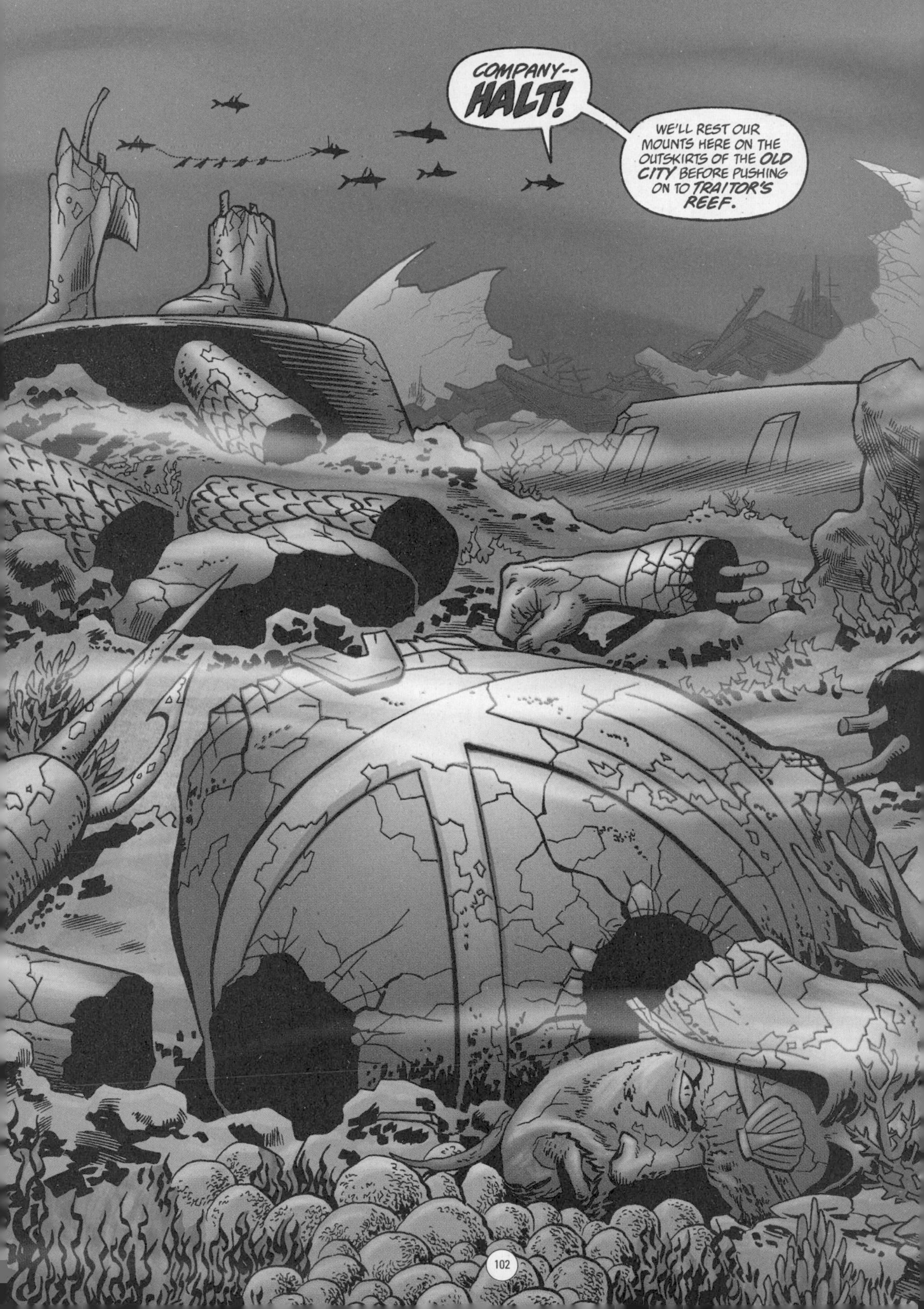
COMPANY-- HALT!
WE'LL REST OUR MOUNTS HERE ON THE OUTSKIRTS OF THE OLD CITY BEFORE PUSHING ON TO TRAITOR'S REEF.

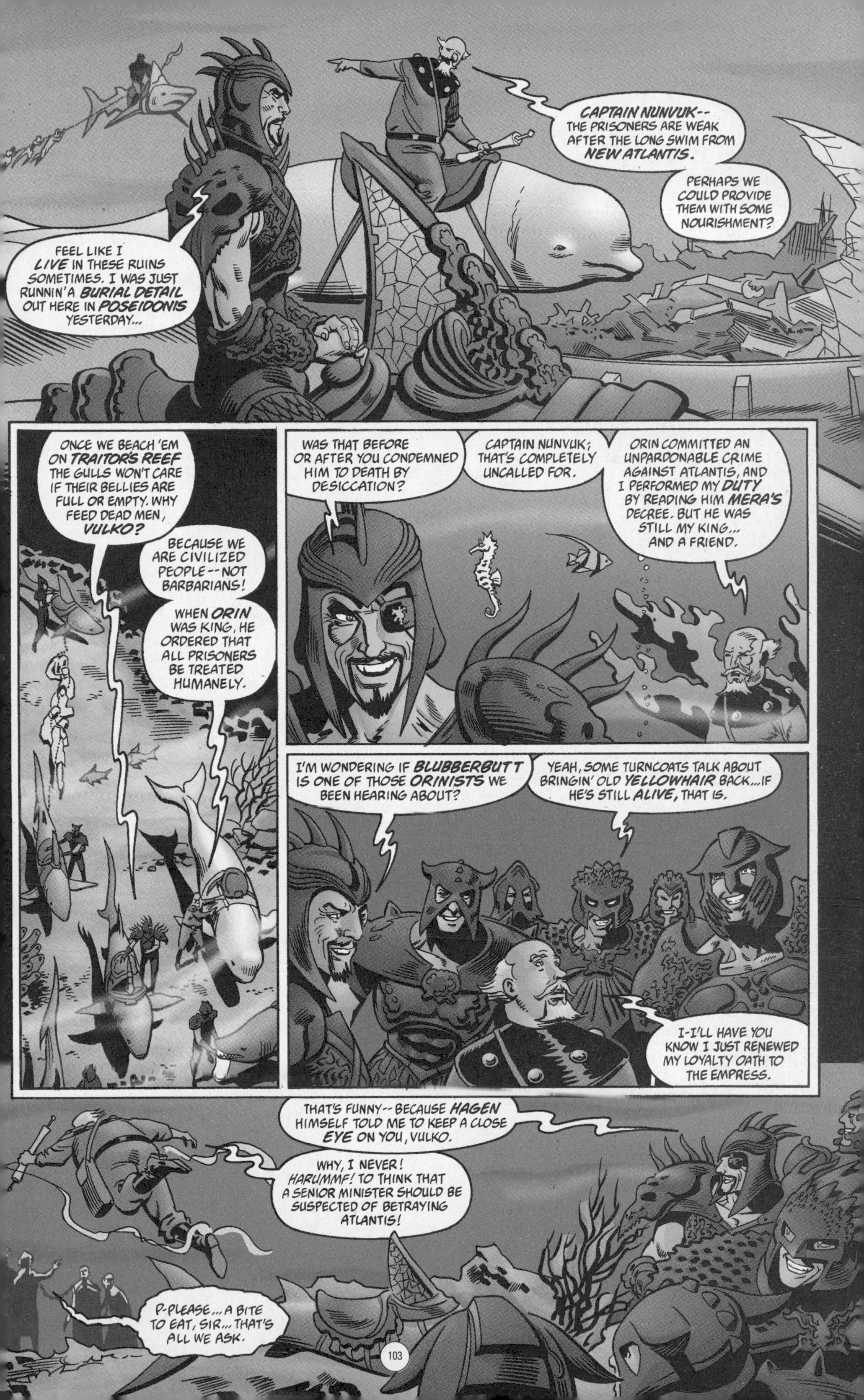
CAPTAIN NUNVUK-- THE PRISONERS ARE WEAK AFTER THE LONG SWIM FROM NEW ATLANTIS.
PERHAPS WE COULD PROVIDE THEM WITH SOME NOURISHMENT?
FEEL LIKE I LIVE IN THESE RUINS SOMETIMES. I WAS JUST RUNNIN' A BURIAL DETAIL OUT HERE IN POSEIDONIS YESTERDAY...
ONCE WE BEACH 'EM ON TRAITOR'S REEF THE GULLS WON'T CARE IF THEIR BELLIES ARE FULL OR EMPTY. WHY FEED DEAD MEN, VULKO?
BECAUSE WE ARE CIVILIZED PEOPLE--NOT BARBARIANS!
WHEN ORIN WAS KING, HE ORDERED THAT ALL PRISONERS BE TREATED HUMANELY.
WAS THAT BEFORE OR AFTER YOU CONDEMNED HIM TO DEATH BY DESICCATION?
CAPTAIN NUNVUK; THAT'S COMPLETELY UNCALLED FOR.
ORIN COMMITTED AN UNPARDONABLE CRIME AGAINST ATLANTIS, AND I PERFORMED MY DUTY BY READING HIM MERA'S DECREE. BUT HE WAS STILL MY KING... AND A FRIEND.
I'M WONDERING IF BLUBBERBUTT IS ONE OF THOSE ORINISTS WE BEEN HEARING ABOUT?
YEAH, SOME TURNCOATS TALK ABOUT BRINGIN' OLD YELLOWHAIR BACK...IF HE'S STILL ALIVE, THAT IS.
I-I'LL HAVE YOU KNOW I JUST RENEWED MY LOYALTY OATH TO THE EMPRESS.
THAT'S FUNNY--BECAUSE HAGEN HIMSELF TOLD ME TO KEEP A CLOSE EYE ON YOU, VULKO.
WHY, I NEVER! HARUMMF! TO THINK THAT A SENIOR MINISTER SHOULD BE SUSPECTED OF BETRAYING ATLANTIS!
P-PLEASE... A BITE TO EAT, SIR... THAT'S ALL WE ASK.

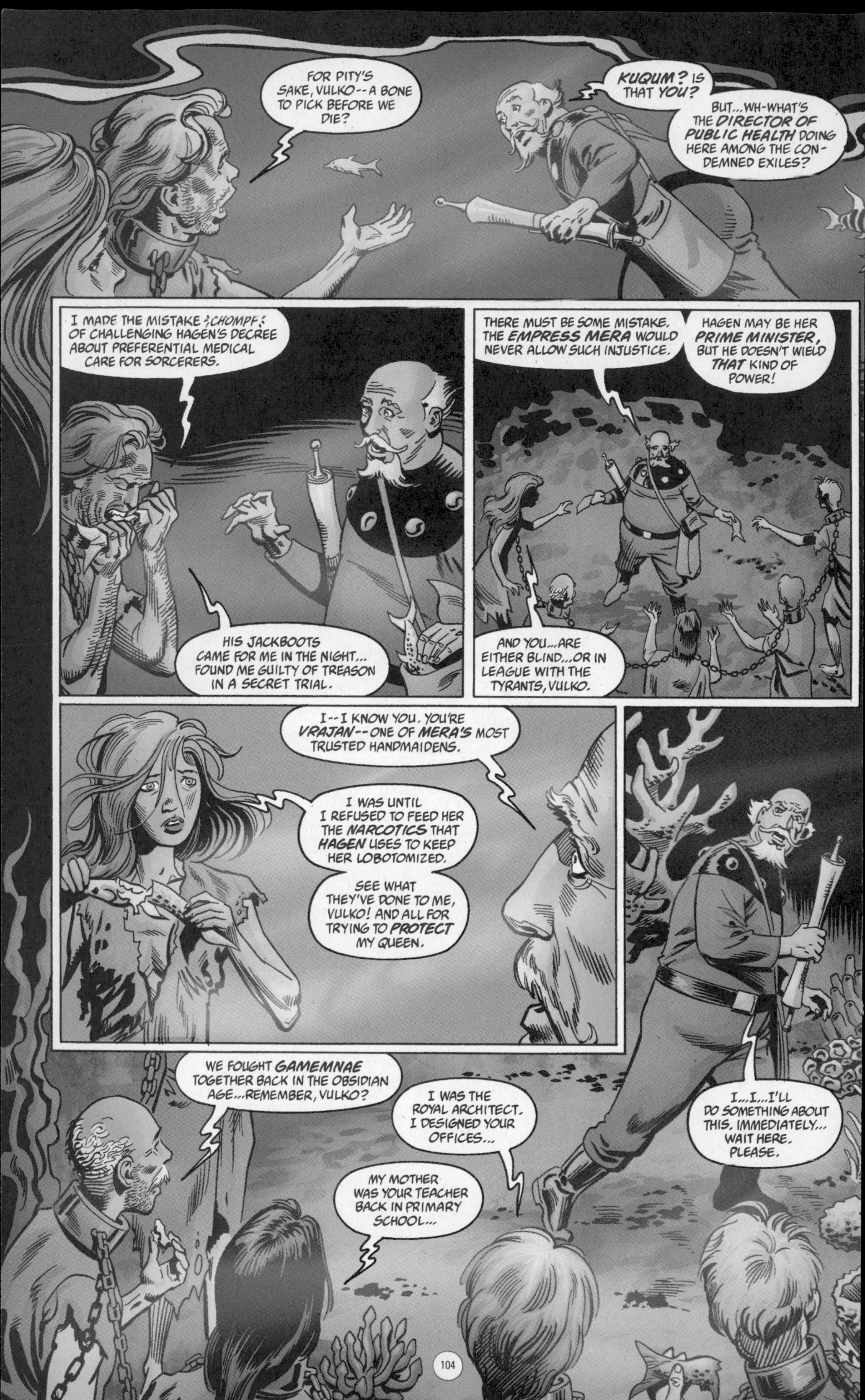
FOR PITY'S SAKE, VULKO--A BONE TO PICK BEFORE WE DIE?
KUQUM? IS THAT YOU?
BUT...WH-WHAT'S THE DIRECTOR OF PUBLIC HEALTH DOING HERE AMONG THE CONDEMNED EXILES?
I MADE THE MISTAKE ;CHOMPF; OF CHALLENGING HAGEN'S DECREE ABOUT PREFERENTIAL MEDICAL CARE FOR SORCERERS.
HIS JACKBOOTS CAME FOR ME IN THE NIGHT... FOUND ME GUILTY OF TREASON IN A SECRET TRIAL.
THERE MUST BE SOME MISTAKE. THE EMPRESS MERA WOULD NEVER ALLOW SUCH INJUSTICE.
HAGEN MAY BE HER PRIME MINISTER, BUT HE DOESN'T WIELD THAT KIND OF POWER!
AND YOU...ARE EITHER BLIND...OR IN LEAGUE WITH THE TYRANTS, VULKO.
I--I KNOW YOU. YOU'RE VRAJAN--ONE OF MERA'S MOST TRUSTED HANDMAIDENS.
I WAS UNTIL I REFUSED TO FEED HER THE NARCOTICS THAT HAGEN USES TO KEEP HER LOBOTOMIZED.
SEE WHAT THEY'VE DONE TO ME, VULKO! AND ALL FOR TRYING TO PROTECT MY QUEEN.
WE FOUGHT GAMEMNAE TOGETHER BACK IN THE OBSIDIAN AGE...REMEMBER, VULKO?
I WAS THE ROYAL ARCHITECT. I DESIGNED YOUR OFFICES...
MY MOTHER WAS YOUR TEACHER BACK IN PRIMARY SCHOOL...
I...I...I'LL DO SOMETHING ABOUT THIS. IMMEDIATELY... WAIT HERE. PLEASE.

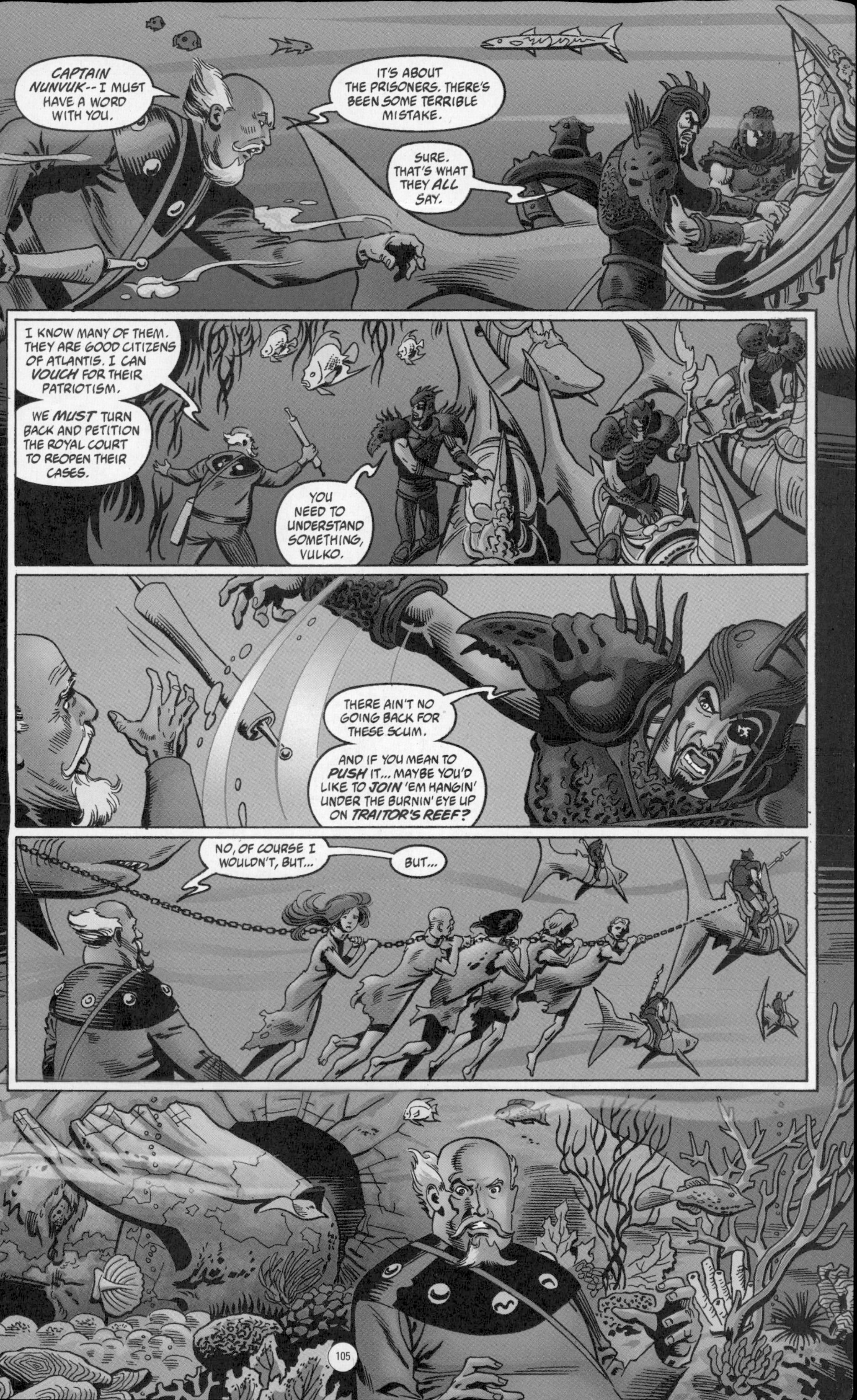

CAPTAIN NUNVUK-- I MUST HAVE A WORD WITH YOU.
IT'S ABOUT THE PRISONERS. THERE'S BEEN SOME TERRIBLE MISTAKE.
SURE. THAT'S WHAT THEY ALL SAY.
I KNOW MANY OF THEM. THEY ARE GOOD CITIZENS OF ATLANTIS. I CAN VOUCH FOR THEIR PATRIOTISM.
WE MUST TURN BACK AND PETITION THE ROYAL COURT TO REOPEN THEIR CASES.
YOU NEED TO UNDERSTAND SOMETHING, VULKO.
THERE AIN'T NO GOING BACK FOR THESE SCUM.
AND IF YOU MEAN TO PUSH IT... MAYBE YOU'D LIKE TO JOIN 'EM HANGIN' UNDER THE BURNIN' EYE UP ON TRAITOR'S REEF?
NO, OF COURSE I WOULDN'T, BUT...
BUT...

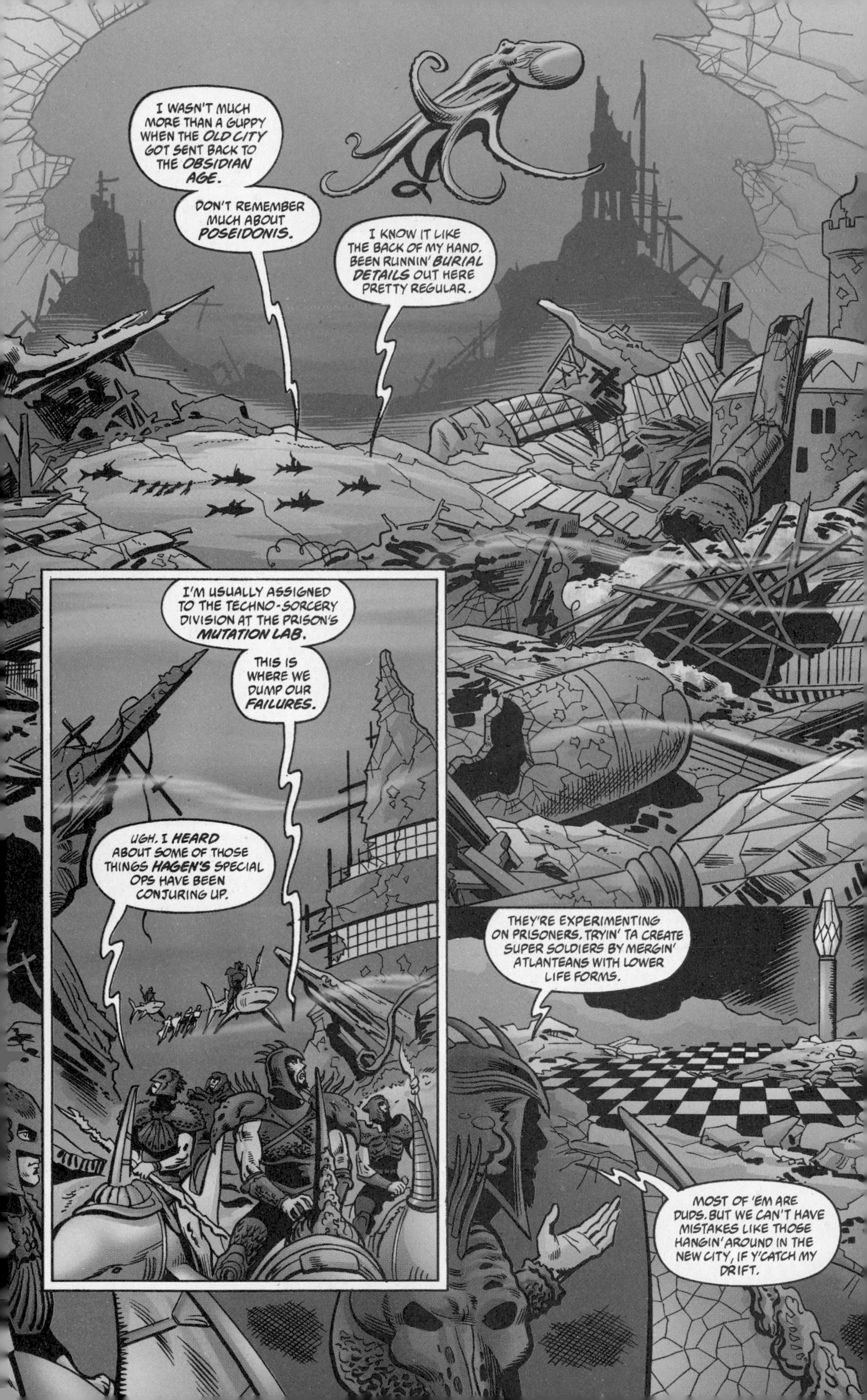
I WASN'T MUCH MORE THAN A GUPPY WHEN THE OLD CITY GOT SENT BACK TO THE OBSIDIAN AGE.
DON'T REMEMBER MUCH ABOUT POSEIDONIS.
I KNOW IT LIKE THE BACK OF MY HAND. BEEN RUNNIN' BURIAL DETAILS OUT HERE PRETTY REGULAR.
I'M USUALLY ASSIGNED TO THE TECHNO-SORCERY DIVISION AT THE PRISON'S MUTATION LAB.
THIS IS WHERE WE DUMP OUR FAILURES.
UGH. I HEARD ABOUT SOME OF THOSE THINGS HAGEN'S SPECIAL OPS HAVE BEEN CONJURING UP.
THEY'RE EXPERIMENTING ON PRISONERS. TRYIN' TA CREATE SUPER SOLDIERS BY MERGIN' ATLANTEANS WITH LOWER LIFE FORMS.
MOST OF 'EM ARE DUDS. BUT WE CAN'T HAVE MISTAKES LIKE THOSE HANGIN' AROUND IN THE NEW CITY, IF Y'CATCH MY DRIFT.

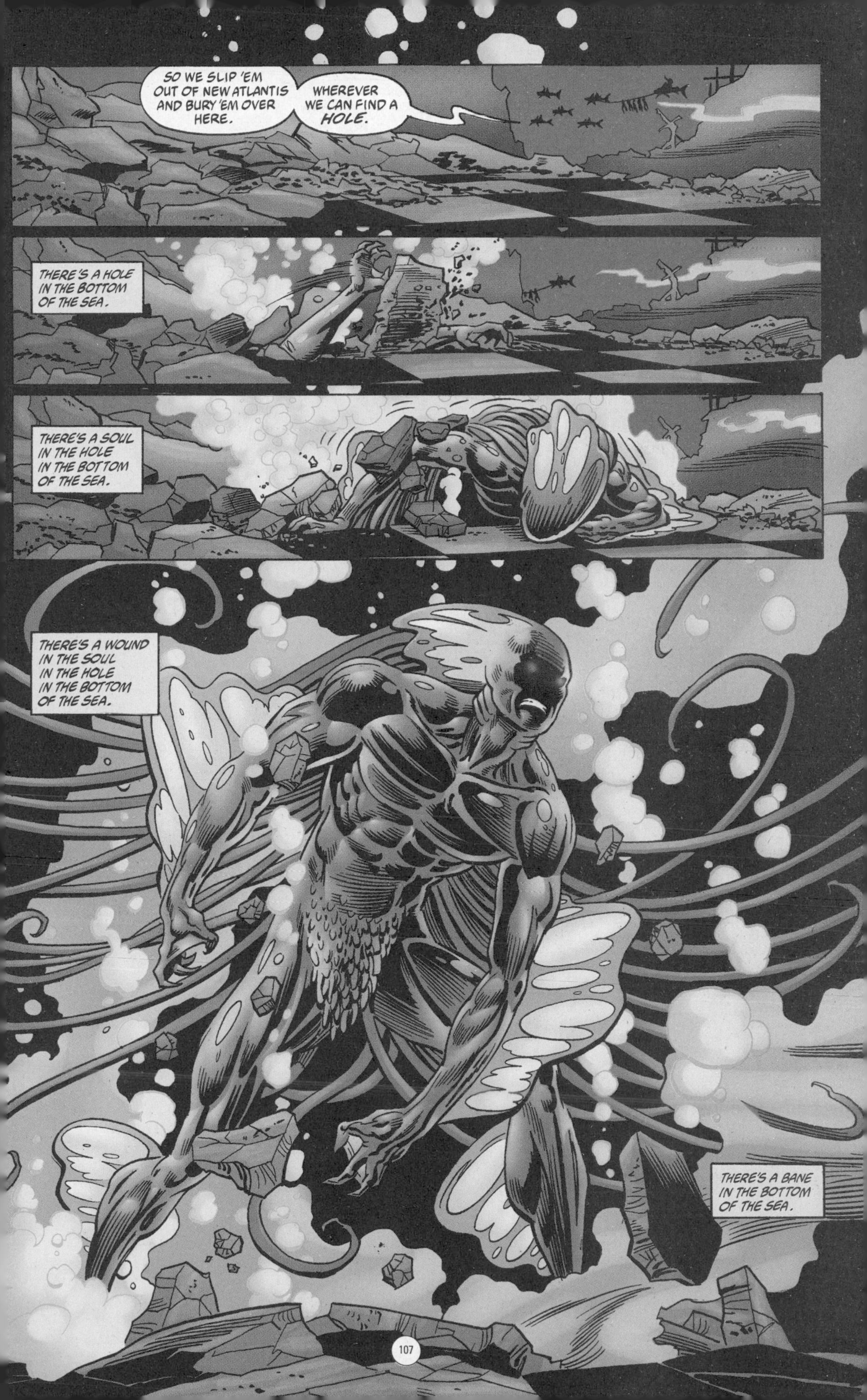
SO WE SLIP 'EM OUT OF NEW ATLANTIS AND BURY 'EM OVER HERE.
WHEREVER WE CAN FIND A HOLE.
THERE'S A HOLE IN THE BOTTOM OF THE SEA.
THERE'S A SOUL IN THE HOLE IN THE BOTTOM OF THE SEA.
THERE'S A WOUND IN THE SOUL IN THE HOLE IN THE BOTTOM OF THE SEA.
THERE'S A BANE IN THE BOTTOM OF THE SEA.

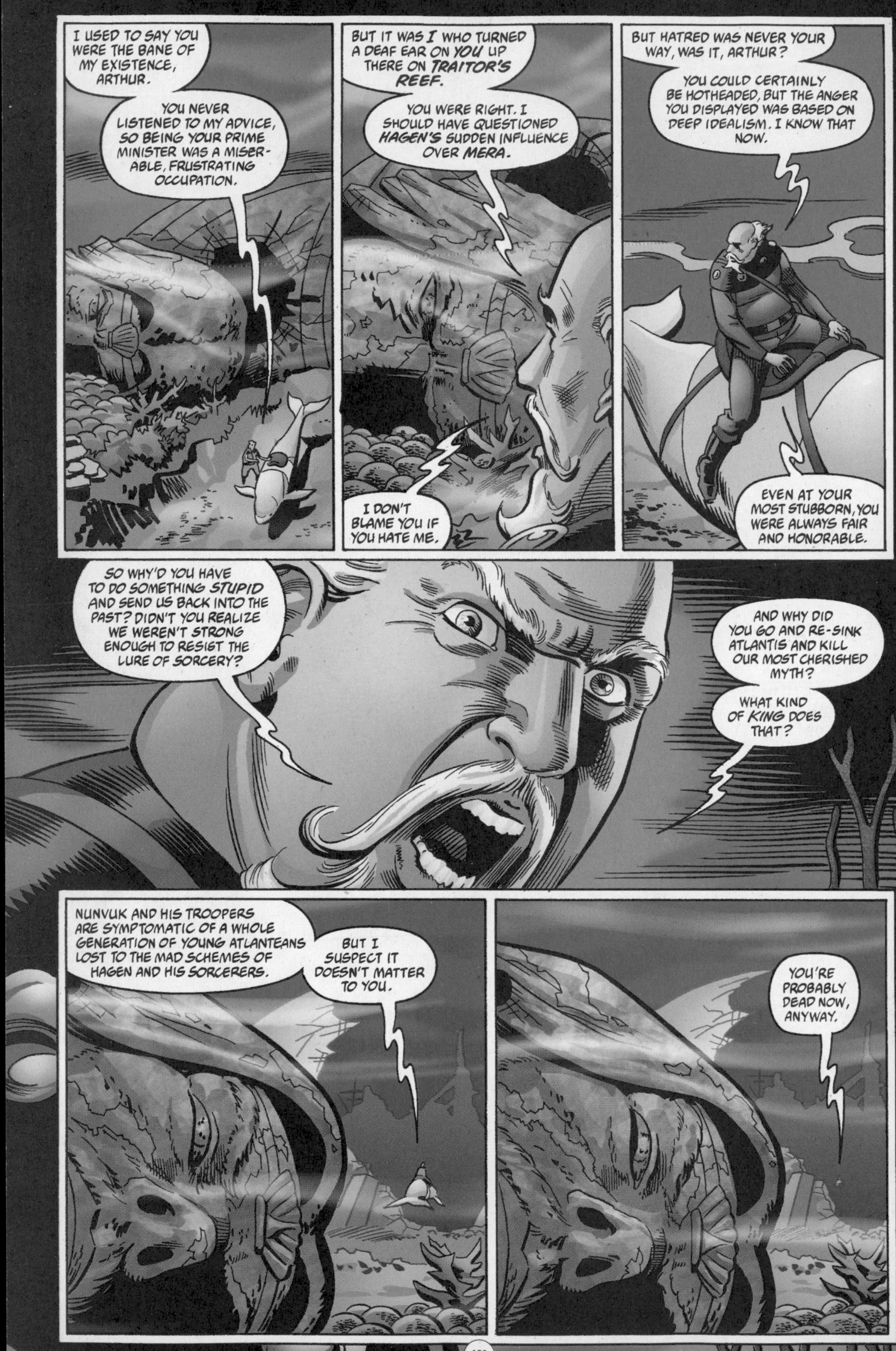

I USED TO SAY YOU WERE THE BANE OF MY EXISTENCE, ARTHUR.
YOU NEVER LISTENED TO MY ADVICE, SO BEING YOUR PRIME MINISTER WAS A MISERABLE, FRUSTRATING OCCUPATION.
BUT IT WAS I WHO TURNED A DEAF EAR ON YOU UP THERE ON TRAITOR'S REEF.
YOU WERE RIGHT. I SHOULD HAVE QUESTIONED HAGEN'S SUDDEN INFLUENCE OVER MERA.
I DON'T BLAME YOU IF YOU HATE ME.
BUT HATRED WAS NEVER YOUR WAY, WAS IT, ARTHUR?
YOU COULD CERTAINLY BE HOTHEADED, BUT THE ANGER YOU DISPLAYED WAS BASED ON DEEP IDEALISM. I KNOW THAT NOW.
EVEN AT YOUR MOST STUBBORN, YOU WERE ALWAYS FAIR AND HONORABLE.
SO WHY'D YOU HAVE TO DO SOMETHING STUPID AND SEND US BACK INTO THE PAST? DIDN'T YOU REALIZE WE WEREN'T STRONG ENOUGH TO RESIST THE LURE OF SORCERY?
AND WHY DID YOU GO AND RE-SINK ATLANTIS AND KILL OUR MOST CHERISHED MYTH?
WHAT KIND OF KING DOES THAT?
NUNVUK AND HIS TROOPERS ARE SYMPTOMATIC OF A WHOLE GENERATION OF YOUNG ATLANTEANS LOST TO THE MAD SCHEMES OF HAGEN AND HIS SORCERERS.
BUT I SUSPECT IT DOESN'T MATTER TO YOU.
YOU'RE PROBABLY DEAD NOW, ANYWAY.

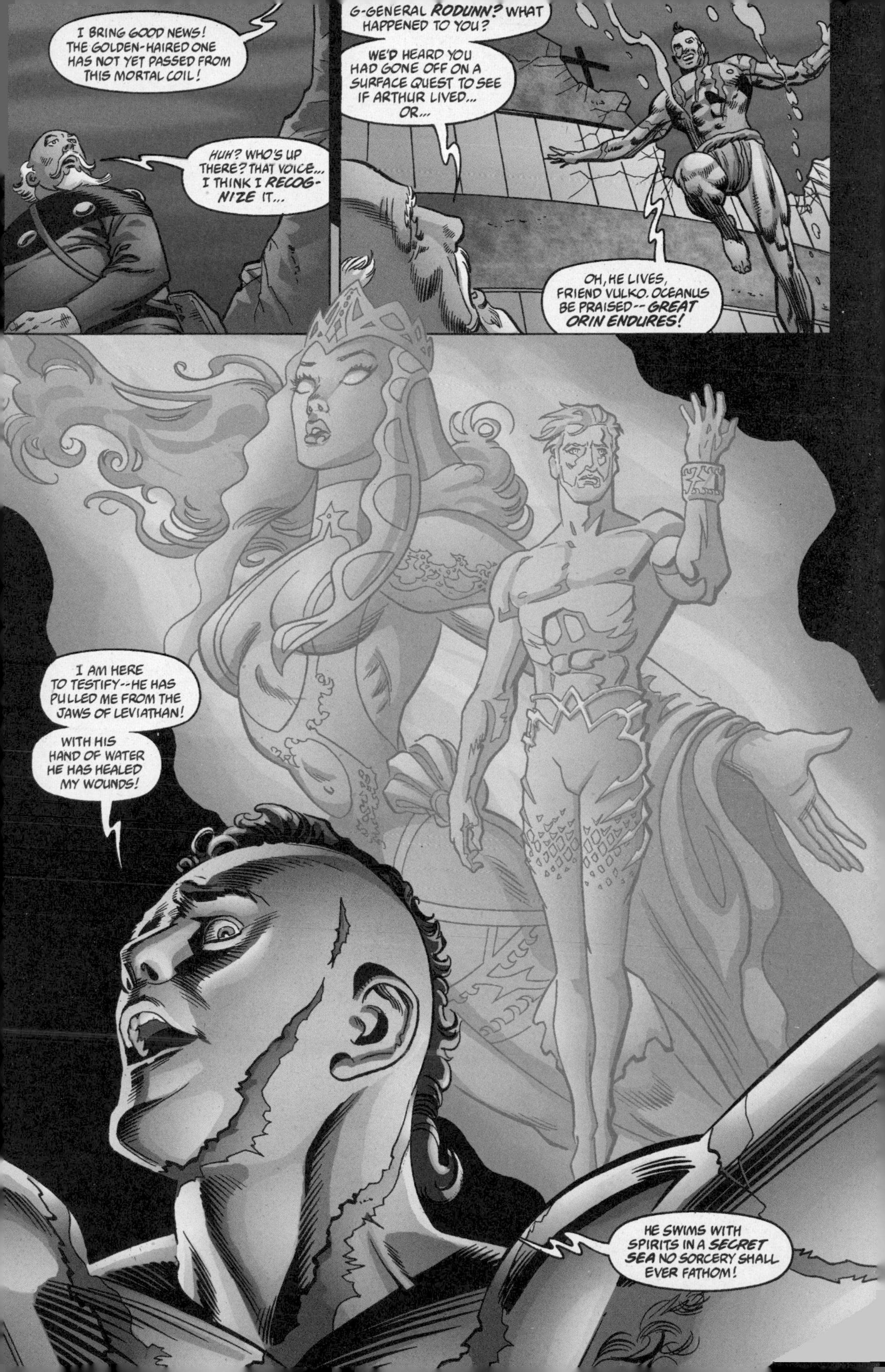
I BRING GOOD NEWS! THE GOLDEN-HAIRED ONE HAS NOT YET PASSED FROM THIS MORTAL COIL!
HUH? WHO'S UP THERE? THAT VOICE... I THINK I RECOGNIZE IT...
G-GENERAL RODUNN? WHAT HAPPENED TO YOU?
WE'D HEARD YOU HAD GONE OFF ON A SURFACE QUEST TO SEE IF ARTHUR LIVED... OR...
OH, HE LIVES, FRIEND VULKO. OCEANUS BE PRAISED-- GREAT ORIN ENDURES!
I AM HERE TO TESTIFY--HE HAS PULLED ME FROM THE JAWS OF LEVIATHAN!
WITH HIS HAND OF WATER HE HAS HEALED MY WOUNDS!
HE SWIMS WITH SPIRITS IN A SECRET SEA NO SORCERY SHALL EVER FATHOM!

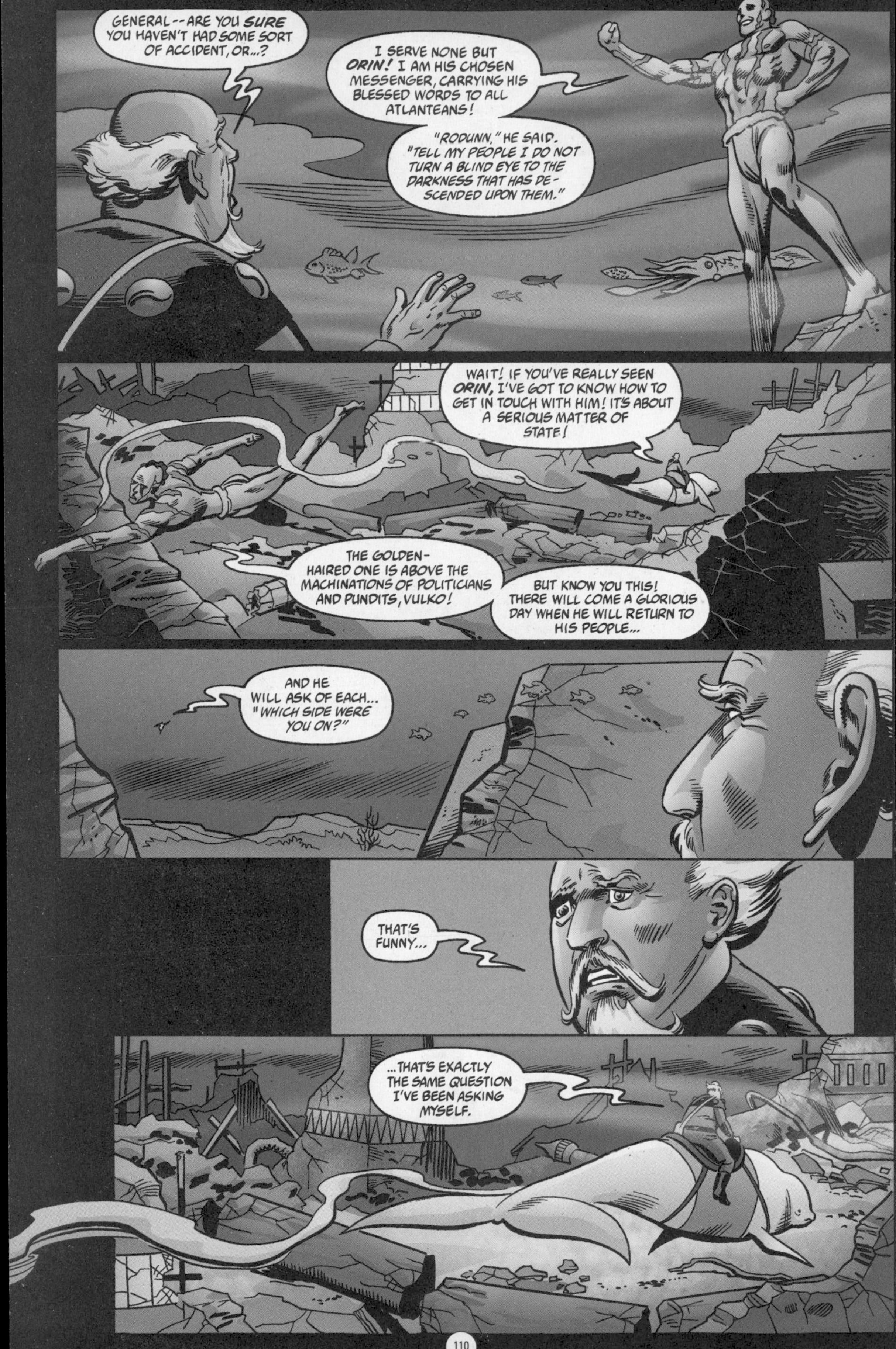
GENERAL--ARE YOU SURE YOU HAVEN'T HAD SOME SORT OF ACCIDENT, OR...?
I SERVE NONE BUT ORIN! I AM HIS CHOSEN MESSENGER, CARRYING HIS BLESSED WORDS TO ALL ATLANTEANS!
"RODUNN," HE SAID. "TELL MY PEOPLE I DO NOT TURN A BLIND EYE TO THE DARKNESS THAT HAS DE-SCENDED UPON THEM."
WAIT! IF YOU'VE REALLY SEEN ORIN, I'VE GOT TO KNOW HOW TO GET IN TOUCH WITH HIM! IT'S ABOUT A SERIOUS MATTER OF STATE!
THE GOLDEN-HAIRED ONE IS ABOVE THE MACHINATIONS OF POLITICIANS AND PUNDITS, VULKO!
BUT KNOW YOU THIS! THERE WILL COME A GLORIOUS DAY WHEN HE WILL RETURN TO HIS PEOPLE...
AND HE WILL ASK OF EACH... "WHICH SIDE WERE YOU ON?"
THAT'S FUNNY...
...THAT'S EXACTLY THE SAME QUESTION I'VE BEEN ASKING MYSELF.

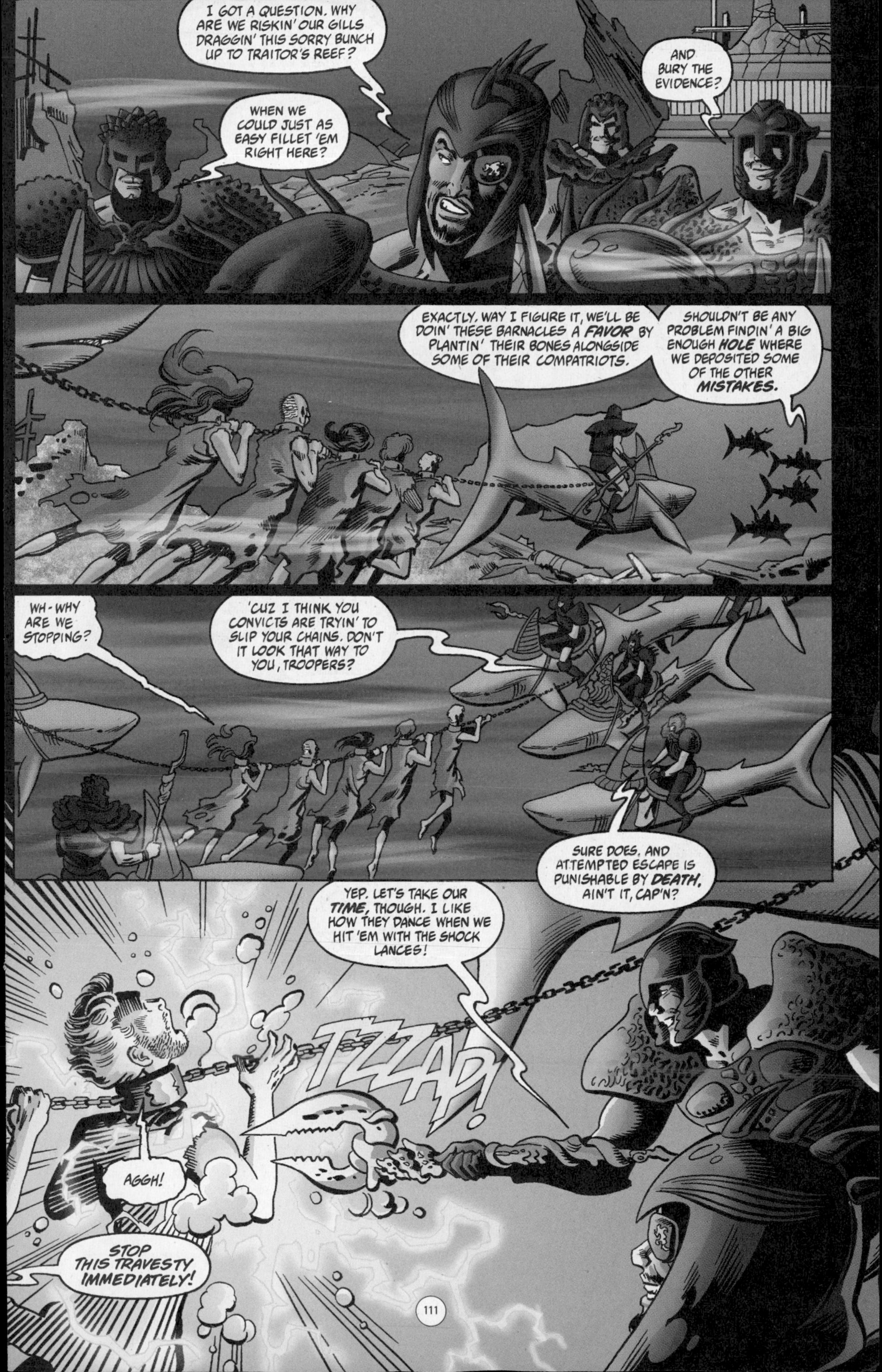
I GOT A QUESTION. WHY ARE WE RISKIN' OUR GILLS DRAGGIN' THIS SORRY BUNCH UP TO TRAITOR'S REEF?
WHEN WE COULD JUST AS EASY FILLET 'EM RIGHT HERE?
AND BURY THE EVIDENCE?
EXACTLY. WAY I FIGURE IT, WE'LL BE DOIN' THESE BARNACLES A FAVOR BY PLANTIN' THEIR BONES ALONGSIDE SOME OF THEIR COMPATRIOTS.
SHOULDN'T BE ANY PROBLEM FINDIN' A BIG ENOUGH HOLE WHERE WE DEPOSITED SOME OF THE OTHER MISTAKES.
WH-WHY ARE WE STOPPING?
'CUZ I THINK YOU CONVICTS ARE TRYIN' TO SLIP YOUR CHAINS. DON'T IT LOOK THAT WAY TO YOU, TROOPERS?
SURE DOES. AND ATTEMPTED ESCAPE IS PUNISHABLE BY DEATH, AIN'T IT, CAP'N?
YEP. LET'S TAKE OUR TIME, THOUGH. I LIKE HOW THEY DANCE WHEN WE HIT 'EM WITH THE SHOCK LANCES!
TZZZAP!
AGGH!
STOP THIS TRAVESTY IMMEDIATELY!

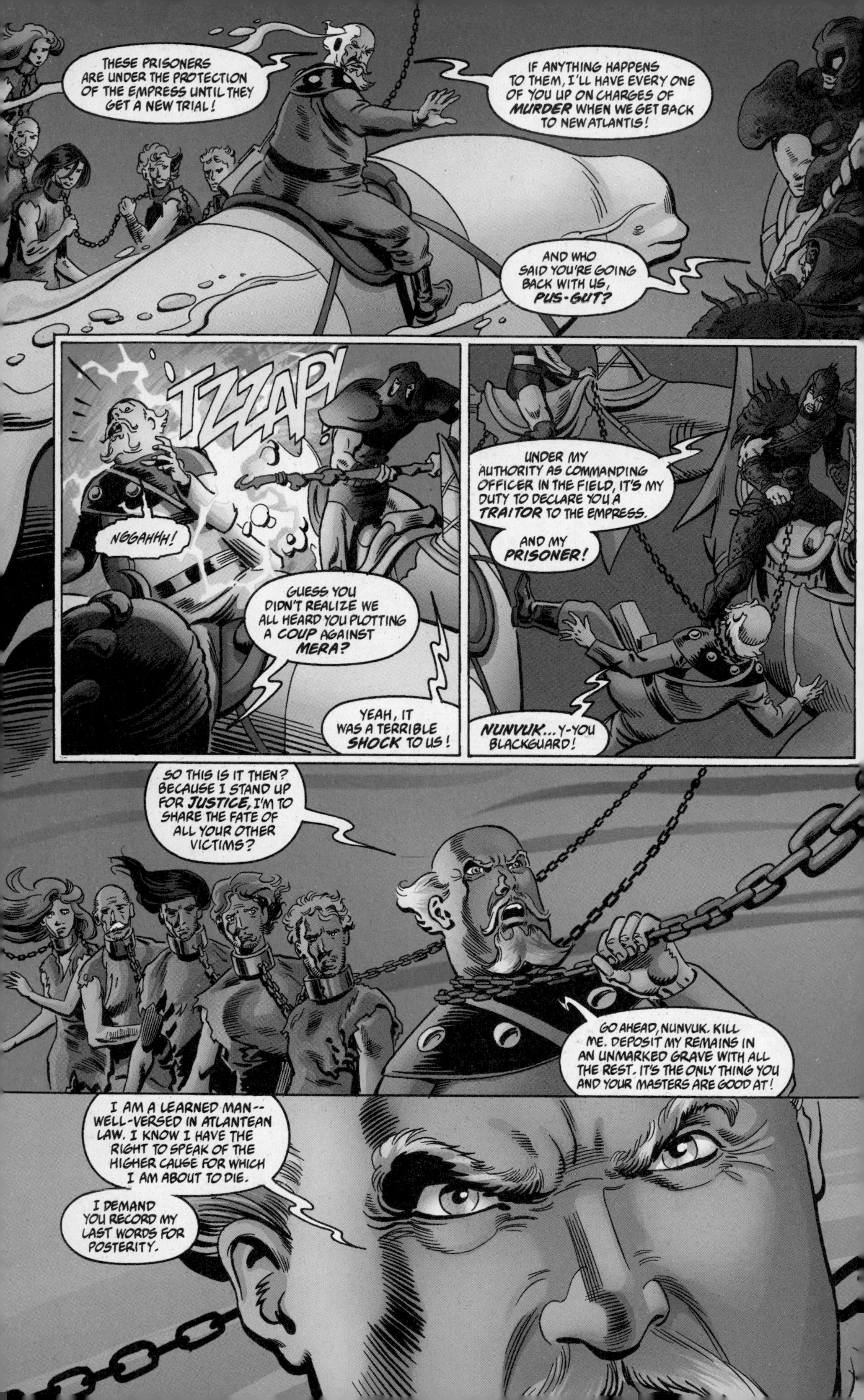
THESE PRISONERS ARE UNDER THE PROTECTION OF THE EMPRESS UNTIL THEY GET A NEW TRIAL!
IF ANYTHING HAPPENS TO THEM, I'LL HAVE EVERY ONE OF YOU UP ON CHARGES OF MURDER WHEN WE GET BACK TO NEW ATLANTIS!
AND WHO SAID YOU'RE GOING BACK WITH US, PUS-GUT?
TZZAP!
NGGAHHH!
GUESS YOU DIDN'T REALIZE WE ALL HEARD YOU PLOTTING A COUP AGAINST MERA?
YEAH, IT WAS A TERRIBLE SHOCK TO US!
UNDER MY AUTHORITY AS COMMANDING OFFICER IN THE FIELD, IT'S MY DUTY TO DECLARE YOU A TRAITOR TO THE EMPRESS.
AND MY PRISONER!
NUNVUK... Y-YOU BLACKGUARD!
SO THIS IS IT THEN? BECAUSE I STAND UP FOR JUSTICE, I'M TO SHARE THE FATE OF ALL YOUR OTHER VICTIMS?
GO AHEAD, NUNVUK. KILL ME. DEPOSIT MY REMAINS IN AN UNMARKED GRAVE WITH ALL THE REST. IT'S THE ONLY THING YOU AND YOUR MASTERS ARE GOOD AT!
I AM A LEARNED MAN-- WELL-VERSED IN ATLANTEAN LAW. I KNOW I HAVE THE RIGHT TO SPEAK OF THE HIGHER CAUSE FOR WHICH I AM ABOUT TO DIE.
I DEMAND YOU RECORD MY LAST WORDS FOR POSTERITY.

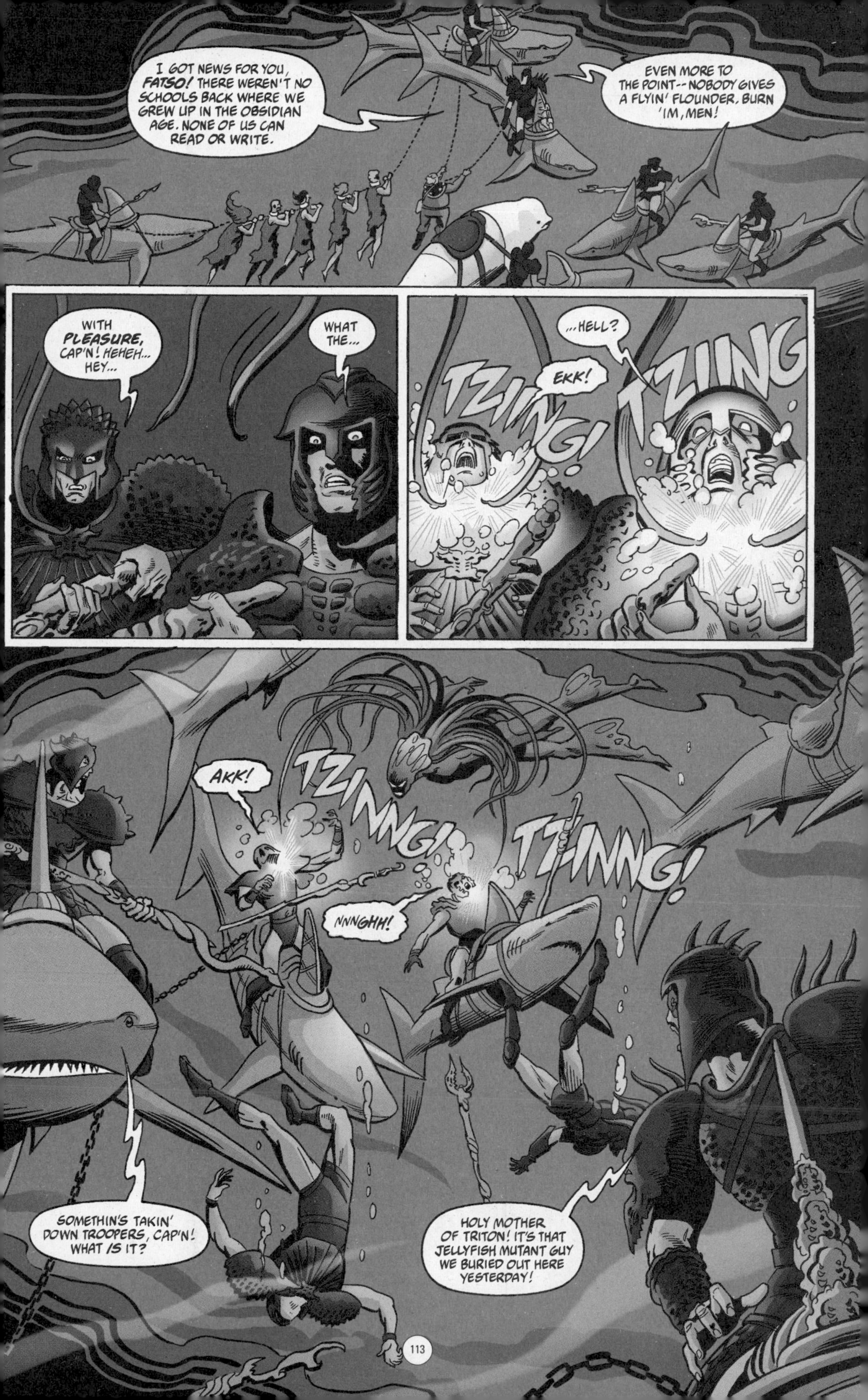
I GOT NEWS FOR YOU, FATSO! THERE WEREN'T NO SCHOOLS BACK WHERE WE GREW UP IN THE OBSIDIAN AGE. NONE OF US CAN READ OR WRITE.
EVEN MORE TO THE POINT-- NOBODY GIVES A FLYIN' FLOUNDER. BURN 'IM, MEN!
WITH PLEASURE, CAP'N! HEHEH... HEY...
WHAT THE...
...HELL?
TZING!
EKK!
TZING
AKK!
TZINNG!
TZHNNG!
NNNGHH!
SOMETHIN'S TAKIN' DOWN TROOPERS, CAP'N! WHAT IS IT?
HOLY MOTHER OF TRITON! IT'S THAT JELLYFISH MUTANT GUY WE BURIED OUT HERE YESTERDAY!

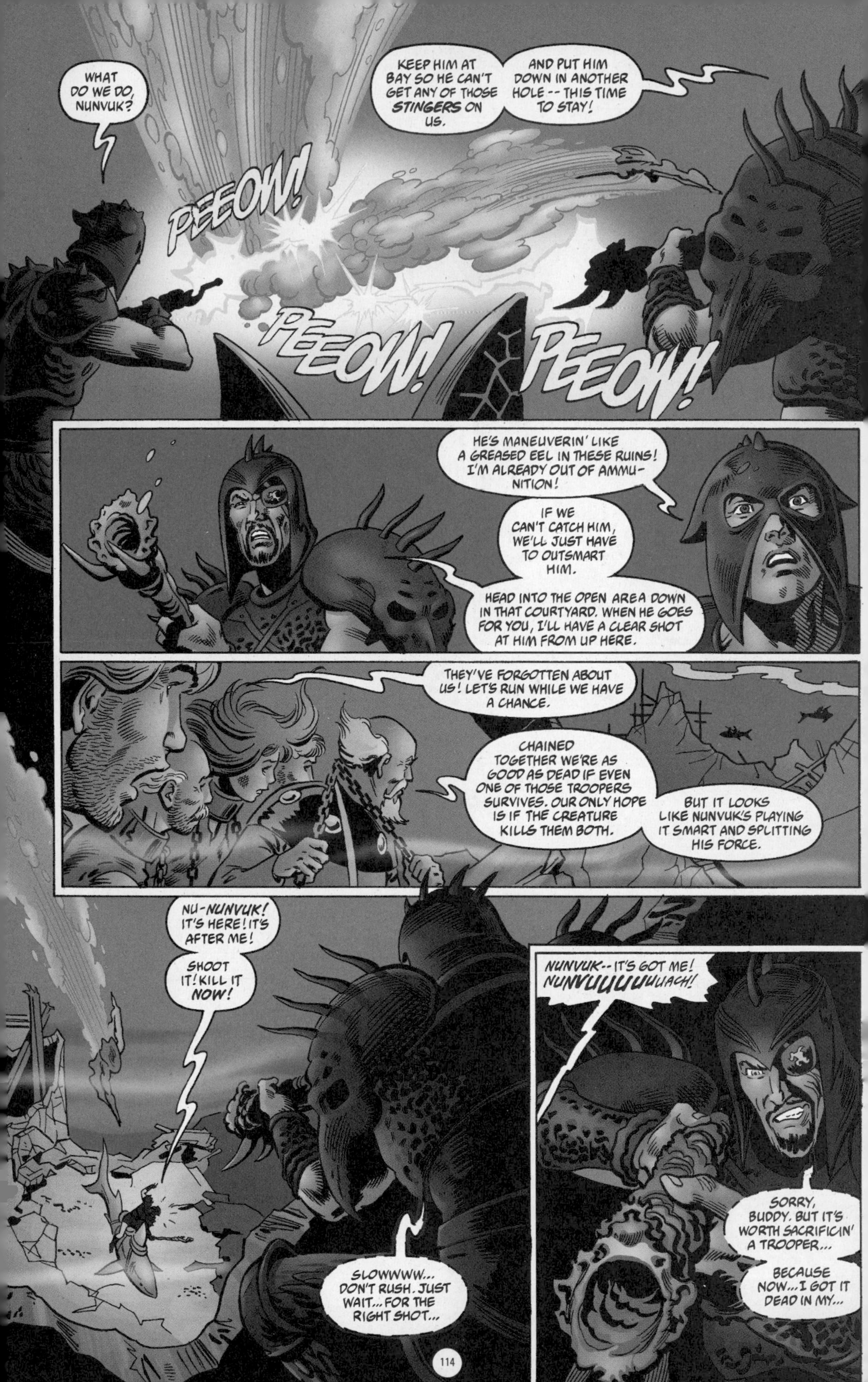
WHAT DO WE DO, NUNVUK?
KEEP HIM AT BAY SO HE CAN'T GET ANY OF THOSE STINGERS ON US.
AND PUT HIM DOWN IN ANOTHER HOLE -- THIS TIME TO STAY!
PEEOW!
PEEOW!
PEEOW!
HE'S MANEUVERIN' LIKE A GREASED EEL IN THESE RUINS! I'M ALREADY OUT OF AMMUNITION!
IF WE CAN'T CATCH HIM, WE'LL JUST HAVE TO OUTSMART HIM.
HEAD INTO THE OPEN AREA DOWN IN THAT COURTYARD. WHEN HE GOES FOR YOU, I'LL HAVE A CLEAR SHOT AT HIM FROM UP HERE.
THEY'VE FORGOTTEN ABOUT US! LET'S RUN WHILE WE HAVE A CHANCE.
CHAINED TOGETHER WE'RE AS GOOD AS DEAD IF EVEN ONE OF THOSE TROOPERS SURVIVES. OUR ONLY HOPE IS IF THE CREATURE KILLS THEM BOTH.
BUT IT LOOKS LIKE NUNVUK'S PLAYING IT SMART AND SPLITTING HIS FORCE.
NU-NUNVUK! IT'S HERE! IT'S AFTER ME!
SHOOT IT! KILL IT NOW!
SLOWWWW... DON'T RUSH. JUST WAIT... FOR THE RIGHT SHOT...
NUNVUK-- IT'S GOT ME! NUNVUUUUUUUACH!
SORRY, BUDDY. BUT IT'S WORTH SACRIFICIN' A TROOPER...
BECAUSE NOW... I GOT IT DEAD IN MY...

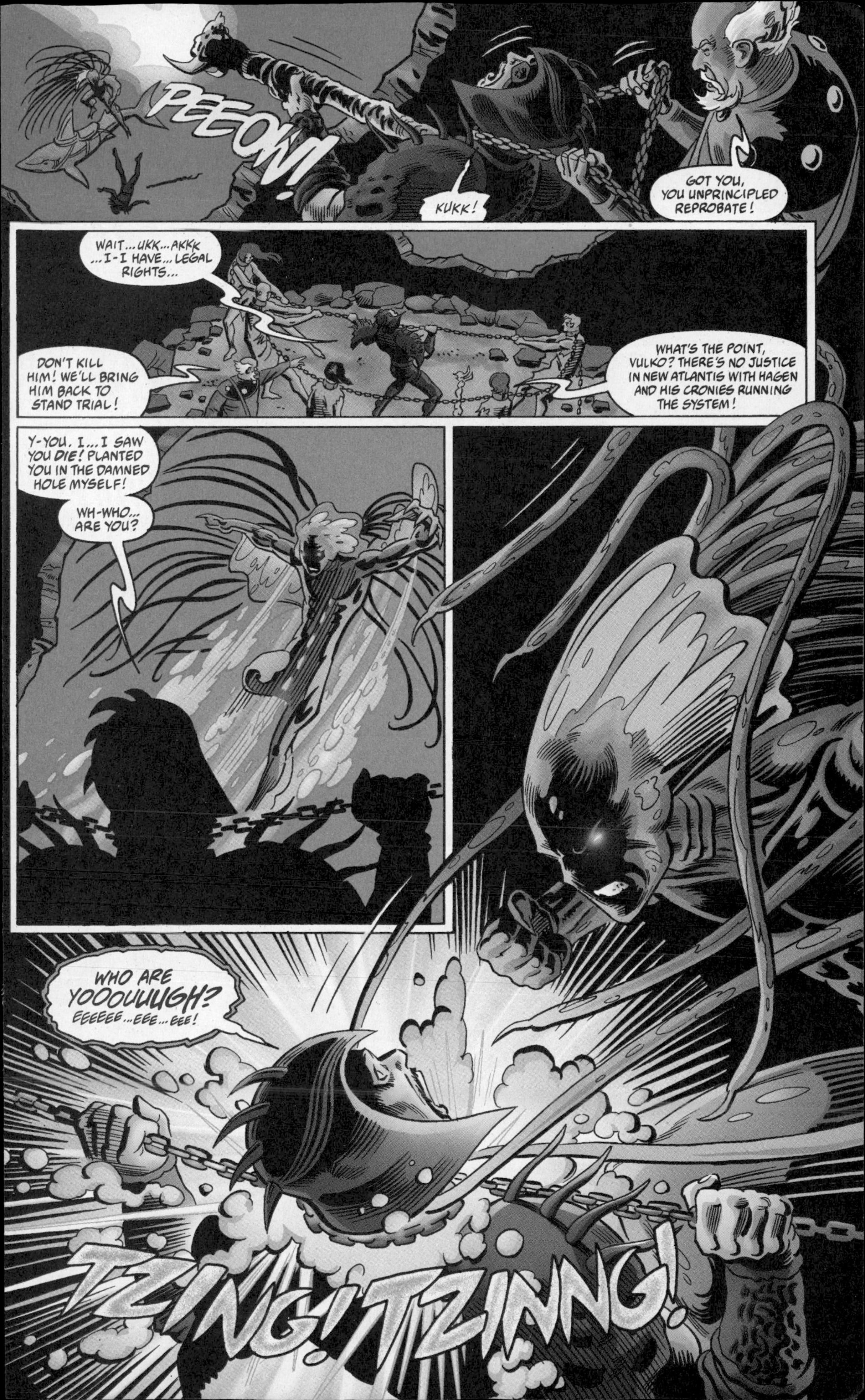
PEEOWM
KUKK!
GOT YOU, YOU UNPRINCIPLED REPROBATE!
WAIT... UKK... AKKK ...I-I HAVE... LEGAL RIGHTS...
DON'T KILL HIM! WE'LL BRING HIM BACK TO STAND TRIAL!
WHAT'S THE POINT, VULKO? THERE'S NO JUSTICE IN NEW ATLANTIS WITH HAGEN AND HIS CRONIES RUNNING THE SYSTEM!
Y-YOU. I... I SAW YOU DIE! PLANTED YOU IN THE DAMNED HOLE MYSELF!
WH-WHO... ARE YOU?
WHO ARE YOOOUUUGH? EEEEEE... EEE... EEE!
TZING! TZINNG!

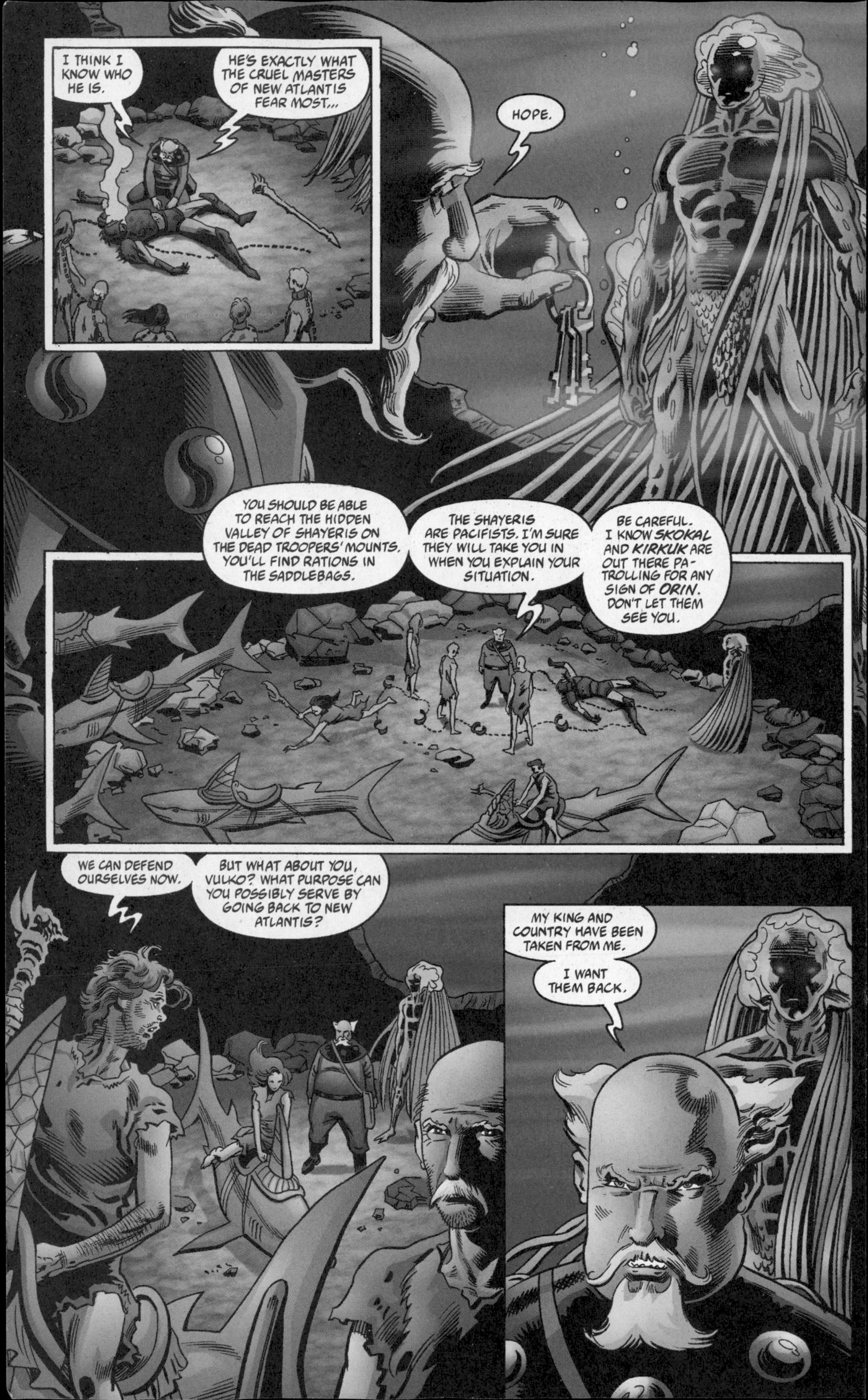

I THINK I KNOW WHO HE IS.
HE'S EXACTLY WHAT THE CRUEL MASTERS OF NEW ATLANTIS FEAR MOST...
HOPE.
YOU SHOULD BE ABLE TO REACH THE HIDDEN VALLEY OF SHAYERIS ON THE DEAD TROOPERS' MOUNTS. YOU'LL FIND RATIONS IN THE SADDLEBAGS.
THE SHAYERIS ARE PACIFISTS. I'M SURE THEY WILL TAKE YOU IN WHEN YOU EXPLAIN YOUR SITUATION.
BE CAREFUL. I KNOW SKOKAL AND KIRKUK ARE OUT THERE PATROLLING FOR ANY SIGN OF ORIN. DON'T LET THEM SEE YOU.
WE CAN DEFEND OURSELVES NOW.
BUT WHAT ABOUT YOU, VULKO? WHAT PURPOSE CAN YOU POSSIBLY SERVE BY GOING BACK TO NEW ATLANTIS?
MY KING AND COUNTRY HAVE BEEN TAKEN FROM ME.
I WANT THEM BACK.

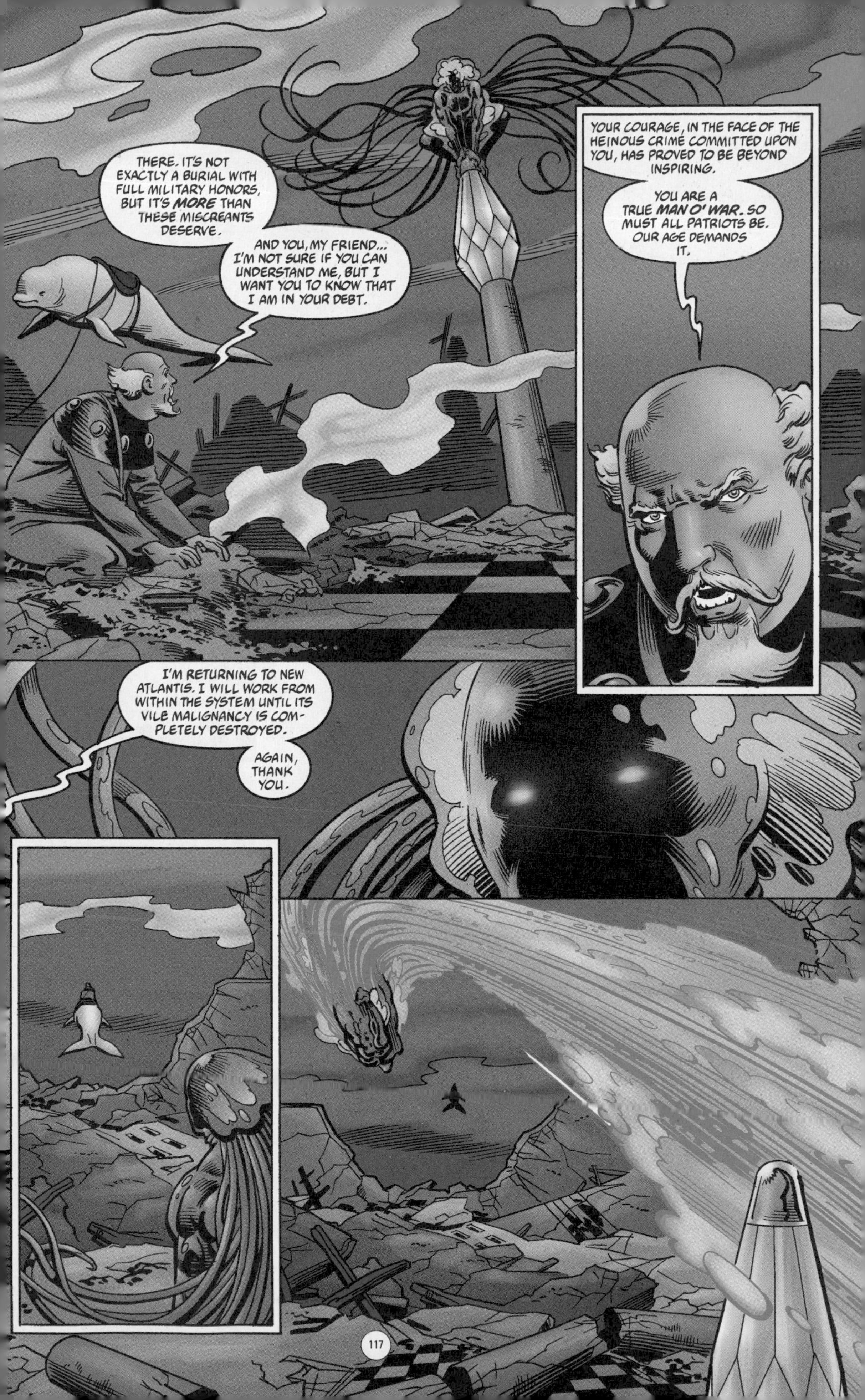
THERE. IT'S NOT EXACTLY A BURIAL WITH FULL MILITARY HONORS, BUT IT'S MORE THAN THESE MISCREANTS DESERVE.
AND YOU, MY FRIEND... I'M NOT SURE IF YOU CAN UNDERSTAND ME, BUT I WANT YOU TO KNOW THAT I AM IN YOUR DEBT.
YOUR COURAGE, IN THE FACE OF THE HEINOUS CRIME COMMITTED UPON YOU, HAS PROVED TO BE BEYOND INSPIRING.
YOU ARE A TRUE MAN O' WAR. SO MUST ALL PATRIOTS BE. OUR AGE DEMANDS IT.
I'M RETURNING TO NEW ATLANTIS. I WILL WORK FROM WITHIN THE SYSTEM UNTIL ITS VILE MALIGNANCY IS COMPLETELY DESTROYED.
AGAIN, THANK YOU.

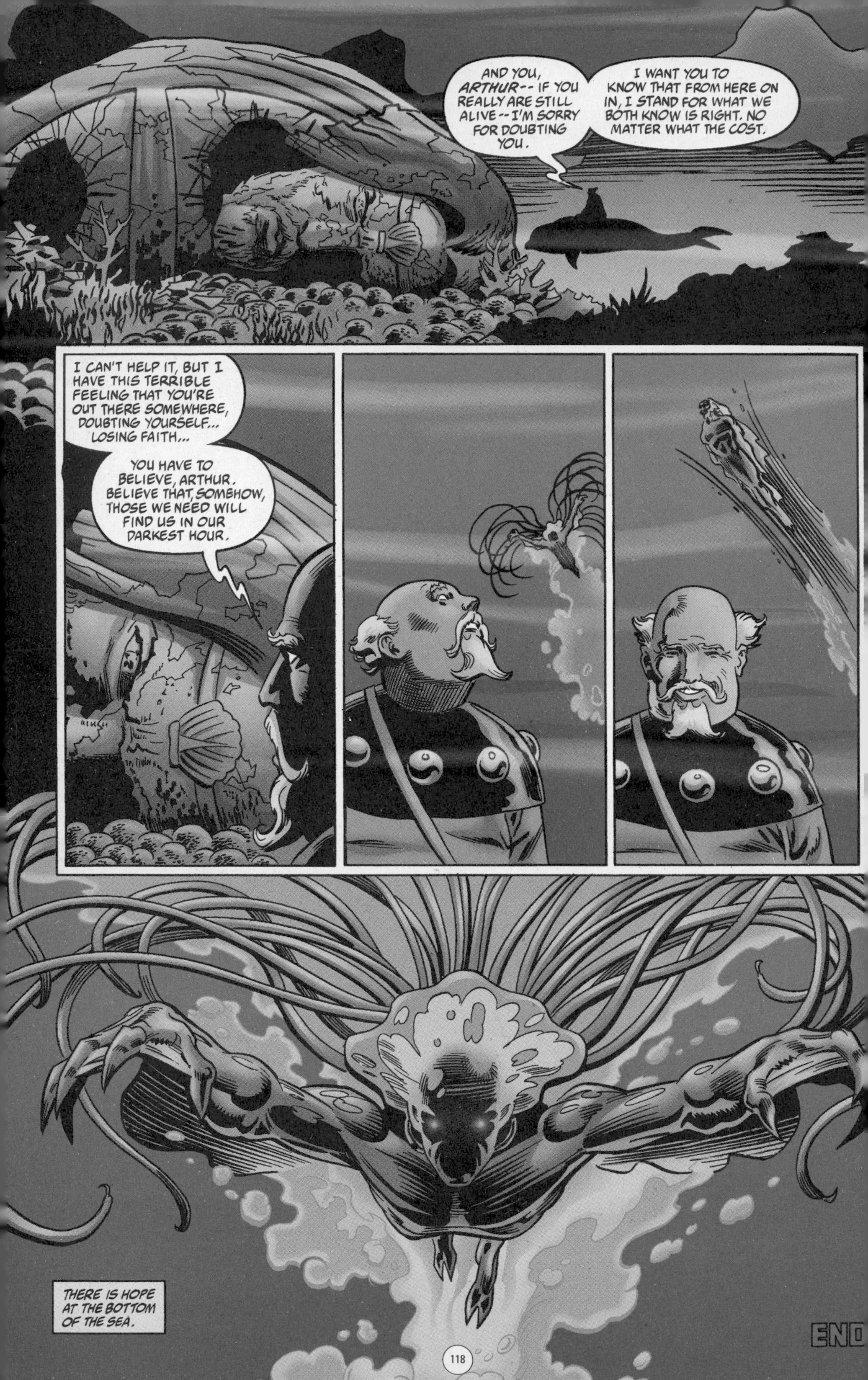
AND YOU, ARTHUR-- IF YOU REALLY ARE STILL ALIVE--I'M SORRY FOR DOUBTING YOU.
I WANT YOU TO KNOW THAT FROM HERE ON IN, I STAND FOR WHAT WE BOTH KNOW IS RIGHT. NO MATTER WHAT THE COST.
I CAN'T HELP IT, BUT I HAVE THIS TERRIBLE FEELING THAT YOU'RE OUT THERE SOMEWHERE, DOUBTING YOURSELF... LOSING FAITH...
YOU HAVE TO BELIEVE, ARTHUR. BELIEVE THAT, SOMEHOW, THOSE WE NEED WILL FIND US IN OUR DARKEST HOUR.
THERE IS HOPE AT THE BOTTOM OF THE SEA.
END

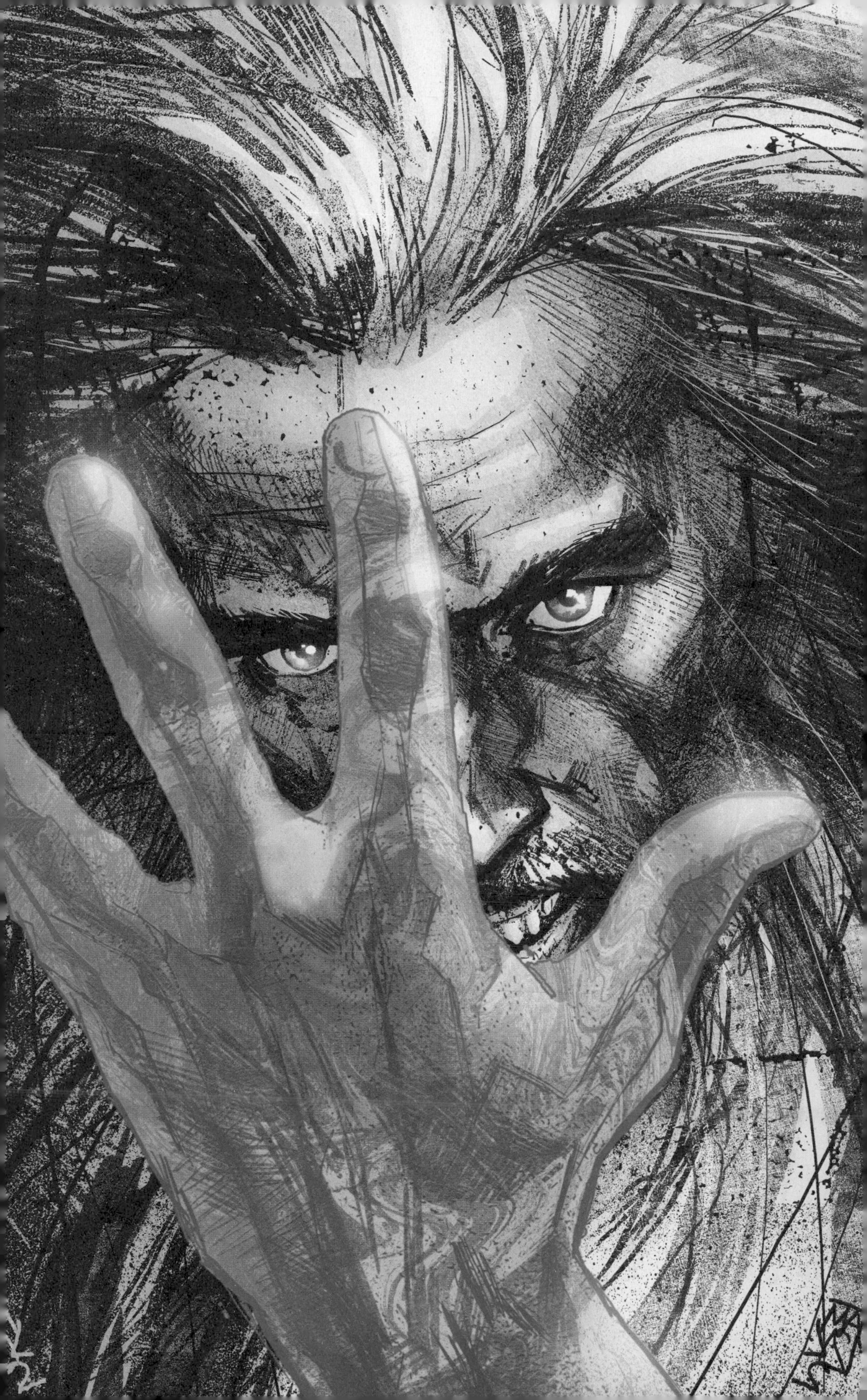

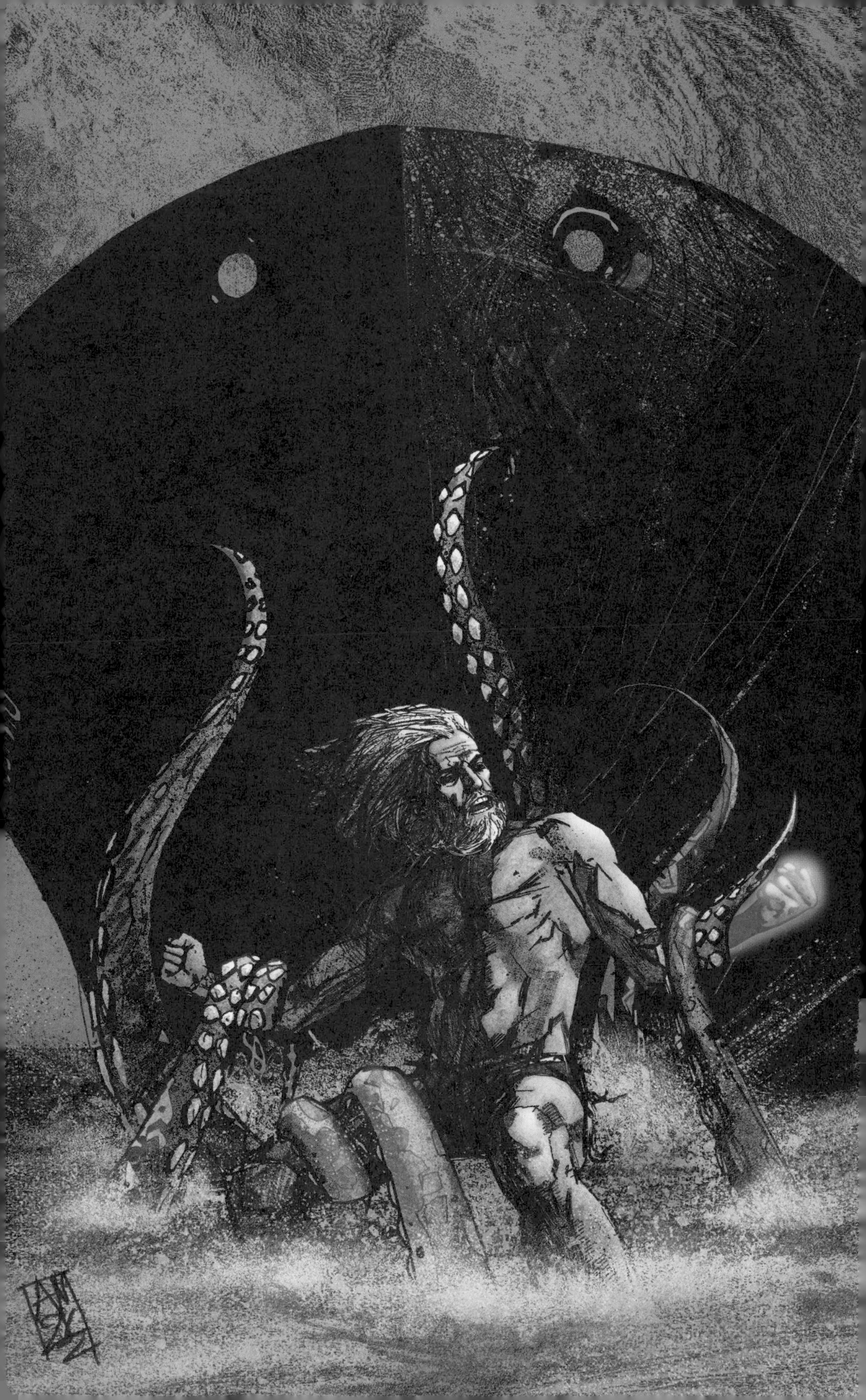

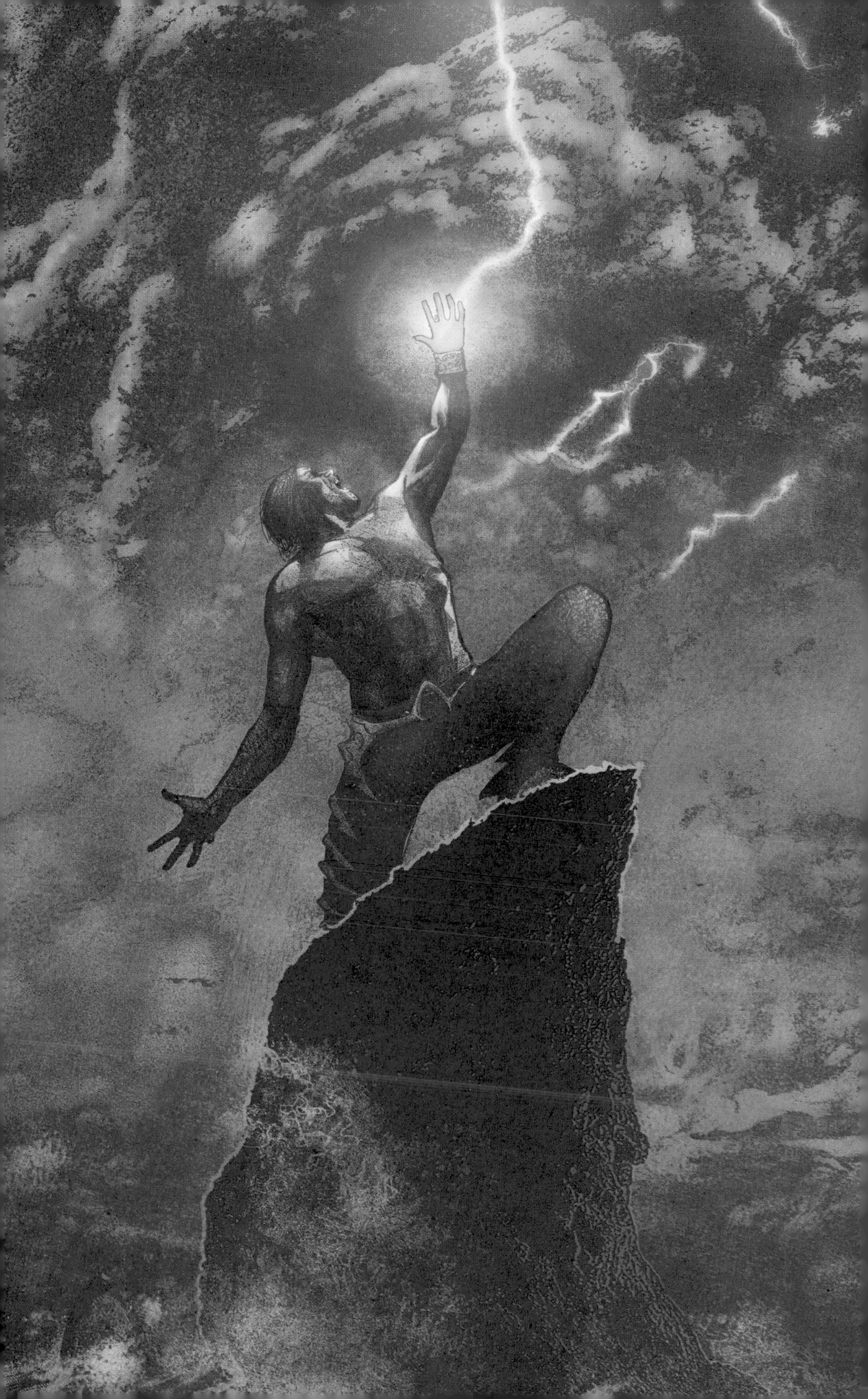

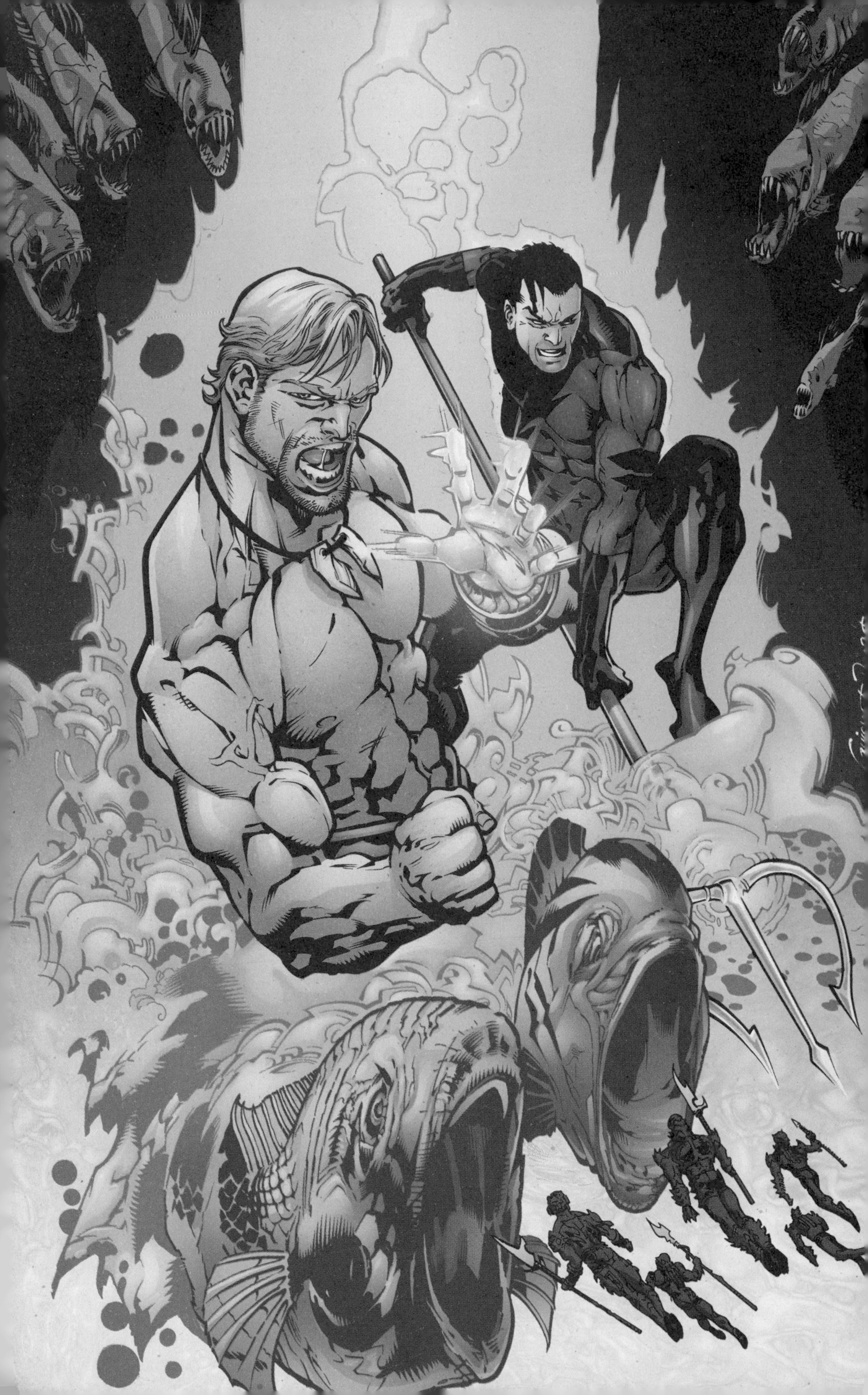

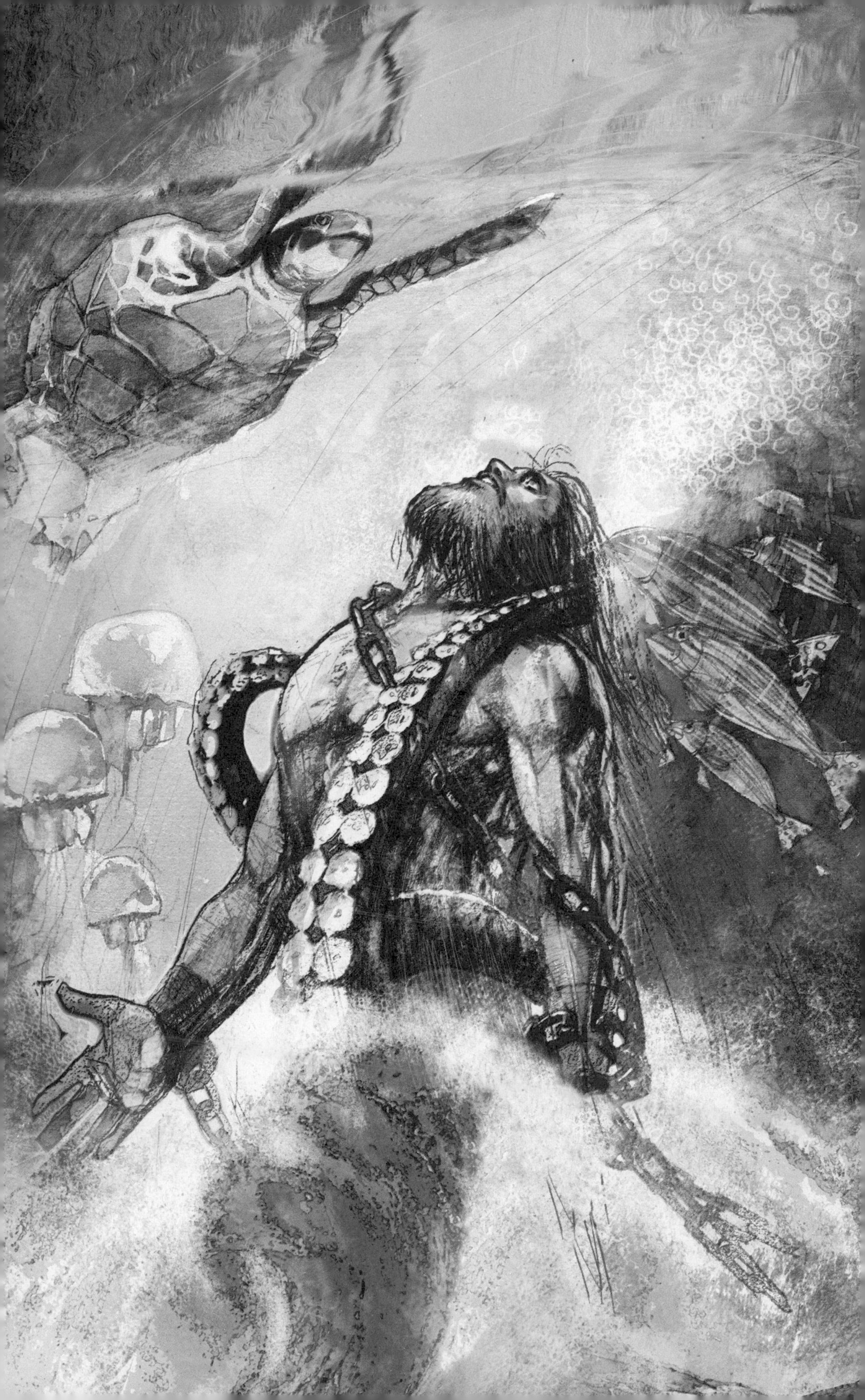

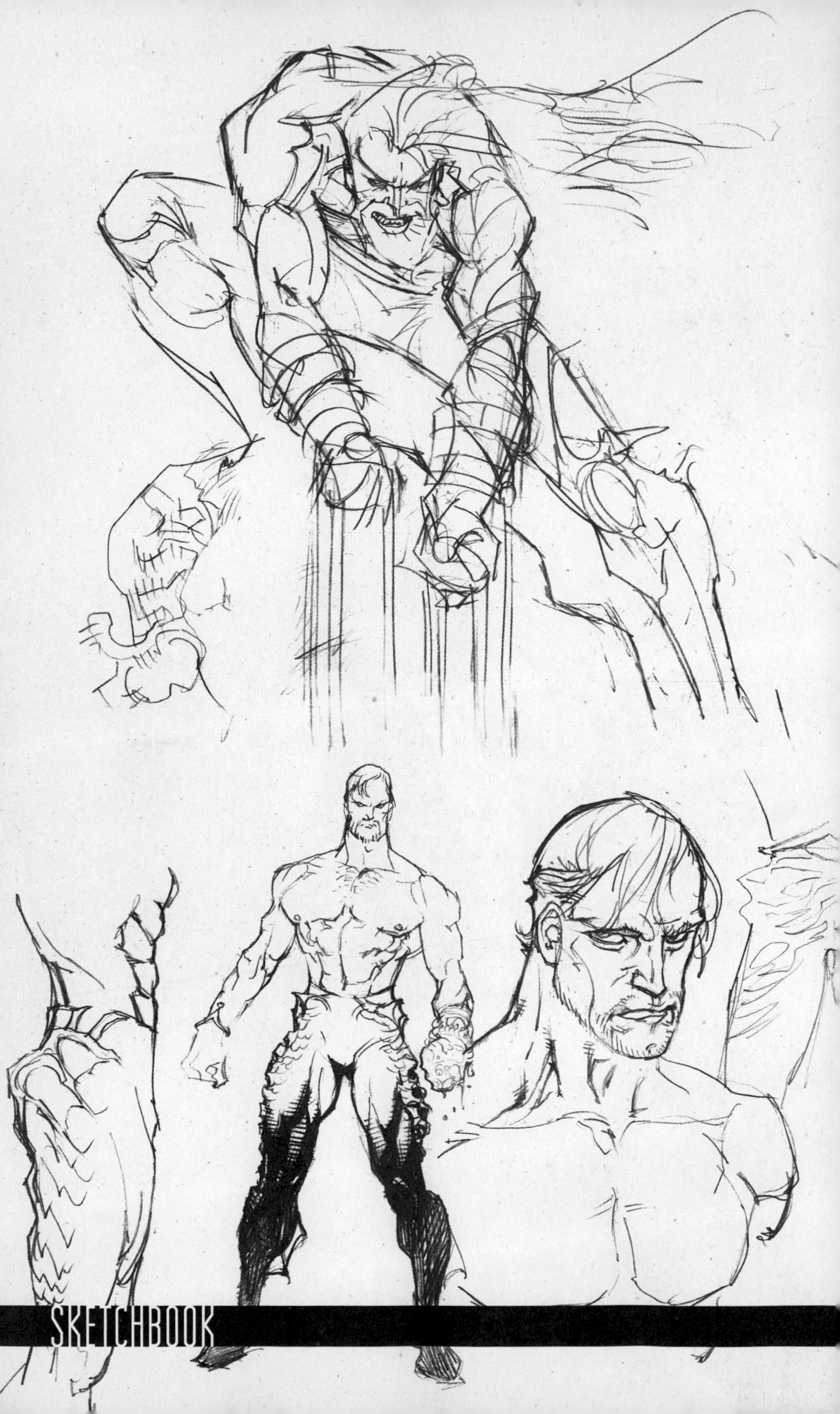

SKETCHBOOK

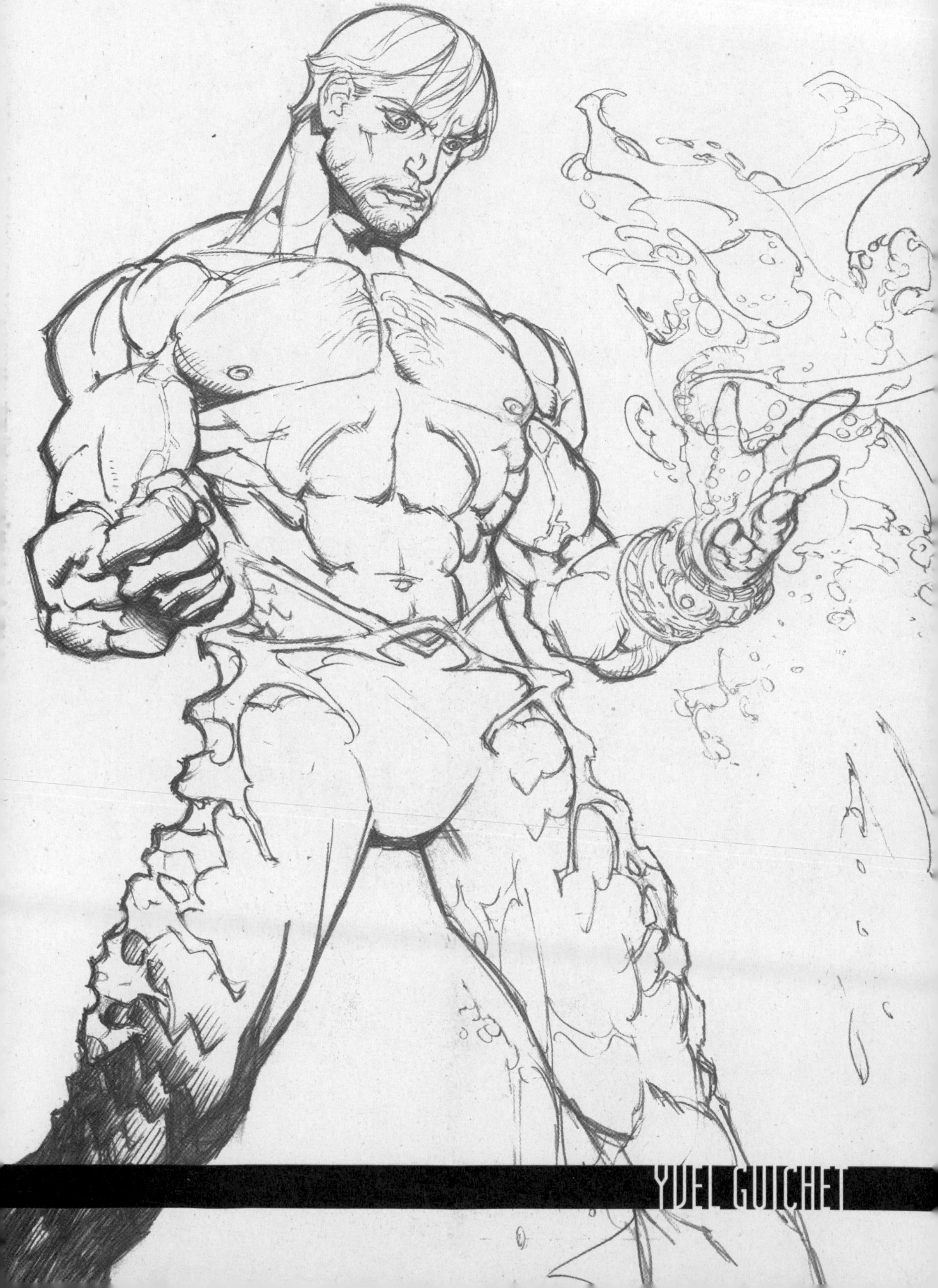
YVEL GUICHET

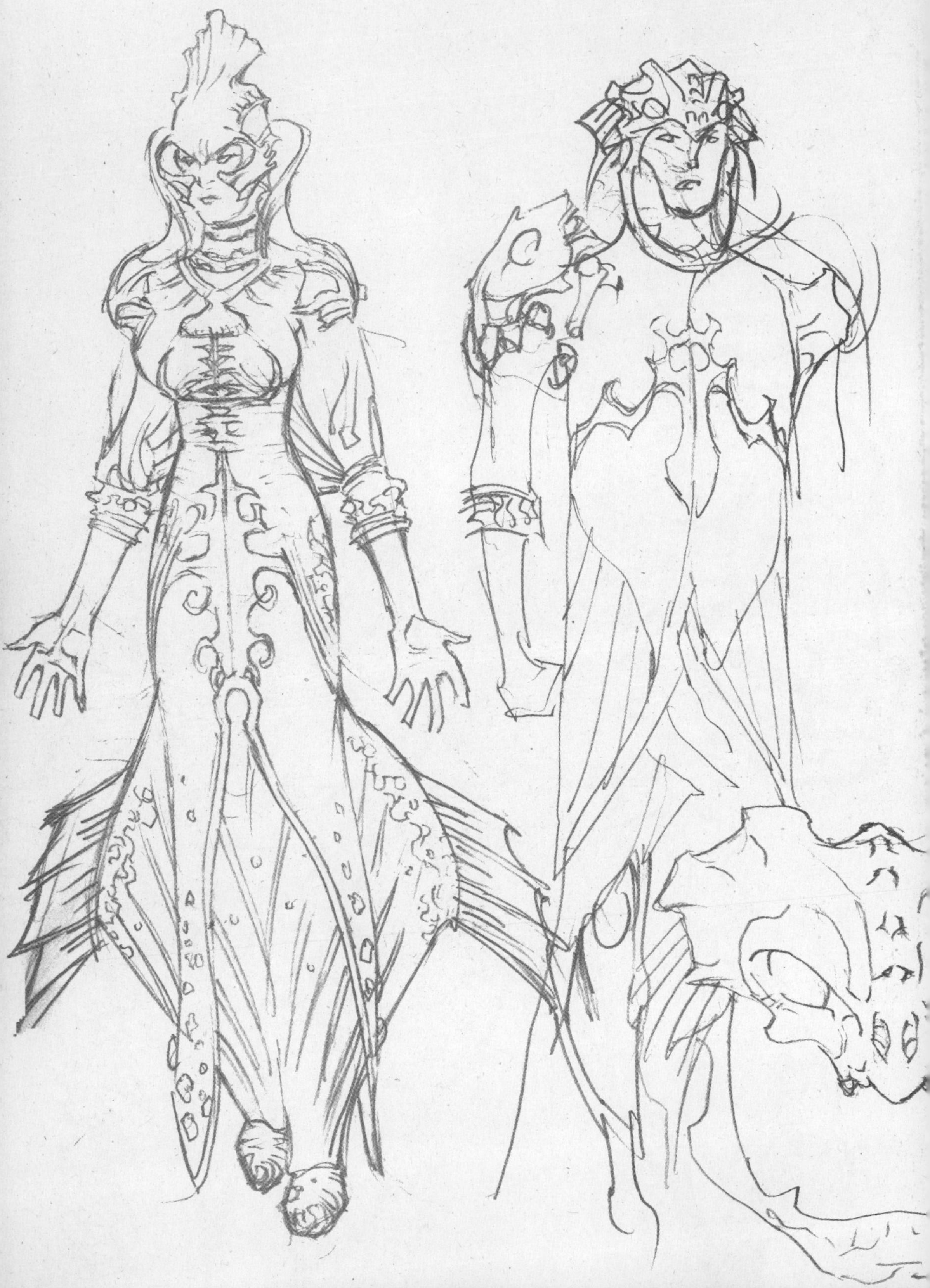